PLANTING

for **visual impact** and **scent** in **borders** and **containers**

PLANTING

for **visual impact** and **scent** in **borders** and **containers**

- A complete guide to choosing and using annuals, perennials, shrubs, bulbs and decorative foliage for instant colour and delicious scent
- With practical step-by-step sequences and 580 fabulous photographs

richard bird, jackie matthews
and andrew mikolajski

HH
HERMES
HOUSE

This edition is published by Hermes House

Hermes House is an imprint of
Anness Publishing Ltd
Hermes House, 88–89 Blackfriars Road,
London SE1 8HA
tel. 020 7401 2077; fax 020 7633 9499
www.hermeshouse.com;
www.annesspublishing.com

A CIP catalogue record for this book is available from the British Library.

All rights reserved. No part of this publication may be reproduced, stored in a retrieval system, or transmitted in any way or by any means, electronic, mechanical, photocopying, recording or otherwise, without the prior written permission of the copyright holder.

10 9 8 7 6 5 4 3 2 1

Publisher: Joanna Lorenz
Editorial Director: Helen Sudell
Editors: Valerie Ferguson, Simona Hill and Elizabeth Woodland
Photographers: Peter Anderson, Sue Atkinson, Jonathan Buckley, Derek Cranch, Sarah Cuttle, David England, John Freeman, Michelle Garrett, Jerry Hapur, Janine Hosegood, Jacqui Hurst, Andrea Jones, Simon McBride, Peter McHoy, Andrew Mikolajski, Marie O'Hara, David Parmiter, Debbie Patterson, Howard Rice, Derek St Romaine, Barbara Segall, Brigitte Thomas, Juliette Wade, David Way, Jo Whitworth, Polly Wreford
Text Contributors: Pattie Barron, Susan Berry, Richard Bird, Steve Bradley, Valerie Bradley, Kathy Brown, Jo Chatterton, Joan Clifton, Ted Collins, Stephanie Donaldson, Tessa Evelegh, Lin Hawthorne, Hazel Key, Gilly Love, Jackie Matthews, Peter McHoy, Andrew Mikolajski, Barbara Segall
Garden Designers: Declan Buckley, Lara Copley-Smith, Sally Court, Dennis Fairweather, Jacqui Gordon, Alan Gray, Bernard Hickie, Jennifer Jones, Elsie Josland, Robert Kite, Shari Lawrence Garden Design, Christina Oates, Antony Paul, Wendy and Michael Perry, Ben Pike, Graham Robeson, Lucy Summers, Paul Thompson, Mrs Winkle-Howarth, Diane Yakely
Designer: Andrew Heath
Cover Designer: Balley Design Associates
Production Controller: Steve Lang

Previously published as part of a larger volume, *The Handbook of Gardening*.

Page 1: Tulipa *'White Virgin' and purple-blue pansies.*
Page 2: Zantedeschia *(arum lily) displayed in tall, silver containers.*
Page 3 left to right: Kniphofia *'Alcazar' (red hot poker, torch lily);* Verbena bonariensis; Lilium *'Royal Class' (lily).*
Page 4: Iris *'George'.*
Page 5 left to right: Muscari armeniacum *'Blue Spike' (grape hyacinth); Mixed border of tulips and blue forget-me-nots (*Myosotis sylvatica*).*

Contents

6 Introduction

8 Shade, Tone & Hue
10 Visual Delight
14 Choosing a Colour Scheme
16 Colour in the Garden
24 Year-round Plants
28 Spring
32 Summer
38 Autumn
42 Winter
46 Plants for Seasonal Colour

50 Annual Attraction
52 Beautiful Borders
56 Using Annuals Effectively
62 Planning Annuals for Colour
64 Choosing Annuals

68 Perennials
70 Everlasting Perennials
74 Perennials in the Garden
80 Perennials for Different Conditions
84 Choosing Perennials with Special Qualities
90 Seasonal Splendour
100 Perennials for Colour
102 Best Perennials for Your Garden

106 Scent in the Garden
108 Delicate Aromas
116 Scented Plants in the Garden
132 Scent for All Seasons
144 Scent for Every Style
154 Plants for Scent

158 Hanging Baskets
160 Miniature Gardens
164 Getting Started
176 Baskets for All Seasons
188 Satisfying the Senses
210 Seasonal Tasks
212 Best Hanging Basket Plants

216 Window Boxes
218 Dressing up Windows
222 Getting Started
230 Seasonal Splendour
244 Satisfying the Senses
256 Seasonal Tasks
258 Best Window Box Plants

262 Indoor Plants
264 Living with Houseplants
270 Getting Started
274 Caring for Houseplants
280 Troubleshooting
282 A–Z of Houseplants

314 Common Names of Plants

318 Index

Introduction

The key element in creating any successful garden must be the plants. They provide shape and structure, whilst producing wonderful colour and scent. Here, you will find everything you need in order to create a fragrant and colourful, indoor and outdoor environment. The wealth of informative material has been divided into seven chapters that will help you through the gardening basics.

The first section of the book, *Shade, Tone & Hue,* explains how colour works, so that you can make choices for harmonizing your planting schemes. Advice on when particular plants are at their best and a quick-reference chart show how you can ensure glorious colour in the garden at all times of the year.

The next two chapters, *Annual Attraction* and *Perennials*, focus on those plants that are jointly responsible for so much colour in our gardens. Advice is given on how to use both types of plant effectively – temporary annuals in seasonal bedding schemes and mixed borders, perennials as permanent planting – and which plants will do best in different situations. Useful charts provide at-a-glance information on the best choices by colour and season of interest.

Below: *Blue* Agapanthus *with* Hemerocallis *(day lily) and pink alliums make a colourful summer border.*

Right: *This attractive basket of* Viola *'Bowles Black' and 'Johnny Jump Up'*, Viola x wittrockiana *(pansy) and* Muscari armeniacum *(grape hyacinth) has been planned for maximum impact.*

Scent in the Garden shows how your garden can be filled with delightful perfume at any time of the year. Scented plants can be found in every category, so you can choose some to suit any planting and to complement any garden style. A useful checklist at the end of the chapter provides a seasonal reference for scented plants.

Hanging baskets are like miniature gardens. Suspended at eye-level, they can receive much scrutiny and so need to always look their best. The *Hanging Baskets* chapter lets you into all the secrets for planting up and maintaining magnificent fragrant baskets for every season of the year. A chart lists the best plants for baskets, to inspire you to experiment with your own combinations.

Before rushing out to buy a window box you need to think about the style of the container and the type of planting you want to achieve. In *Window Boxes*, you will find everything you need to know, including information on different types of container, composts (soil mixes) and mulches as well as tips on planting and maintenance. There is also advice on keeping an arrangement looking good through the year. Readers with culinary interests will appreciate the section on growing herbs, fruit and vegetables. A seasonal task list plus a reference chart will help you to keep up appearances.

The *Indoor Plants* chapter completes the picture with valuable advice on selecting and growing plants within your home.

However ambitious your gardening plans, this wonderful guide will help them to become a flourishing reality.

SHADE, TONE & HUE

Knowing how colour works and how to match hues to create visual harmony or eye-catching contrasts is fundamental to planning a successful scheme for any garden, no matter what its size. This chapter includes information on year-round plants as well as more seasonal performers that will enable you to sustain or subtly alter a scheme as the year progresses.

Visual Delight

We expect to find colour in our gardens, but to create stunning effects and ensure a continuous show throughout the year will require some understanding of how colour behaves and when plants are at their best. With planning, even the smallest gardens can provide year-round colour.

Year-round Colour

As the year progresses, different types of plant come into their own. Using the right mix of plants and blends of colour will ensure that a garden has plenty of colour the year round. In mixed borders, shrubs provide the basis of any planting, giving it structure as well as colour. These can be in-filled with a multitude of other types of plants, mostly herbaceous perennials, bulbs, and annuals, their seasonal time and colour chosen to complement the more permanent plants. Beds devoted to particular types of plants can be planted up on a rotation basis.

Above: *Yellows and creams blend to create a restful feel to this summer border.*

Borders

Spring-flowering bulbs can be planted in borders used for summer bedding, providing colour early in the year. Herbaceous and mixed borders also benefit from a generous scattering of bulbs to help provide colour and interest until the late spring, when the early summer plants take over.

Left: *Irises and primulas dominate this late-spring border for a striking effect.*

Certainly, the flowers of some bulbs are short-lived compared with summer flowers (often no more than a couple of weeks at their peak), but this short-coming is easily rectified by inter-planting with spring bedding plants such as winter-flowering pansies, forget-me-nots and polyanthus. They ensure a superb display for more than a month, by which time the beds will probably have to be cleared when the ground is prepared for summer flowers. They also help to fill in around the base of tall bulbs such as tulips that can otherwise look rather stalky.

Make sure that mixed borders include shrubs that flower at different times of the year.

The planting schemes used by your local parks department can provide some useful ideas for successful colours and plants, especially if your plant knowledge is limited.

Above: *The colourful bark of* Salix *is at its best in the winter months.*

Containers

An ideal way to ensure a display of plants at their peak is to plant them in containers. This allows plants to be moved about as they come into flower and fade. Tubs, troughs, window boxes, and even hanging baskets can all be replanted for spring colour.

Permanent Colour

Annuals and perennials are wonderful for providing successional colour, but growing them does involve work – sowing, potting on, planting out, deadheading, dividing and clearing away dead matter. So some gardeners prefer to create most of their colour using more permanent plants such as heathers and evergreen shrubs, including conifers and ivies which require less maintenance.

Left: *Dahlias provide strong colours for the autumn border.*

The Effects of Colour

Colour has a strong influence on mood and you can use it in your garden to create different effects. Reds are restless and passionate, blues can be calming, yellows are cheerful. Colours also affect the tones of other colours next to them, creating slight changes in their appearance. The way colours work is explored in more detail later in the chapter.

Nothing in a garden is static and whatever effect you create will undergo changes through the day and according to the season. The colour of a flower or leaf will change as it develops, from bud to fall.

Light

Each season has a different type of light, and this affects the hues of plants. Light also changes throughout the day. Pale flowers stand out in shade and at dusk, while bright ones seem to bleach out in the midday sun.

Above: *The copper-tinted leaves of the* Phormium *make an interesting contrast with small, vivid geranium flowers.*

Using Foliage

Most foliage is green, but the number of different greens is almost infinite. Careful arrangement of these various greens will enhance the display, but even more can be achieved by incorporating into the garden the large number of plants, especially shrubs, that have foliage in other colours, including yellow, gold, silver, white, purple and blue.

To enjoy coloured foliage at its best, remember that purple and silver-leaved plants need the sun to retain their colour; golden and yellow foliage, however, often need a dappled shade

Left: *Many of the smoke bushes (*Cotinus*) have excellent purple foliage. They look especially effective when they are planted so that the evening sun shines through the leaves.*

***Above:** The variegated* Hosta *'Golden Tiara', with its creamy-edged leaves, brightens a shaded corner.*

as too much sun can scorch the leaves and too much shade causes them to turn greener.

Variegated Foliage

Some plants have leaves in two or more colours, known as "variegated" foliage. There are many different types of variegation. In shrubs most variagations are gold, followed closely by cream and white. These have the effect of lightening any group of plants they are near. Green-on-green variegations also have a lightening effect, but variegations involving purples often introduce a more sombre mood.

Variegated plants should be used with discretion. They can become too "busy", and if several are planted together they tend to clash. Reserve them for use as accent plants, to draw the eye. They are useful in shade or in a dark corner because they shine out and create interest in an otherwise unpromising or dull situation.

Although many variegated shrubs will tolerate full sun, many prefer a light, dappled shade, out of hot sun.

How to Use This Chapter

Begin by reading *Choosing a Colour Scheme* which explains how colours work together. It is possible to install permanent colour in the garden, which remains constant through the changing seasons. The section entitled *Year-round Plants* describes the plants to use for this effect.

The following sections are each devoted to a season of the year. They look at which plants are at their best in each season and explore successful colour combinations.

To plan for colour through the year, you can refer to the plant charts in this book.

***Right:** The purple foliage of* Canna *'Roi Humber' is eyecatching against red, yellow and green.*

Choosing a Colour Scheme

PLANTS ARE AVAILABLE IN A WONDERFUL RANGE OF COLOURS, WHICH GIVES GARDENERS TREMENDOUS SCOPE WHEN DESIGNING AN AREA. START BY PLANNING YOUR COLOUR SCHEME ON GRAPH PAPER USING COLOURED PENCILS, TO GIVE YOU A BETTER IDEA OF THE END RESULT.

USING COLOUR

There is such vast choice of colour in plants, that with a little imagination it is possible to paint any picture you like and create any mood you desire.

Not all colours mix well, so rather than randomly scattering colours, it is better to use them in drifts, placing plants so that each has a harmonious relationship with its neighbour. When this is done, the eye can move effortlessly along a border, enjoying inherent subtleties as it passes over a thoughtfully blended whole.

If in doubt about colour combinations, bear in mind that white or blue will go with almost any other colour, and look good. Pastel shades are forgiving colours. The ones to be careful with are brilliant orange and strong magenta, which could look disconcerting when placed together.

BLENDING COLOURS

Unless you want a monochromatic scheme, the basic principle is to blend colours. If you want to use two different colours that oppose each other on the colour wheel in close proximity, you can sometimes find another colour that will link them. Blue and red are in stark contrast to each other, and you may prefer to keep them apart by placing a purple plant between them, which will greatly improve the appearance of the flower border. Incorporating areas of interesting foliage in suitable colours is often an excellent way of linking and separating blocks of colour.

***Left:** Silver leaves, a dusty pink and the crimson flowers of* Digitalis *are unified by the purple* Aquilegia *and* Ajuga *which both stimulate and please the eye.*

Above: The hot yellow and reds of the primulas contrast perfectly with the blue Myosotis.

Leaf Colour

Foliage plays an important part in any colour scheme and wonderful effects can be created by placing a stunningly different coloured flower against an interesting leaf colour. For instance the delicate pink of an opium poppy *(Papaver somniferum)* is beautifully set off against silver-grey leaves.

Hot and Cool Colours

When you are decorating the whole mood of a room can change depending on whether you are using hot or cool colours. It is exactly the same when you are designing and planning a garden.

Hot colours – the flame reds and oranges – are lively and will bring a dash of excitement to a border. Intense blues will definitely cool things down, and white imparts a general sense of purity and tranquillity. Each colour has many tones and shades and all of these can be found in flowers and the many varieties of foliage.

Pastel colours have a romantic quality, and are often suitable for a dull, grey climate. However, a garden devoted entirely to pale colours such as these can be rather boring.

THE COLOUR WHEEL

Artists and designers use what is known as a colour wheel, in which colours that are situated next to each other on the wheel have a sympathetic bond and will work well together. Purple and blue as well as blue and green, for example, look good together. Colours on opposite sides of the wheel are contrasting and may clash with each other. Orange, for instance, will stand out quite starkly against blue.

There are occasions, however, when combining opposing colours can be used to create a focal point or to add life in an otherwise bland scheme.

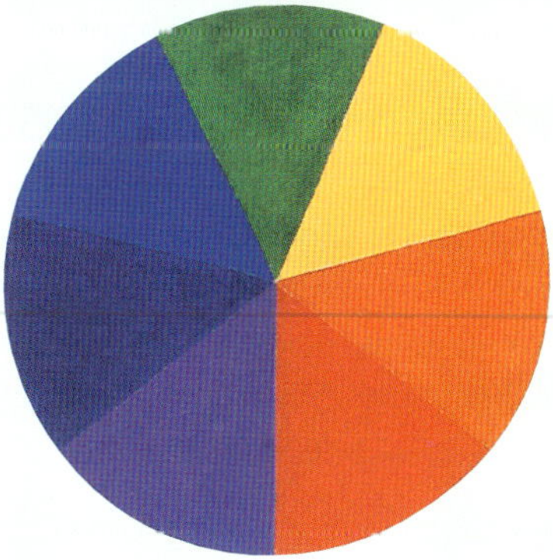

Colour in the Garden

As you plan for colour in the garden, decide which effect you wish to achieve. You can use calming, soft colours or include a bright, vibrant focal point or a hot border. You may even choose to create peace and tranquillity with a completely white border.

Using Hot Colours

Confine hot colours to one border, possibly as a centrepiece, but use softer colours in the other beds to ring in the changes and to provide a more tranquil planting area. It is possible to create a border containing nothing but red flowers, but it is always more interesting to have one that incorporates other hot colours as well. However, many people prefer to use a limited number of hot-coloured perennials in a cooler-coloured border, where they will act as a strong focal point and make a dramatic statement. Red or yellow flowers are the strongest colours for impact.

Above: *Kniphofias have several alternative names, of which "red-hot poker" aptly describes the colour of many of them. These shafts of hot colours are useful not only for their brightness, but also for their shape.*

Hot colours have a tendency to "advance" – that is, they seem much closer than they really are – so if you want to make a long border appear shorter than it is, plant the hot colours at the far end.

Use the different hues of foliage to link the hot colours with cool colours in the border.

Above: *The glorious ruby-red flowers of* Rhododendron *'Dopey'.*

Using Cool Colours

Although blues are, in theory, cool colours, those blues that are tinged with red are warm. Combined with the warm pinks, the overall effect is

***Above:** The cool colours of* Nemophila menziesii *(Californian bluebell).*

one of cool calm. Use blues, purples and pinks, including many of the pastel shades, to achieve this effect.

Pastel colours create a misty effect, which means that they can be mixed together or dotted around. An even better effect can be achieved by using drifts of colour, merging the drifts.

***Above:** Use bright-red plants, such as* Dahlia *'Bishop of Llandaff', as a bold focal point.*

RED FLOWERS

Amaranthus caudatus
Antirrhinum 'Scarlet Giant'
Begonia semperflorens 'Volcano'
Canna
Cleome hassleriana 'Cherry Queen'
Crocosmia 'Lucifer'
Dahlia
Geum 'Mrs. J. Bradshaw'
Impatiens (various varieties)
Kniphofia (red hot poker)
Lobelia erinus 'Red Cascade'
Monarda 'Cambridge Scarlet'
Paeonia
Papaver rhoeas
Pelargonium (various varieties)
Penstemon barbatus
Petunia 'Red Star'; P. 'Scarlet'
Tropaeolum majus 'Empress of India'
Verbena (various varieties)

Red

The fiery reds are hot, exciting colours. They combine well with oranges, and golden and orange-yellows, but don't generally mix well with blue-reds, which are more subdued. Use them wherever you want to inject some vibrancy into your garden designs – in beds and borders or in hanging baskets and other containers. But remember that too much of a good thing can become monotonous, so use these strong colours sparingly.

Hot reds can be found in many perennials, but are especially well represented in summer annuals, which are so useful for adding dramatic patches of colour between other plants.

***Above:** This brilliant bright orange* Osteospermum *makes a strong contrast against green foliage.*

ORANGE

A warm, friendly colour, orange has quite a wide range of shades. At the deeper end of the spectrum it is quite definitely a hot colour, exciting and vibrant, but at the golden end it is warm rather than hot and can be used more freely.

Orange mixes well with most colours although the redder shades are not so complementary with the bluer reds, including purple and pink, unless you like to combine colours that clash. It shows up well against green foliage and can be picked out at a distance.

Autumn gardens often display orange tones, not only in flowers, such as chrysanthemums, but in trees and shrubs with coloured foliage and brightly coloured berries.

ORANGE FLOWERS

Antirrhinum
Canna 'Orange Perfection'
Crocosmia
Dahlia
Eccremocarpus scaber
Erysimum
Euphorbia griffithii
Geum 'Borisii'
Hemerocallis
Kniphofia
Ligularia
Papaver orientale
Potentilla 'William Robinson'
Primula bulleyana
Rudbeckia hirta
Tagetes erecta
Tropaeolum
Trollius
Zauschneria californica

***Above:** This* Calceolaria, *with its flame-orange flowers, is a striking annual to use in the border.*

Many annuals and biennials can add a vibrant orange note throughout the year, including winter-flowering pansies followed by wallflowers (*Erysimum*), snapdragons (*Antirrhinum*) and pot marigolds (*Calendula*). During summer, nasturtiums (*Tropaeolum*) and African marigolds (*Tagetes erecta*) will follow.

***Above:** The yellow heads of* Achillea *'Coronation Gold' float above its delicate foliage.*

Yellow

There are three distinct yellows within this part of the spectrum, all exhibiting different qualities in a planting scheme. One side is tinged with green and may be described as a cool colour, while the other side is tinged with orange, making it very much a hot colour. These hot yellows have a warm, cosy feeling about them, and go well with flame-reds, oranges and creams. In between the two yellows are pure clear yellows. These will blend happily with most other colours.

The green or lemon yellows look much better when associated with greens blues and white. They can be bright, but create a fresher effect than the warmer yellows.

***Above:** The stately yellow spires of* Verbascum *add height to a traditional summer border.*

YELLOW FLOWERS

Achillea
Aurinia saxatilis
(syn. *Alyssum saxatile*)
Canna
Centaurea macrocephala
Chrysanthemum
Coreopsis verticillata
Dahlia
Erysimum 'Jubilee Gold'
Geum 'Lady Statheden'
Helianthus
Heliopsis
Hemerocallis
Inula
Ligularia
Primula
Rudbeckia

Green

Foliage can provide an effective link in borders and beds. Dark green is good used with hot colours, whereas soft green and silver suit cool colours, especially pink, pale blue and pale, greeny yellow. Blue foliage, which can be found in some grasses and hostas, can also be useful in linking or separating blocks of colour.

Blue

The different shades of blue can be bright, clean-cut colours with a great intensity, or softened to such an extent that they only have a whisper of colour left, creating a very soft, hazy image. Intense blues can be used in a bold way in the garden, but the softer blues are good for romantic container arrangements, especially those in large stone pots or urns.

BLUE FLOWERS

Agapanthus praecox subsp. *orientalis*
Ageratum houstonianum
Brachyscome iberidifolia
Campanula medium
Centaurea cyanus
Consolida ambigua
Eryngium x *oliverianum*
Felicia bergeriana
Lathyrus odoratus
Limonium sinuatum 'Blue Bonnet'
Lobelia erinus
Myosotis
Nigella damascena
Nolana paradoxa 'Blue Bird'
Salvia farinacea 'Victoria'

Above: *Use the delicate* Nigella damascena, *with its blue flowers and feathery fronds, in a cool border.*

Blues are versatile and can be combined with most colours. They create a rather rich, luxurious combination with purple-reds, but avoid mixing them with orange-reds. With orange, however, the effects can be startling, so use this combination sparingly.

Blue and yellow is another exciting combination, giving a fresh, clean-looking contrast. The pale blues and yellows, however, are more hazy and have a soft, romantic image, but still retain a distinctive, fresh quality.

Blues set against silver or grey foliage create an interesting combination that is distinct yet soft.

Purple and Violet

Even a patch of purple appears as a strong block of colour, never as a misty haze. Over-use of this solid colour can have a deadening effect. As purple

Above: Digitalis *creates wonderfully elegant spires of flowers, bringing height to a planting scheme. These flowers vary in colour from a light pink to purple.*

tends to sink back into green foliage, it is better to contrast it with foliage that is silver or grey.

Violet is a more lively colour, and has still more vibrancy when on the dark side. Nonetheless, it should still be used with care and discretion.

Both purple and violet can be used more extensively if they are mixed with other colours. Lighter colours, such as yellows and whites, contrast with and stand out against purple. Purple also harmonizes well with purple-reds and purple-blues, but if these are too dark, the colours tend to blend too much, creating a leaden effect. Lime-green flowers such as lime zinnias and the lime foliage of *Helychrysum petiolare* 'Limelight' make excellent border companions.

Lavenders combined with pinks are a delightfully romantic combination and have the bonus of a delightful scent. When used with creamy-yellow they have a soothing effect.

Pink

This colour can be quite bright, even startling and brash, particularly when tinged with purple and moving towards cerise and magenta shades. On the other hand it can be very soft and romantic. You have to be careful

Above: The delicate pink flowers of Oenothera speciosa rosea *have creamy white centres.*

PINK FLOWERS
Anemone hupehensis
Astilbe x *arendsii* 'Venus'
Centaurea Cyanus
Cleome hasslerianna 'Colour Fountain'
Cosmos bipinnatus 'Sensation'
Dicentra spectabilis
Geranium x *oxonianum* 'Wargrave Pink'
Impatiens
Lathyrus odoratus
Matthiola, Brompton Series
Penstemon
Petunia, Resisto Series

Above: Cream blended with soft mauve and gently variegated foliage creates a soothing effect.

in choosing the right colour for the effect you want to achieve. Pinks tend to mix best with lavenders and soft blues. But they can be used with reds to tone them down slightly. Pinks do not mix harmoniously with bright yellows and oranges.

Cream

White mixed with a little yellow makes the sensuous and luxurious shade of cream. It goes well with most colours, adding a slightly mellow hue and often blending in sympathetically with hot colours.

Left: The large pompom heads of creamy yellow Tagetes *'French Vanilla'.*

White

Long associated with purity, peace and tranquillity, white flowers add sophistication to a scheme. White goes well with most other colours, and it can be used to lighten a colour scheme. Used with hot oranges and reds, pure white can create a dramatic effect. White and blue is always a popular combination and it can be particularly effective to combine different shades of white with a mixture of pastel colours.

White is visible until well after dark, and so it is a good colour to plant where you eat evening meals. It also can be used to illuminate dark corners of the garden. White busy Lizzies (*Impatiens*), for example, in a hanging basket against a dark background or in shade, will shine out.

A disadvantage with white flowers is that they often look unsightly when they die. To keep such displays at their best, deadhead once a day.

Some gardeners devote whole borders, even whole gardens, to white flowers. Although these are referred to as white gardens, there are usually at least two colours present, because most white-flowered plants have green leaves. A third colour, in the form of grey or silver foliage, is also often added.

There are many different shades of white, and they do not always mix sympathetically. On the whole, therefore, it is better to plant pure whites since the creamier ones tend to "muddy" the picture. Many white and cream flowers have bright yellow centres, and it is best to avoid these if you are planning a white border.

Above: The tiny flowers of Gypsophila elegans *make a delicate display in any summer border.*

WHITE FLOWERS

Alcea rosea
Anaphalis margaritacea
Clarkia pulchella 'Snowflake'
Cosmos bipinnatus 'Purity'
Gypsophila elegans 'Giant White'
Impatiens 'Super Elfin White'
Lathyrus odoratus
Lobelia erinus 'Snowball'
Lobularia maritima
(syn. Alyssum maritimum)
Matthiola (white varieties)
Nicotiana alata
Osteospermum 'Glistening White'
Pelargonium (various white forms)
Petunia (various white forms)
Viola x *wittrockiana* (white varieties)

Left: This white Osteospermum *will lighten any scheme, from hot oranges to misty blues.*

Year-round Plants

BY SELECTING PLANTS WITH YEAR-ROUND INTEREST, IT IS POSSIBLE TO ACHIEVE CONTINUOUS COLOUR WITH MINIMUM EFFORT. HEATHERS, GRASSES AND EVERGREENS, INCLUDING CONIFERS AND IVIES, ARE ALL INVALUABLE SOURCES OF RICH COLOUR.

***Above:** The genus* Calluna *consists of one species,* C. vulgaris, *but this has over 500 cultivars in a wide range of colours.*

HEATHERS

Multi-coloured heathers are enduring garden performers. Tough and hardy, most can withstand extreme conditions, and some even put on their finest performance when the weather is at its most severe. One of the many advantages of heathers is that they provide year-round colour. Not only is there a heather in flower every month of the year, but some have coloured foliage that can itself be a strong, year-round feature, the leaf colour often changing with the seasons. For gardens without acid soil, many heathers need to be grown in raised beds or containers with the correct acidity.

Heathers are most highly rated as plants for the winter garden. Choose from varieties of *Erica carnea* and *E.* x *darleyensis*, perhaps mixing in selections of *Calluna vulgaris*.

> COLOURFUL HEATHERS
>
> *Calluna vulgaris:*
> 'Beoley Gold', golden-yellow
> 'Golden Feather', gold/orange red
> 'Multicolor', yellowish green, orange and coral tips
> 'Red Fred', dark green/vivid red tips
> 'Roland Haagen', gold/orange-red
> 'Sister Anne', grey-green/bronze
> 'Sunset', golden-yellow/orange/red
>
> *Erica:*
> *E. carnea* 'Ann Sparkes', golden-yellow, bronze tips
> 'Foxhollow', yellow/slightly orange
> 'Golden Starlet', lime-green/yellow
> 'Westwood Yellow', yellow
> *E. cinerea* 'Fiddler's Gold', golden-yellow/red
> 'Lime Soda', lime green
> 'Windlebrooke', golden yellow/orange-red
> *E.* x *darleyensis*
> 'J.W. Porter', red and cream tips
> *E. vagans* 'Valerie Proudley', bright yellow

In summer, varieties of *Calluna vulgaris*, *Erica cinerea* and *E. vagans* dominate the scene, and are all effective with other acid-loving plants.

As an edging to a shrub border, heathers provide a softer line than the more conventional *Buxus sempervirens*.

Above: *A collection of grasses in containers makes a versatile display for a small garden terrace or balcony.*

Grasses

A wide variety of ornamental grasses is available, ensuring that there is usually at least one type for every garden situation. Grasses look good when grouped together, or used as single specimens. They often work particularly well when associated with other plants. Their airy form and movement contrast effectively with larger-leaved plants, and their vertical accent lifts and lightens dense groupings. They are particuarly useful for adding winter interest.

In shady areas, the variegated foliage of *Carex hachijoensis* 'Evergold' will shine out all year round. Other shade-tolerant variegated grasses include *Molinia caerulea* ssp. *caerula* 'Variegata', *Hakonechloa macra* 'Alboaurea' and 'Aureola' and *Phalaris arundinacea* var. *picta* 'Picta'. They complement other shade-loving plants such as hostas, ferns and hydrangeas.

Areas of dry shade are difficult to plant successfully but *Stipa arundinacea* copes with these inhospitable conditions. Shady woodland areas can be carpeted with the golden foliage of *Milium effusum* 'Aureum', or with varieties of *Deschampsia cespitosa*, which have elegant flower spikes that catch the light beautifully.

Left: *Use grasses, such as this* Stipa calamagrostis, *as architectural plants in your scheme.*

EVERGREENS

Brachyglottis (Dunedin Group) 'Sunshine'
Choisya
Daphne tangutica
Euonymus fortunei
Hebe cupressoides
Ligustrum lucidum
Pieris japonica
Rhododendron
Santolina chamaecyparis
Vinca

***Above:** Many of the hebes are evergreen. This one,* H. cupressoides, *has striking violet flowers and small leaves.*

Evergreens

The great feature of evergreens is that they hold on to their leaves throughout the year. They can be used as a permanent part of the structure of any border or garden. Unless they are carefully sited, however, evergreens can become a bit dull, so plan your planting with care.

Many evergreens have dark green leaves, but using plants with variegated leaves, or clever planting combinations, will add colour and interest. Try *Eleagnus pungens* 'Maculata' with its yellow-centred leaves or *Ligustrum lucidum* 'Excelsior Superbum', which has a golden variegation in the open, although in shade it glows with a bright yellowish green.

Lots of evergreens have the bonus of glorious flowers. Rhododendrons and azaleas in particular, many of the evergreen hebes and camellias, are prized for their gorgeously coloured blooms. *Choisya* is a good example. The shiny leaves catch the sun and it produces masses of fragrant white flowers in spring and often again later in the year.

Conifers

Dwarf conifers are especially useful for providing year-round interest. Planted close together they will grow into each other, assuming a sculptural quality, besides making excellent ground cover. Some form dense mats,

DWARF CONIFERS

Abies Cephalonica 'Meyer's Dwarf'
Chamaecyparis lawsoniana 'Minima Aurea'
Juniperus communis 'Compressa'
Taxus baccuta 'Elegantissima'
Thuja orientalis 'Aurea Nana'
Thuja plicata 'Irish Gold'
Picea glauca var. *albertiana* 'Conica'
Picea pungens 'Globosa'

Above: Conifers provide a wonderful selection of shapes and textures. This juniper produces an attractive "sea of waves" effect that can never become boring.

particularly the prostrate junipers such as *Juniperus horizontalis*, *J squamata* and *J. procumbens*.

Most dwarf conifers are suitable for rock gardens and containers, and also look good planted with heathers. Choose upright conifers, to provide height.

Ivies

One of the great features of ivies is their ability to cover and conceal unsightly structures or eyesores. They will thrive in different locations.

The classic situation for ivy is growing up a wall. *Hedera helix* 'Buttercup' is spectacular against a sunny wall. *H. h.* 'Goldheart', which has green-

IVIES

Hedera 'Bruder Ingobert'
Hedera helix 'Goldheart'
Hedera hibernica
Hedera 'Merion Beauty'

edged, gold-centred leaves, retains its colour on a shaded wall. Don't grow different ivies too closely together on walls or they will cover each other.

Some designers use mixed ivies for mass bedding, but these do require pruning once or twice a year. Ivy also makes excellent edging to a flower border. It can be grown along the edge of a garden path or planted on a terrace garden to great effect.

Ivies make excellent ground cover and can completely cover large areas quickly. One of the best for this is *Hedera hibernica*. Many *Hedera helix* cultivars are also suitable, especially the dark green 'Ivalace' or 'Shamrock'.

Above: Here a golden ivy rambles happily over a wall intermingled with a rose and underplanted with complementary flowers.

Spring

FRESHNESS AND VITALITY ARE THE KEYNOTES OF SPRING. FOLIAGE AND FLOWERS ARE BRIGHTLY COLOURED, WITH SUNNY YELLOW ONE OF THE MOST PREVALENT COLOURS.

PLANTS AT THEIR BEST

After the short, dark days of winter, spring begins tentatively with a few jewel coloured bulbs and occasional perennial flowers. Flower buds on trees and shrubs begin to open. Before long plants are bursting into colour all around. The spring light makes everything in the garden look new and fresh.

Above: Spring in the cottage garden is a glorious jumble of colours with primulas, Myosotis *(forget-me-nots) and* Dicentra.

Bulbs

This is a wonderful season for bulbs and corms of all kinds. There is a multitude of crocuses, daffodils, tulips, hyacinths, fritillaries, dog's tooth violet *(Erythronium)*, irises, snowflake *(Leucojum)*, grape hyacinths and trilliums, coming into flower in grass, borders and containers. These are all hardy plants, unharmed by frosts.

Left: Hyacinthus orientalis *'Pink Pearl' interspersed with* Viola *makes a beautiful, scented display.*

Perennials

Some herbaceous plants have been around all winter. Lungworts (*Pulmonaria*), for example, have been in full leaf constantly, but now produce masses of blue, red, pink or white flowers. Hellebores are flowering as are primulas, of which the primrose is perhaps the best loved. As the days continue to lengthen and the air and ground become warmer, early flowers move into the background as other herbaceous perennials begin to emerge. Among the next phase are bleeding hearts (*Dicentra spectabilis*) and other dicentras, which need light shade and will grow happily under trees that have yet to open their leaves. Wood anemones (*Anemone nemorosa*), in a range of white and delicate blues, pinks and yellow, also make use of the temporary light under deciduous trees and shrubs. Among the brightest flowers are the brilliant golden daisies of leopard's bane (*Doronicum*), and buttery kingcup (*Caltha*) flowers, which are essential for any bog or waterside planting. *Paeonia mlokosewitschii*, one of the earliest peonies to flower, has delicate yellow flowers.

Above: Euphorbia polychroma *creates a perfect dome which is effective in any spring border.*

Shrubs

Many shrubs flower early in the year. Rhododendrons, azaleas, magnolias, pieris, camellias and many others provide outstanding spring colour.

Spiraea 'Arguta' is among the earliest to flower, producing frothy pure white flowers over quite a long period. One of the best-loved shrubs is *Magnolia stellata* with its mass of delicate, star-like flowers in glistening white or tinged with pink. The effect is enhanced because the flowers appear before the leaves develop. *Exochorda* x *macrantha* 'The Bride' is so covered in pure white flowers that the leaves are barely visible.

Forsythia creates one of the biggest splashes of spring colour. It should be cut back immediately after flowering to ensure that new flowering shoots grow in time for next season. Lilac (*Syringa*), prized for its colour and perfume, flowers late in the season. The white forms especially can look untidy when the flowers die, so they should be removed.

Rhododendrons and azaleas, especially, have such a vast range of glorious colours and flower sizes, that perhaps the best way to make a choice for your own garden is to see as many as you can in flower and then discover the names of the ones you like.

Left: *Rhododendrons grow into large shrubs which burst into colour in late spring.*

Colour Combinations

In lawns and under shrubs and trees, naturalized bulbs flower in cheerful multi-coloured carpets without constraint. In many spring borders, however, regularity and uniformity of planting are often preferred. Spring light has a softening effect and so strong opposing colours, such as primary red and blue, seem to go together better at this time of year.

Formal Beds

In formal beds you can interplant spring bulbs with bushy bedding plants, for example late-flowering tulips with pansies, forget-me-nots, polyanthus, double daisies *(Bellis perennis)* or dwarf wallflowers. These bedding plants hide the bare soil and make tall-stemmed bulbs like tulips less ungainly and vulnerable to wind damage. Pink tulips with blue forget-me-nots is a classic combination that can be enlivened by the occasional dot of a red tulip.

Such schemes offer scope for colour coordination and combinations that vary from the subtle to the gaudy. For example, pale pink hyacinths and white or pale yellow *Polyanthus* make a restful, receding combination, while deep yellow *Polyanthus* makes an arresting sight. Try planting two different kinds of spring bulbs together, such as bright blue *Scilla siberica* among 'Pink Pearl' hyacinths.

Such a border, recreated at the home of Monet in Giverney, France, combines a number of favourites – tall bearded blue-and-white iris fronting masses of Siberian wallflowers (*Erysimum hieracaciifolium*), scented wallflowers and *Hesperis matronalis*. All of this display could be edged with purple-flowered *Lobularia maritima* 'Royal Carpet'.

Informal Borders

Planting an informal border is easier. Generally, bold clumps of a single variety work best in a border, and if the clumps or drifts are used to fill gaps they will probably be well spaced out with little risk of colour clashes. It is often possible to plant bulbs between perennials that will hide the dying foliage as they emerge.

Above: *The variegated* Weigela florida *'Albomarginata' is seen here against a* Spiraea. *The striped leaves blend well with the white flowers of the* Spiraea *in spring.*

Above: Dainty yellow primroses are charmingly set off by their own green foliage and enhanced by a fountain of yellow grass.

Natural Effect

For a natural effect in borders, try a mass planting of spring-flowering bulbs and perennials. Purple crocus and yellow aconites could be planted to flower above the marbled leaves of *Arum italicum pictum*, with the rich mauve flowers of hellebores atop leafless stems. Around these could perhaps be scattered the green-tipped white bells of snowdrops.

The strong blue of grape hyacinths with the pale yellow of primroses is another time-honoured spring combination. Or you could try a mix of hyacinths, compact tulips and narcissi. Planted closely for maximum impact, these would be as colourful as any summer bedding.

PLANTS AT THEIR BEST

EARLY SPRING

Bergenia (non-woody evergreen)
Camellia (shrub)
Crocus (bulb)
Eranthis hyemalis (bulb)
Helleborus orientalis (perennial)
Hyacinthus (bulb)
Iris reticulata (bulb)
Magnolia stellata (shrub)
Primula x *polyantha* (perennial)
Tulipa kaufmanniana (bulb)

MID-SPRING

Amelanchier (shrub/tree)
Cytisus, various (shrub)
Dicentra (perennial)
Doronicum (perennial)
Magnolia x *soulangiana* (tree)
Magnolia stellata (shrub)
Narcissus (bulb)
Prunus 'Kwanzan' (tree)
Rhododendron, various (shrub)
Ribes sanguineum (shrub)

LATE SPRING

Azalea (shrub)
Bergenia (non-woody evergreen)
Cheiranthus (wallflower)
Choisya ternata (shrub)
Clematis montana (shrubby climber)
Cytisus, various (shrub)
Dicentra (perennial)
Fritillaria (bulb)
Laburnum (tree)
Malus (tree)
Paeonia (perennial and shrub)
Phlox subulata (rock plant)
Pulsatilla vulgaris (rock plant)
Rhododendron, various (shrub)
Saxifraga, various (rock plant)
Syringa (shrub)
Tulipa, various (bulb)
Wisteria (shrubby climber)

Summer

THE ARRIVAL OF SUMMER ALWAYS SEEMS SUDDEN. ONE MINUTE IT IS SPRING, THE NEXT IT IS SUMMER, AND THE GARDEN IS BURSTING WITH LIFE, HEADY WITH AROMAS AND VIBRANT WITH COLOUR.

PLANTS AT THEIR BEST

Although often regarded as a continuation in gardening terms there is quite a difference between early, mid- and late summer.

Early summer carries on where spring left off, with plenty of fresh-looking foliage and bright, rich colours. Lupins, poppies, peonies and delphiniums are vital players in any display at this time of the year.

As midsummer approaches, the colours change subtly and flowers with more muted tones unfurl. Among these are *Phlox*, *Catanache* (sometimes known as Cupid's dart), penstemons and *Gypsophila*.

By late summer colours are fading and foliage is starting to look a little tired. Autumnal tones become evident with the deep golds and russet-reds of perennials such as achilleas, heleniums and inulas.

Perennials

Summer is the height of the perennial year. The hardy geraniums (cranesbills) are one of the mainstays of the summer border. There is a vast range to choose from.

Above: *A variety of different shades of yellow are broken up by contrasting splashes of red in this summer garden.*

Cranesbills are widely grown for their pink or purple flowers. They are generally trouble-free, coming back each year with little or no attention.

Dahlias are useful for borders as they last for months, come in many different heights and provide lots of flowers for cutting.

Tuberous-rooted begonias, used for both bedding and container display, come in shades of pink, red, yellow and white. Seed-raised begonias that flower quickly, such as Non-stop, are also popular. They flower all summer, until cut back by frost, and are suitable for massed bedding. These are all low growing, reaching 23–30cm (9–12in) in height.

The tall – up to 1.8m (6ft) – exotic-looking cannas come into bloom early and continue until the first frost. They combine spectacular red, orange or yellow flowers with interesting foliage, mostly dark or purple bronze but some brightly variegated.

Bulbs

Summer-flowering bulbs are exceptionally good for adding highlights to a traditional herbaceous border, and can be useful for brightening up areas between shrubs that have finished flowering. It is difficult to imagine a traditional herbaceous border, for example, without groups of lilies or a clump or two of crocosmias. The crocosmia corms multiply freely, and after a year or two most plantings make a bold show in late summer with arching sprays of red, orange or yellow flowers.

Above: *Yellow achillea and the streaked leaves of* Canna *'Striata' make an effective backdrop for* Crocosmia *'Lucifer'.*

Above: *The pink globes of* Allium christophii *contrast successfully with* Salvia sylvestris.

The round, colourful heads of alliums make stunning statements in the summer border. There are many forms including dwarf ones like the yellow *Allium moly*, *A. christophii*, with its 15cm (6in) spheres of starry, lilac flowers, and tall, majestic species such as the 1.8m (6ft) *A. giganteum* with its huge bloom. *A. sphaerocephalon* has drumstick heads of pinkish-purple flowers on thin 75cm (2½ft) tall stems. It is best grown mid-border, where other border plants can hide and support the stems. The seedheads are another delight. They can be enjoyed in the garden or used indoors in dried flower arrangements.

Shrubs

From midsummer onwards, many shrubs begin to flower. These include brightly flowering shrubs such as *Hypericum calycinum*, which, with its brilliant yellow flowers, will even flourish in shade. For a sunny spot, the bright pinks and oranges of helianthemums, or the soft-pink shades of *Cistus* are a delight. Use white-flowering shrubs such as *Cistus laurifolius* or *Philadelphus* to break up bold masses of colour and act as a backdrop to vivid shades.

Hydrangeas, with their huge mounds of blooms, prefer shady positions, where the whites will brighten up their surroundings. The delicate lace-caps are popular because of the shape of the flowers. *Hydrangea quercifolia* combines white flowers, which become tinged pink with age, with mid-green leaves which will turn bronze in autumn. *H. aspera* 'Villosa' has mauvish-blue and pink flowers. Mophead varieties (*H. macrophylla*) bear blue flowers on acid soil, red ones on neutral soil and pink ones on alkaline soil.

***Above:** A white* Hydrangea *thrives in a shaded border.*

***Above:** The glorious cascading flowers of* Fuchsia *'Prosperity' would be a delightful addition to the summer scheme.*

Few other plants smother themselves so completely or over such a long period as fuchsias. Ranging from almost white, through pastel pink to rich purples, reds and oranges, the flower shapes and colours of fuchsias offer unlimited possibilities. Tender types have become prized bedding plants, while the often less showy hardy types can be integrated into mixed borders, where they can give years of pleasure. Some hardy fuchsias

Above: Clematis *'Purpurea Plena Elegans' provides the interest now that its host plant,* Rosa *'Cécile Brünner, climbing', has all but finished flowering.*

make elegant plants that can stand alone as specimens in a bed or in a suitable container.

Roses are at their best in summer. Some are once-flowering and do so in the early summer, but many go on flowering throughout the whole season. Some gardeners prefer to have a separate garden or special beds for roses, while others like to mix them in with other plants.

Climbers

Interesting effects can be created using climbing roses. The rambling 'Albertine', for example, can be grown to produce a glorious fountain of salmon-pink flowers up to 6m (20ft) high.

Like climbing roses, clematis can be grown in a variety of ways, on pergolas, against walls and fences. The more vigorous types will reach into trees to provide glorious colour and height. There are many startling colours to choose from, ranging from deep rose-pink through crimson and wine red to bright purple, in small or large flower sizes. You can select from the three different groups to ensure colour throughout the summer.

PLANTS AT THEIR BEST

EARLY SUMMER

Allium
Dianthus
Geranium
Iris germanica hybrids
Paeonia
Papaver orientale
Philadelphus

MID-SUMMER

Clematis
Digitalis
Geranium
Hardy annuals
Hydrangea
Hypericum
Lavandula
Lilium
Rosa

LATE SUMMER

Dahlia
Fuchsia
Helenium
Hibiscus syriacus
Hypericum
Lavatera
Perovskia atriplicifolia
Romneya
Solidago
Summer bedding

***Above:** Orange and blue are both powerful colours. Used together in a planting scheme, they produce an agreeable tension as is shown by the bright* Agapanthus *and orange* Crocosmia.

Colour Combinations

With all the colour that is around during summer, some stunning plantings are possible.

Beds and Borders

At this time of year blues can be tinged with pink, making them work well with mauves and violets. For example, *Echium* 'Blue Bedder', which comes in varying shades of blue, combines beautifully with *Penstemon* 'Sour Grapes'. To create a restful mood, try fronting spires of purplish-blue delphiniums with a mass of violet-blue *Geranium ibericum*.

Including white flowers in a planting with a lot of soft blues and pinks will soothe the whole effect; blue and pink with occasional pure white highlights is a favourite scheme for the summer border.

While some gardeners will relish a totally hot composition, most will want to use red with some discretion at this time of the year. Even a combination of bright red and blue, achieved perhaps by planting red oriental poppies with blue anchusas, can be too strong for some. If you prefer a pink-and-pastel summer mix, do include the occasional hot red such as *Penstemon, Kniphofia* or *Crocosmia* to add some spice.

***Above:** The stunning white bloom of the Easter or Bermuda lily* (Lilium longiflorium).

A White Border

Cool white summer plantings can be centred on white lilies, perhaps combining them with 'Iceberg' roses, hazy *Gypsophila* and white *Penstemon*. Lilies make a good focal point in the border, and will flower above a sea of

Above: The glorious white flowers of Rosa *'Madame Hardy' will enhance a traditional cottage garden.*

herbaceous plants. The Madonna lily *(Lilium candidum)* is a traditional cottage garden plant that blends well with old-fashioned roses. You could fill out such a scheme with *Hebe rakaiensis* and grey-green leaved *Anaphalis triplinervis*, both white flowered. You could also include silvery-leaved plants.

Effects with Climbers

The evergreen foliage of the many types of conifers provides a superb foil for the bright blooms of summer-flowering climbers. Climbers can also be allowed to scramble through formally trained plants, creating different effects. Mixing violet-blue *Clematis* 'Ascotiensis' with the creamy white old-fashioned *Rosa* 'Albéric Barbier', for instance, produces a cool, striking result and will provide colour over a long period.

Late-flowering clematis can be encouraged to meander through heathers. The less vigorous, small-flowered viticella or texensis types of clematis, in the same colour range as the heathers, are best for this purpose (summer-flowering species would be too rampant). The flowers of *Clematis* 'Royal Velours' glow like rubies against the velvety old-gold foliage of *Erica carnea* 'Foxhollow', for instance. If you plant a clematis among winter-flowering *Erica*, however, you will have to cut it back in late autumn rather than late winter, as is generally recommended, so that the clematis does not smother the heather flowers. Clematis can also be grown up small trees to add interest to the lower section, which is without leaves.

Above: Climbers planted together prolong the colour in an area. Here Rosa *'Iceberg' is grown with* Clematis tangutica.

Autumn

AUTUMN MAY WELL SIGNIFY THE END OF SUMMER, BUT IT COMPENSATES WITH A FLUSH OF GLORIOUS COLOUR. WARM YELLOWS, BURNING ORANGES AND BRONZE, AND FIERY REDS AND PURPLES ARE NEVER BETTER THAN NOW.

PLANTS AT THEIR BEST

Mellowed by the slanting autumn light, colours at this time of year become more muted, but there are still plenty of bright flowers around. Additionally, the tints and hues of foliage, berries and other fruit make this season a celebration of reds and browns which glow in the light and bring a warmth to the garden.

Above: *The magnificent autumn flowering bulb* Crinum x powellii *is also known as the Cape Lily.*

Above: *The foliage of an* Acer *tree is at its best in the autumn.*

Bulbs

Autumn-flowering bulbs are a delight, with exotic dahlias and cannas vying for attention with strident colours and bold foliage. Nerines bear their large heads of frilly, bright pink, trumpet-shaped flowers. Colchicums are found in various shades of lilac, pink and white and will grow in borders or grass in sun or partial shade. Other autumn highlights include the sternbergias, with their bright yellow, crocus-like flowers and crinums, which produce a wonderful array of large, pink, funnel-shaped flowers.

The open, cup-shaped flowers of the kaffir lily (*Schizostylis coccinea*) are available in shades of pink or red.

Perennials

Many perennial plants run on into autumn from summer but true autumn has its own distinctive flora. Michaelmas daisies (*Aster*) are one of the mainstays of the season, as are chrysanthemums, while vibrantly coloured sedums are invaluable for attracting the last of the butterflies and bees.

Yellows, oranges and bronzes are plentiful, with coneflowers *(Rudbeckia)* and sunflowers *(Helianthus)* in full flower, but there are also deep purple ironweeds *(Vernonia)*. Lilyturf *(Liriope)* has blue spikes of flowers and is useful because it is one of the few autumn-flowering plants that will grow in shade.

***Above:** Many shrubs have stunning berries in the autumn. Here* Pyracantha *is covered with glowing orange berries.*

***Above:** The autumn border will look glorious with a display of* Aster x frikartii.

Shrubs

Fuchsias, buddlejas, hibiscus and hydrangeas all continue to bloom in autumn. One of the few true autumn-flowering shrubs is *Osmanthus heterophyllus*, with fragrant white flowers. *Ceratostigma willmottianum* has piercingly blue flowers that continue well into autumn and *Eucryphia glutinosa* bears glistening white flowers with a central boss of stamens.

Foliage and Berries

The true glory of autumn, of course, belongs to foliage. Paramount for autumn beauty are the acers, trees and shrubs, which have a stunning range of leaf shades. Berries and other fruit are an added bonus; they are attractive and supply birds and other animals with a valuable food resource.

Above: *The red leaves of* Acer palmatum *'Sakazuki' make a fiery climax to the year.*

Colour Combinations

The abundance of plant material and vibrant colour in the garden during autumn can provide some stimulating effects. Autumn flower colours can be arranged to harmonize with the season's colourful berries and changing leaves.

Beds and Borders

Whilst daisy-like plants such as chrysanthemums, dendranthemas, asters and the yellow-flowered *Rudbeckia* 'Goldsturm' are the mainstay of autumn borders, there are other plants that can be utilized, too.

Daisy plants can be combined with late-flowering dazzlers such as the white-flowered *Anemone japonica* 'Honorine Jobert'. *Achillea ptarmica* 'The Pearl', also white flowered, and *Campanula lactiflora*, are also good choices to extend the late summer border well into autumn.

Sedums take on some glowing hues now. At the front of a border, the pink-mauve flowers of the iceplant *Sedum* x *spectabile* 'Brilliant' planted with an eye-catching daisy plant like *Dendranthema* 'Raquel' would provide a long period of strong colour. Hostas could be substituted for sedums to edge a border. *Hosta* 'Honeybells' and *H.* 'Green fountain' both provide particularly glowing foliage as well as useful flowers. *Cephalaria gigantea* would make a bold display at the back of the border.

Contrasting Shapes

Some interesting effects can be engineered by planting contrasting shapes and textures together. The tall, slender

Above: *The autumn-flowering succulent* Sedum spectabile *is a seasonal highlight.*

Above: Cortaderia selloana *'Sunningdale Silver' is at its most splendid in the autumn months.*

flower spikes of cannas, which rise above their spiralling oval leaves, often brilliantly coloured at this time of year, can be contrasted with the roundness of dahlia flowers. These range from the large open flowers of the single forms to the round, tight balls of the Pompon varieties.

Dahlias also make interesting associations with ornamental grasses. Plant them with grasses such as *Calamagrostis* x *acutifolia*, *Miscanthus sinensis* or *Cortaderia selloana* to create a graceful picture. Try placing the copper-orange spikes of *Canna* 'Wyoming' alongside *Dahlia* 'David Howard' together with the lilac-purple flowers of *Verbena bonariensis*.

Right: *Autumn is renowned for the warm tones of its plants and foliage.* Dahlia *'David Howard' has glowing flowers.*

PLANTS AT THEIR BEST

EARLY AUTUMN
Anemone japonica
Aster novae-angliae
Aster novi-belgii
Chrysanthemum, early-flowering garden type
Dahlia
Hibiscus syriacus
Pyracantha
Rudbeckia
Sedum spectabile
Solidago
Sternbergia lutera

MID-AUTUMN
Acer
Anemone japonica
Aster novi-belgii
Fothergilla
Liriope muscari
Schizostylis coccinea

LATE AUTUMN
Berberis
Cotoneaster
Fothergilla
Gentiana sino-ornata
Liriope muscari
Nerine bowdenii
Pernettya
Pyracantha

Winter

GARDENS CAN BE FULL OF COLOUR AT THIS TIME OF YEAR. THERE IS PLENTY TO SEE AND ENJOY, FROM STRIKING STEMS AND FOLIAGE TO BRIGHT FLOWERS THAT WILL DISPEL THE WINTER GLOOM.

PLANTS AT THEIR BEST

Winter light shows up plants in relief. Silvers and greys are sympathetic to the season, and green takes on new importance. Many evergreen shrubs, especially those with shiny leaves, can look particularly good in the weak winter sunlight.

Bulbs

There are many dainty winter-flowering bulbs and corms, including snowdrop cultivars, winter aconites (*Eranthis hyemalis*), early crocuses, dwarf irises, tiny cyclamen and *Anemone blanda*. The earliest daffodils, such as *Narcissus* 'January Gold', are slightly taller.

***Above:** Winter aconites bring a touch of colour at the end of the year.*

The Algerian iris (*Iris unguicularis*) starts flowering in late autumn and continues until early spring, whatever the weather. Its mauve or purple flowers are deliciously scented.

Perennials

Primroses (*Primula vulgaris*) often flower sporadically at this time of year, and sweet violets (*Viola odorata*) will flower in warm spots. Hellebores (*Helleborus*) are one of the mainstays of the perennial scene in winter.

***Left:** Clump-forming hellebores add colour and architectural interest in winter.*

Above: *Conifers retain their glowing colours throughout the winter.*

Shrubs

Many shrubs provide plenty of interest during winter months. Winter jasmine (*Jasminum nudiflorum*) is truly a winter plant, flowering from the end of autumn through to early spring, untroubled by frost and snow. Jasmine stems taken indoors make attractive winter flower decorations.

Winter hazels (*Corylopsis*), with their lovely yellow catkins, also make excellent winter plants. Witch hazels (*Hamamelis*) produce curious flowers, resembling clusters of tiny ribbons. As well as being attractive, they have a prominent smell that fills the air. Several viburnums flower during winter. *Viburnum tinus* is evergreen and covered with flat heads of small white flowers throughout most of the winter and often right through into spring.

Coloured Stems

Some shrubs are prized for the colours of their bare stems in winter. When planted to catch the low winter sunshine, they make a wonderful display. Dogwoods (*Cornus*) are renowned for the beauty of their stems with colours ranging from red though to yellow. *C. alba* is scarlet. Vibrant *C. stolonifera* 'Flaviramea' has yellowish green bark. *Rubus* 'Golden Veil', which has bright yellow foliage in summer, sports white stems in winter.

Several of the willows (*Salix*) have beautiful winter stems, which bear distinctive catkins at the end of the season. *S. alba* produces some of the best coloured stems, but there are many other good species.

Above: Daphne burkwoodii *has an intense scent as well as delightful pink flowers.*

Colour Combinations

As colour is so precious at this time of year and valued in its own right, planting combinations seem to have less importance than during other seasons. Nonetheless there are some delightful associations to be enjoyed.

Above: A welcome sight in the winter, Cyclamen coum *and snowdrops.*

Brightening the Gloom

The early woodland bulbs and perennials naturally favour locations under bushes and trees where they enjoy precious sunshine before the newly-formed leafy canopy obstructs their light and they cease flowering.

Snowdrops (*Galanthus*) multiply quickly where they are growing, especially in their natural habitat in damp woodland, and will eventually spread to carpet vast areas with white and green. In the garden, you can plant them under shrubs to create a similar, if scaled down, effect. Winter aconites (*Eranthis hyemalis*) grown this way provide welcome splashes of yellow, rather than white, in dark places.

Above: *The bright red stems of* Cornus *lighten a wintery scene when branches are bare.*

WINTER SHRUBS

(Shrubs marked * are best cut back hard each spring for their winter stem effect.)

*Berberis temolacia**
Cornus alba 'Sibirica'*
Cornus sanguinea 'Winter Beauty'*
Cornus stolonifera 'Flaviramea'*
Garrya elliptica
Hamamelis mollis
Mahonia x *media* 'Charity'
Prunus subhirtella 'Autumnalis'
Rubus thibetanus
Salix alba var. vitellina 'Britzensis'*
Salix irrorata
Viburnum x *bodnantense* 'Dawn'
Viburnum tinus

Above: Heather can be relied on to add colour to the winter garden.

Effects with Grasses

The evergreen grass, *Stipa arundinacea*, which thrives in dry shade, can be used in a similar but altogether more stunning way, by being underplanted with a skirt of *Bergenia cordifolia*. The impact of the bergenias' purple-tinged, heart-shaped leaves beneath the arching orange-brown fronds of the grass is heightened when rose-red to dark pink, winter flowers on dark red stems come into play.

Winter Heathers

The glowing colours of winter heathers can be strikingly combined with some of the more colourful shrubs. Varieties of *Erica carnea* and *E.* x *darleyensis* can be mixed with the colourful stems of dogwoods (*Cornus*) and some varieties of willow (*Salix*). Selections of *Calluna vulgaris* with highly coloured foliage, such as 'Beoly Gold' (bright golden yellow) or 'Robert Chapman' (gold turning orange-red) will also complement plants with interesting stems. Many heathers look good when matched with shrubs such as *Viburnum* x *bodnantense* 'Dawn' or white-stemmed birches such as *Betula utilis* var. *jacquemontii*.

PLANTS AT THEIR BEST

EARLY WINTER
Hamamelis mollis
Iris unguicularis
Jasminum nudiflorum
Mahonia 'Charity'
Nerine bowdenii
Pernettya, berries
Prunus x *subhirtella* 'Autumnalis'
Pyracantha, berries
Sarcococca
Viburnum

MID-WINTER
Chimonanthus praecox
Eranthis hyemalis
Erica carnea
Erica x *darleyensis*
Galanthus nivalis
Garrya elliptica
Ilex, berries
Lonicera fragrantissima
Sarcococca

LATE WINTER
Crocus
Daphne mezereum
Eranthis hyemalis
Garrya elliptica
Helleborus
Iris unguicularis
Jasminum nudiflorum
Prunus x *subhirtella* 'Autumnalis'
Viburnum

Plants for Seasonal Colour

*Plants marked * require acid soil; those marked with ^ alkaline soil. Plant positions: (d) free-draining; (m) moist soil; (s) sun; (ps) partial shade; (fs) full shade.*

Botanical name	Sow	Plant out	Season of interest and colour
Acer (s)	N/A	autumn/spring	autumn foliage
Achillea (s)	spring, in situ	N/A	summer, yellow/autumn, pink
Allium (s)	spring	autumn	summer, autumn
Alyssum (s, d)	spring/autumn	summer	summer, yellow or white
Anemone blanda (s, ps, d)	spring	autumn	spring, blue, pink, white
Aster x *frikartii* (s, ps, d)	spring/autumn	autumn/spring	early autumn, violet-purple
Aubrieta (s, d)	autumn/spring	spring/autumn	late spring, mauve
Berberis (s, ps)	N/A	autumn/spring	autumn foliage, berries
Bergenia (s, ps)	spring	summer	spring, pink
Buddleja (s)	N/A	autumn/spring	summer, mauve, pink, white
Calluna vulgaris * (s)	N/A	autumn/spring	summer, autumn, pink, white
Canna (s)	spring/autumn	early summer	summer, autumn, red, yellow
Chimonanthus praecox (s, d)	spring	autumn/spring	winter, yellow
Chionodoxa (s, d)	late spring	autumn	early spring, blue, pink
Choisya ternata (s)	N/A	autumn/spring	late spring, autumn, white
Chrysanthemum (s, m)	early spring	early summer	early autumn, many colours
Clematis summer-flowering (s, ps, d)	N/A	autumn/spring	summer, many colours
Clematis viticella (s, ps, d)	N/A	autumn/spring	summer, autumn, blue, purple
Colchicum autumnale (s)	N/A	summer	autumn, pink
Cortaderia selloana (s, d)	spring	summer	late summer, plumes
Cotinus coggygria 'Royal Purple' (s, ps, m, d)	N/A	autumn/spring	year-round, purple foliage
Crocosmia 'Lucifer' (s, ps, m)	N/A	spring	summer, red

Botanical name	Sow	Plant out	Season of interest and colour
Crocus (s, most d)	N/A	autumn	late winter/early spring, many colours
Dahlia (s, d)	spring	summer	late summer/early autumn, many colours
Delphinium (s, d)	spring	autumn	summer, blue, pink, white
Dianthus (s)	spring	early summer	summer, pink, white, red
Doronicum (ps)	spring	autumn	spring, yellow
Echium vulgare 'Blue Bedder' (s, d)	summer	spring	summer, blue
Eranthis hyemalis (s)	spring	autumn	winter/early spring, yellow
Erica carnea * (s, d)	N/A	autumn	winter, purple-pink
Erica cinerea * (s, d)	N/A	autumn	summer, white, pink, purple
Forsythia (s)	N/A	autumn	spring, yellow
Fuchsia hybrids (s, ps, m)	spring	autumn	summer, pink, mauve
Galanthus nivalis (ps)	spring	autumn	winter, white
Garrya elliptica (s, d)	N/A	autumn/spring	winter, spring catkins
Geranium (s, ps)	spring	autumn	early summer, pink, mauve
Gladiolus (s, d)	spring	early summer	summer, many colours
Gloxinia (ps, m)	spring	autumn	summer, pink, lavender
Gypsophila ^ (s)	spring, in situ	N/A	summer, white, pink
Hamamelis mollis (s, ps, m)	N/A	autumn/spring	winter, yellow, orange
Hedera (s, fs)	N/A	autumn/spring	year-round foliage
Helenium (s)	spring	autumn	summer, orange, yellow
Helleborus niger (ps, m)	N/A	autumn/spring	winter, white

Botanical name	Sow	Plant out	Season of interest and colour
Hosta (fs)	N/A	autumn/spring	year-round foliage
Hyacinthus (s, d)	N/A	autumn	spring, many colours
Hydrangea (s, ps)	N/A	autumn/spring	summer/early autumn, white, blue, pink
Ilex (s)	N/A	autumn/spring	winter, berries
Iris unguicularis (s, d)	N/A	early summer	winter, white, lavender, blue
Jasminum nudiflorum (s, ps)	N/A	autumn	winter, yellow
Juniperus (s, d)	N/A	autumn/spring	year-round foliage
Kniphofia (s, ps)	spring	early summer	summer, red, orange
Lathyrus odoratus (s, m)	spring	early summer	summer, many colours
Lavandula (s)	spring	autumn	summer, lavender
Lilium * (s, ps)	N/A	autumn	summer, many colours
Liriope muscari (fs)	spring	early summer	autumn, winter, purple
Lobelia erinus (ps, m)	spring	early summer	summer, many colours
Lobularia maritima (s, d)	spring	early summer	summer, white, pink
Lonicera fragrantissima (ps, d)	spring	autumn	winter, yellow, pink
Magnolia stellata * (s, ps, m)	N/A	autumn/spring	spring, white
Mahonia (fs)	N/A	autumn/spring	winter/spring, yellow
Miscanthus (s, ps, m)	early spring	autumn	year-round foliage
Muscari armeniacum (s, m)	spring	autumn	late winter, early spring, blue
Myosotis (s, m)	spring, in situ	N/A	early summer, blue
Narcissus (s, m)	N/A	autumn	spring, white, yellow
Nerine bowdenii (s, d, m)	N/A	spring	autumn, pink
Nicotiana (s, ps, m)	spring, in situ	N/A	summer, many colours
Paeonia (s, ps)	N/A	autumn/spring	early summer, many colours
Papaver orientale (s, d)	spring	early summer	early summer, scarlet
Papaver somniferum (s, d)	spring, in situ	N/A	summer, mauve, red, white
Pelargonium (s)	late winter/ early spring	summer	summer, red, pink
Penstemon (s, ps)	spring	early summer	summer, many colours

Botanical name	Sow	Plant out	Season of interest and colour
Perovskia atriplicifolia (s, d)	N/A	autumn/spring	late summer, blue
Petunia (s,d)	spring	summer	summer, pink, purple
Philadelphus (s, ps)	N/A	autumn/spring	early summer, white
Primula Polyanthus Group (s, ps, most m)	early spring	autumn	spring, many colours
Primula vulgaris (ps)	early spring	autumn	spring, purple
Pulsatilla vulgaris (s, d)	N/A	autumn/spring	late winter, yellow
Pyracantha (s, ps)	N/A	autumn/spring	autumn berries
Ranunculus ficaria (fs)	spring	autumn	spring, yellow
Rhododendron * (ps)	N/A	autumn/spring	spring, many colours
Ribes sanguineum (s, d)	N/A	autumn/spring	spring, pinkish white
Romneya coulteri (s, d)	spring	autumn	summer, white
Rosa (s, m)	N/A	autumn/spring	summer, many colours
Rudbeckia (s)	spring	autumn	summer, autumn, yellow
Salvia splendens (s, m)	spring	summer	summer, red
Schizostylis coccinea (s, m)	spring	autumn	autumn, pink, red
Sedum spectabile (s, d)	autumn	spring	early autumn, pink
Solidago (s, d)	N/A	autumn/spring	late summer/early spring, white
Spiraea 'Arguta' (s)	N/A	autumn/spring	spring, white
Stachys byzantina (s, d)	autumn/spring	autumn/spring	summer, purple
Stipa arundinacea (s, ps, d)	spring	autumn	year-round foliage
Tagetes (s)	spring	summer	summer, orange, yellow
Trillium (fs)	spring	autumn	spring, white
Tropaeolum majus (s, d)	spring	summer	summer, orange, red
Tulipa (s, d)	N/A	autumn	spring, many colours
Verbena (s, m)	autumn, spring	summer	summer, pink, purple, white
Viburnum x *bodnantense* (s, ps, m)	N/A	autumn/spring	winter, pink
Viburnum tinus (s, ps, m)	N/A	autumn/spring	winter, white
Viola Universal (s, ps, m)	summer	autumn	winter, many colours
Zinnia (s, d)	spring	summer	summer, orange, yellow

ANNUAL ATTRACTION

They may be short-lived, but annuals and biennials come in just about every shade you could want. Whether you sow them directly into the soil to fill gaps or use them as seasonal bedding schemes, they reward you with abundant colour, in many cases all summer long. Being temporary, these garden fillers allow you to experiment and ring the changes from year to year.

Beautiful Borders

When a garden is in need of an instant face-lift, annuals are the perfect answer. They provide a colourful display over a long period, yet being temporary, they allow you to experiment with different schemes each year.

What is an Annual?

The simple definition of an annual is a plant that grows from seed, then flowers, sets seed and dies all within a year. However, gardening is never that simple, and several other types of plants, including short-lived perennials and tender perennials, are often treated as annuals in the garden. Biennials are a related group which also need to be replaced, but their life cycle takes two years to complete.

Biennials and Tender Perennials

Unlike annuals, biennials are sown in one year, planted out in the autumn and flower during the following year, usually in spring or early summer. Short-lived perennials are plants, such as snapdragons and pansies, which flower best in their first year and so are normally discarded and replaced, but they can have their flowering stems removed in order to produce flowers again in the following

***Above:** A mixture of annuals in a large bedding scheme. Such designs can be scaled down for the small garden.*

Above: *Tender perennials are often treated as annuals. Here both dahlias and verbenas belong to this group.*

summer. Tender perennials are plants, such as geraniums and dahlias, which cannot be overwintered outside in colder climates. These can be kept indoors over winter, but many people prefer to replace them, particularly when using them as bedding plants.

Hardiness

Annuals are also categorized according to their hardiness. Hardy annuals are those that can be sown outside in autumn or spring. Half-hardy annuals will not tolerate frost and are usually sown indoors for planting out when the frosts are over. Those that grow quickly enough, however, can be sown outside at the end of spring for flowering that summer. Tender annuals need to be sown in a greenhouse to ensure a long enough growing season – again, they are planted out when there is no danger of frost.

POPULAR TENDER PERENNIALS

Alcea rosea
Alonsoa warscewiczii
Antirrhinum majus
Argyranthemum
Chrysanthemum
Felicia amelloides
Dahlia
Impatiens
Pelargonium
Salvia splendens
Semperflorens begonias
Verbena x *hybrida*

POPULAR BIENNIALS

Campanula medium
Dianthus barbatus
Digitalis purpurea
Erysimum (*Cheiranthus*)
Matthiola incana
Oenothera biennis
Silybum marianum
Verbascum

Above: *Honesty,* Lunaria annua, *is a versatile, self-sowing biennial.*

Value for Money

The great thing about annuals is their value for money. Many are easy to raise from seed, which can be highly rewarding. Indeed, with those hardy annuals that can be sown in situ, growing them from seed is scarcely any more trouble than buying plants. Some are more difficult to germinate, but small plants can often be bought very cheaply, and in most cases they will flower for a long period, often from late spring right through to the first frosts of winter.

Variety

Annuals have a wide range of attributes which mean that they can be used and appreciated in a number of ways. Colour is obviously one of their main qualities. This can be from dazzling reds to very subtle pinks and blues. Some have very colourful or shapely leaves and are used as foliage plants, others have a mixture of both attractive flowers and foliage. Many have delicious scents – you only have to think of sweet peas or heliotropes.

Annuals in the Garden

There are many situations in the garden where annuals are useful. One of their most popular uses is as container plants. They are perfect for containers of all sorts, from hanging baskets and window boxes to a wide variety of pots, tubs and troughs. They are also frequently used as bedding plants, either in a random, informal way for a cottage-style effect, or in traditional formal bedding schemes with geometrical designs. Some annuals have a more limited flowering period and these tend to mix in with perennials very well. Some gardeners grow annuals in separate beds, often in the vegetable garden, specifically for cutting to use in flower arranging, or for exhibition purposes.

Left: *Annuals are great in containers. They are colourful, long flowering and not difficult to look after.*

How to Use This Chapter

This chapter will introduce you to a wide range of annuals, all of which are relatively easy to grow and will definitely enhance your garden, whether it be simply confined to a couple of hanging baskets or an area the size of a soccer pitch. As well as firing your enthusiasm, there is also plenty of practical information. *Using Annuals Effectively* gives advice on choosing plants that will suit the conditions in your garden, as well as suggestions for a variety of ways of planting annuals, depending on the style of garden you want to create. You will then find useful charts listing annuals by colour and height – invaluable information for designing bedding schemes. In this chapter you will find all you need to know to create a beautiful display of colourful plants that will give you and your friends pleasure throughout the summer.

Above: *Trailing petunias are perfect for hanging baskets, and come in a huge range of colours. Shades of yellow and white are used here to great effect, combined with red geraniums and busy Lizzies.*

Above: *There would not be bedding without annuals. The even height and vivid colour of these geraniums makes them perfect for use in such schemes.*

Using Annuals Effectively

THE TEMPORARY NATURE OF ANNUALS MAKES THEM IDEAL PLANTS FOR EXPERIMENTING WITH INTERESTING EFFECTS. IT IS WORTH TRYING OUT UNUSUAL COMBINATIONS OF COLOUR AND FORM – IF YOU ARE NOT HAPPY WITH THE RESULTS YOU CAN CHANGE THEM NEXT YEAR.

GETTING THE CONDITIONS RIGHT

Many of the annuals grown in gardens are reasonably tolerant of a wide range of conditions, though most will perform best in a sunny, well-drained site. If your soil is very heavy, you can improve the drainage by adding plenty of horticultural grit or sand – this is especially helpful in a very wet or sunless site which might be prone to waterlogging. Shade is more difficult to counteract – light shade is fine for most annuals, but if it is very deep shade, you will be limited in your choice of plants. Foxgloves, for example, may succeed, and busy Lizzies are also worth trying – they are one of the few plants that will give a really colourful show in a shady spot, yet they are also happy in sun.

Above: *Some annuals self-sow freely once they have flowered. Here, they have sown themselves a little too closely together, but if thinned out they should flower again with no further attention.*

Above: *These sweet Williams are a mixture of colours that harmonize together very well. Care would be needed when adding other plants to the scheme, so as not to spoil the effect.*

Getting the Scheme Right

Annuals are versatile plants. You may choose to use them simply as flowering plants mixed in with perennials in the border – this can be a good way to create a cottage-garden effect, particularly if you allow the plants to self-sow randomly. They can also be used as temporary fillers in a more planned mixed border.

Many gardeners, on the other hand, prefer to create bedding schemes made up entirely of annuals, and this is an ideal way to create a formal design. Whichever way you want to use annuals, their ephemeral nature means that you can try out a different scheme each year. Since annuals offer such a wide range of bold, bright colours, as well as more delicate, subtle ones, there is plenty of scope for imaginative self-expression.

***Above:** This delightful spring border, combining deep blue forget-me-nots and pink daisies with delicate tulips, shows a careful use of colour while still creating an attractively informal effect.*

Getting the Plants Right

If you want to make things easy for yourself, particularly if you are new to gardening, you will probably do well to choose from the many plants that are widely available in garden centres, or those that you see flourishing in other people's gardens. The reason for their popularity is usually their reliability – often these are the plants that will flower for a long period, suffering few problems. However, you may wish to be more adventurous. Seed catalogues will offer a far wider range of plants, so if you grow from seed you will be able to create more interesting and unusual effects. Some of the less common plants may have shorter flowering periods, but you can allow for this when planning your scheme. If you do not want to raise seeds, try mail-order plant suppliers – many of these will produce a wider range than you can find at most garden centres.

Bedding Schemes

Many annuals, particularly the smaller varieties, will grow very uniformly in terms of height, size and colour. These are ideal for bedding schemes where blocks or patterns are required.

Above: This design has been created entirely from foliage plants, showing that different leaf colours can produce an effect as striking as flowers.

The possibilities for creativity here are endless – it is a good idea to visit public parks and gardens for inspiration, particularly if you want to make a traditional, formal scheme. However, there is no need to restrict yourself to traditional patterns. Geometrical shapes can also be used in new and striking ways, or you may want to create a softer effect, perhaps with swirling lines or colours subtly merging into one another. If your design contains intricate details, make sure you choose only small, neat plants that will suit the scheme.

Colour and Texture

Bedding plants can be used almost like a paintbox – indeed, you might even find inspiration for your design by visiting an art gallery for colour ideas, as well as the more obvious approach of wandering around garden centres looking at different plants and placing them together to see how they combine. Do not overlook the value of foliage plants – many bedding plants are grown purely for their foliage, and these are often silver-leaved, with interesting furry textures. There are also some with deep red or purple leaves, or variegated plants such as coleus, with many colour variations.

Above: Large triangular blocks of colour, here using geraniums and busy Lizzies in shades of pink and purple, create a vivid impact in this border.

GARDENER'S TIP

Remember that the smaller and neater the plants you use, the more detailed and intricate your design can be.

Above: A neatly clipped box parterre with a filling of summer plants. When these are finished they will be replaced by colourful winter pansies.

Infilling with Colour

Blocks of colours can be used to fill in shapes within an outline, which can be 'drawn' either with a single variety of small annual – foliage plants are often a good choice – or with a line of permanent small hedging plants such as box. The latter is the classic method for creating a traditional parterre. Though this will be a permanent feature, you will still be able to vary the annuals that are planted within the shapes.

Varying the Height

Plants of different heights can be used to great effect in bedding schemes. You need to be careful with detailed patterns – if taller plants are hiding smaller ones the effect can be spoiled. However, by grading the heights so that taller plants are towards the back of a border, or in the centre of an island bed, you can create a design that still looks very neat and regular while gaining extra interest from the added vertical dimension.

Creating the Design

It is often difficult to imagine how a scheme will look when it is planted out, and it can be helpful to draw it on paper first, using crayons or coloured pencils. If you make your drawing to scale, you can also use it to work out how many plants you are likely to need – this is particularly useful if you are covering a large area.

Mixing It

Many of the annuals work well in a mixed border with perennials, in an informal cottage-garden style. This is particularly good for more subtle and unobtrusive flowers, such as the soft blue or white love-in-a-mist, or toad-flax in various delicate colours. These also have short flowering seasons, making them less suitable for bedding schemes, but in an informal border they can come and go, and can be allowed to self-sow. It is less easy to fit in some of the more strongly-coloured annuals, such as busy Lizzies, so choose your plants carefully.

Above: *The pale pink shades of* Cleome *blend in well with the perennials in this mixed border.*

Above: *The temporary gaps between these young shrubs are being planted with nasturtiums, which will soon spread out and fill the space.*

Temporary Fillers

Annuals are perfect candidates for filling gaps in a border. If for example you have just planted a number of shrubs, then it will be several years before they have filled their allotted space and during that time the gaps can be filled by annuals. In the perennial border, early season plants finish flowering and their remains, often unattractive, can be hidden by planting annuals in front of them. Winter annuals can be used to fill beds that will be planted up permanently in the following spring. Filling temporary gaps with annuals not only improves the appearance of the garden, avoiding boring expanses of bare soil, but the plants can also act as a useful ground cover, especially if planted relatively close together. This will reduce the occurrence of weeds, as well as preventing erosion of the empty soil by the weather.

Going Up in the World

There are a handful of annuals which are climbing plants, the best-known being sweet peas and nasturtiums. Some tender perennial climbers are also used as annuals, such as *Cobaea scandens* – this could also be grown in a tub and overwintered indoors. Climbers can be used to scramble up through other plants, perhaps providing colourful blooms after the host plant's flowers have finished. They can be grown up sticks in the centre of a bedding scheme, trained up trellising or allowed to spread out to make colourful ground cover.

Above: *No cottage garden would be complete without the delicious scent of sweet peas.*

Above: *Climbing annuals, such as this* Ipomoea lobata, *can be used to fill vertical space in a border. They help to relieve boring flat spaces.*

POPULAR ANNUAL CLIMBERS

Asarina erubescens
Cobaea scandens
Convolvulus tricolor
Eccremocarpus scaber
Ipomoea
Lablab purpureus
(syn. *Dolichos lablab*)
Lathyrus odoratus
Lathyrus sativus
Mikania scandens
Rhodochiton atrosanguineum
Thunbergia alata
Tropaeolum majus
Tropaeolum peregrinum

Planning Annuals for Colour

WITH SO MANY PLANTS TO CHOOSE FROM, PLANNING A SCHEME FOR A GARDEN CAN SEEM A DAUNTING PROSPECT. HOWEVER, WITH ANNUALS YOU CAN TRY SOMETHING DIFFERENT EACH YEAR, AND YOU WILL SOON FIND OUT WHAT WORKS WELL IN TERMS OF STYLE AND COLOURING.

RED ANNUALS
Adonis aestivalis
Alcea rosea 'Scarlet'
Cosmos bipinnatus 'Pied Piper Red'
Dianthus chinensis 'Fire Carpet'
Impatiens Tempo Burgundy
Lathyrus odoratus 'Winston Churchill'
Linum grandiflorum
Lobelia erinus 'Rosamund'
Papaver rhoeas
Pelargonium (many red varieties)
Petunia 'Mirage Velvet'
Salvia splendens
Semperflorens begonias
Tagetes patula 'Scarlet Sophie'
Verbena 'Blaze'

ORANGE ANNUALS
Alonsoa warscewiczii
Antirrhinum majus (various varieties)
Calceolaria (various varieties)
Calendula officinalis (various varieties)
Emilia javanica
Erysimum (*Cheiranthus*) 'Fire King'
Eschscholzia californica
Helichrysum bracteatum (various varieties)
Impatiens 'Mega Orange Star'
Mimulus (various varieties)
Nemesia 'Orange Prince'
Rudbeckia hirta (various varieties)
Tagetes erecta (various varieties)
Tithonia rotundifolia 'Torch'
Tropaeolum majus (various varieties)
Zinnia (various varieties)

BLUE ANNUALS
Ageratum houstonianum
Borago officinalis
Brachyscome iberidifolia
Campanula medium
Centaurea cyanus
Cynoglossum amabile
Echium 'Blue Bedder'
Echium vulgare
Felicia bergeriana
Gilia
Godetia bottae 'Lady in Blue'
Legousia pentagonica
Limonium sinuatum 'Azure'
Limonium sinuatum 'Blue Bonnet'
Linanthus liniflorus
Lobelia erinus
Myosotis
Nemophila menziesii
Nigella damascena
Nolana paradoxa 'Blue Bird'
Petunia
Primula (blue varieties)
Salvia farinacea 'Victoria'
Viola x *wittrockiana*

VIOLET AND PURPLE ANNUALS
Antirrhinum 'Purple King'
Callistephus chinensis (various varieties)
Centaurea cyanus 'Black Ball'
Cleome spinosa 'Violet Queen'
Eschscholzia californica 'Purple-Violet'
Eustoma grandiflora
Heliotropium
Hesperis matronalis
Impatiens (purple varieties)
Lathyrus odoratus (various varieties)
Limonium sinuatum 'Midnight' or 'Purple Monarch'
Lunaria annua
Malva sylvestris subsp. *mauritanica*
Orychiophragmus violaceus
Papaver somniferum (purple varieties)
Petunia (purple varieties)

PINK ANNUALS
Alcea rosea 'Rose'
Antirrhinum majus (numerous varieties)

Centaurea cyanus (pink forms)
Dianthus (numerous varieties)
Diascia (numerous varieties)
Godetia grandiflora 'Satin Pink'
Helichrysum bracteatum 'Rose'
Impatiens Impact Rose
Lathyrus odoratus (numerous varieties)
Lavatera trimestris 'Mont Rose'
Nicotiana 'Domino Salmon-Pink'
Nigella damascena 'Miss Jekyll Pink'
Papaver somniferum
Pelargonium (numerous varieties)
Petunia (numerous varieties)
Semperflorens begonias

WHITE ANNUALS
Anoda cristata 'Silver Cup'
Clarkia pulchella 'Snowflake'
Cleome spinosa 'Helen Campbell'
Cosmos bipinnatus 'Purity'
Digitalis purpurea f. *albiflora*
Gypsophila elegans 'Covent Garden'
Helianthus annuus 'Italian White'
Hibiscus trionum
Impatiens Tempo White
Lathyrus odoratus (various varieties)
Lavatera trimestris 'Mont Blanc'
Limonium sinuatum 'Iceberg'
Lunaria annua var. *albiflora*
Malope trifida 'Alba'
Malope trifida 'White Queen'
Nemesia 'Mello White'
Nemophila maculata
Nicotiana sylvestris
Nigella damascena 'Miss Jekyll Alba'
Osteospermum 'Glistening White'
Papaver somniferum (various varieties)
Pelargonium (various varieties)

YELLOW ANNUALS
Alcea rosea 'Yellow'
Anoda cristata 'Buttercup'
Antirrhinum majus (yellow varieties)
Argemone mexicana
Argyranthemum frutescens 'Jamaica Primrose'
Calendula officinalis 'Kablouna'
Chrysanthemum segetum
Cladanthus arabicus
Coreopsis 'Sunray'
Glaucium flavum
Helianthus annuus
Limnanthes douglasii
Limonium sinuatum 'Forever Moonlight'
Limonium sinuatum 'Goldcoast'
Lonas annua
Mentzelia lindleyi
Mimulus (various varieties)
Sanvitalia procumbens
Tagetes erecta (yellow varieties)
Tagetes patula (yellow varieties)
Tripleurospermum inodora 'Gold Pompoms'
Tripleurospermum inodora 'Santana Lemon'
Tropaeolum majus (yellow varieties)
Tropaeolum peregrinum
Viola x *wittrockiana* (yellow varieties)

MIXED-COLOURED ANNUALS
Antirrhinum majus
Linaria maroccana
Dianthus barbatus
Dianthus chinensis
Lathyrus odoratus
Nemesia
Primula
Salpiglossis
Schizanthus
Tagetes
Viola x *wittrockiana*

ANNUALS FOR FOLIAGE
Brassica oleracea
Canna
Coleus blumei
Euphorbia marginata
Galactites tomentosa
Helichrysum petiolare
Ocimum basilicum 'Purple Ruffles'
Onopordum acanthium
Ricinus communis
Senecio cinerea
Silybum marianum
Tropaeolum majus 'Alaska'

ANNUAL GRASSES
Agrostis nebulosa
Briza maxima
Chloris barbata
Hordeum jubatum
Lagurus ovatus
Panicum miliaceum
Tricholaena rosea
Zea mays

Choosing Annuals

THIS QUICK REFERENCE SECTION CAN BE USED TO HELP SELECT THE MOST SUITABLE ANNUALS FOR A VARIETY OF DIFFERENT PURPOSES AND CONDITIONS. IT INCLUDES ANNUALS AND BIENNIALS AS WELL AS TENDER AND SHORT-LIVED PERENNIALS THAT ARE USED AS ANNUALS.

Plant Name	Height	Flower Colour
Ageratum HH/A or B b (t) C	up to 30cm (12in)	blue, pink and white
Alonsoa HH/A b t hb w C	up to 45cm (18in)	scarlet and orange
Amaranthus HH/A b mb C S	up to 1.5m (5ft)	red-purple
Antirrhinum H or HH/SP b t mb C	up to 45cm (18in)	wide range (not blue)
Arctotis H or H/A TP b C	up to 60cm (2ft)	most colours except blue
Argemone HH/A b mb C F	up to 1m (3ft)	white and yellow
Argyranthemum TP b mb t hb w C	up to 60cm (2ft)	pink and yellow
Atriplex H/A b mb F	up to 1.2m (4ft)	foliage red
Begonia Semperflorens TP ps/s b t hb w C	up to 15cm (6in)	white, pink, orange, red and yellow
Bidens ferulifolia HH/SP b t hb w C	up to 90cm (3ft)	yellow
Borago officinalis HH/A b C F He	90cm (3ft)	blue and white
Brachyscome iberidifolia H/A b t hb w C	23cm (9in)	blue, pink and white
Calceolaria HH/A b t hb w C	up to 30cm (12in)	yellow and orange
Calendula officinalis H/A b C He	45cm (18in)	orange, yellow and cream
Callistephus chinensis HH/A b t C Sc	up to 60cm (2ft)	all colours
Canna TP b mb C F	up to 1.5m (5ft)	orange and red, purple foliage (some)
Centaurea cyanus H/A b C	60cm (2ft)	blue, pink and white
Cerinthe major H/A b t C	30cm (12in)	purple flowers, grey foliage
Cheiranthus cheiri H/B b (t) mb C Sc	45cm (18in)	orange, yellow and red

Calceolaria

Lathyrus odoratus

Chrysanthemum TP b t w C Sc Cu	1.2m (4ft)	all except true blue
Clarkia HH/A b t hb w C	up to 50cm (20in)	pink, red and mauve
Cleome HH/A b mb C S	up to 1.2m (4ft)	pink, white and purple
Collinsia H/A b tolerates ps C	up to 30cm (12in)	bicoloured in pink and purple
Consolida HH/A b (t) C	up to 45cm (18in)	blue, white, pink and purple
Convolvulus tricolor HH/A b hb C	up to 30cm (12in)	tricoloured mainly blue with white and yellow
Coreopsis tinctoria H/A b (t) C	up to 1.2m (4ft)	yellow, red, purple and brown forms
Cosmos HH *or* H/A b mb C	90cm (3ft)	red, pink and white
Dahlia TP b C Cu	1.2m (4ft)	all colours except true blue
Dianthus chinensis H/A b (t) mb e C	up to 23cm (9in)	pink, red and white
Echium H/A or B b t w C	up to 60cm (2ft)	blue, purple and pink
Eschscholzia HH/A b mb C	up to 15cm (6in)	orange, cream and yellow
Eustoma grandiflorus T/A or B b C	up to 45cm (18in)	blue, purple, pink and white
Felicia HH/A b t hb w C	up to 60cm (2ft)	blue and white
Gomphrena globosa T/A b C	up to 60cm (2ft)	red, pink, purple and white
Helianthus H/A b C S	up to 2.5m (8ft)	yellow
Helichrysum HH/A or TP b t hb w C F	up to 60cm (2ft)	white, pink and yellow
Heliotropium HH/A b (t w) C Sc	45cm (18in)	violet
Hesperis matronalis H/B b mb C Sc	1.2m (4ft)	mauve and white
Hordeum jubatum H/A grass b C S	up to 45cm (18in)	
Iberis H/A b e t C	up to 30cm (12in)	white and pink
Impatiens TP b t hb w tolerates ps C	up to 30cm (12in)	red, orange, purple, pink and white
Ipomoea T/A b C	up to 5m (15ft) climber	blue, pink, purple and red
Isatis tinctoria H/B b C He	up to 1.2m (4ft)	yellow
Lathyrus odoratus H/A b C Sc Cu	up to 1.8m (6ft) climber	red, pink, mauve and white
Lavatera trimestris H/A b C	up to 1.2m (4ft)	pink and white
Limnanthes douglasii H/A b e C Be	15cm (6in)	bicoloured yellow and white

Dahlia

Hesperis matronalis

Linum grandiflorum H/A b mb C	up to 75cm (30in)	red
Lobelia erinus HH/A b e t hb w C	up to 15cm (6in) some trailing	blue, purple and white
Lobularia maritima H/A b e t hb w C	15cm (6in)	white and pink
Lunaria annua H/B b tolerates sh Sp C F	up to 1m (3ft)	purple and white, also variegated foliage forms
Matthiola HH or H/A b t C Sc	up to 45cm (18in)	pink, mauve and white
Melianthus TP b mb F C S	up to 3m (10ft)	red, foliage silver
Moluccella laevis HH/A b C	up to 1m (3ft)	green
Myosotis H/A b t hb w mb tolerates ps C	up to 30cm (12in)	blue
Nemesia HH/A b t hb w C	up to 30cm (12in)	white, blue, yellow and purple
Nicandra physalodes H/A b C F	up to 1m (3ft)	blue
Nicotiana HH/A b t hb w C Sc (some)	up to 2.1m (7ft)	white and pink
Nigella H/A b mb C	60cm (2ft)	blue and white
Oenothera H/B b mb C Sc	90cm (3ft)	yellow, orange and pink (in evening)
Omphalodes linifolia H/A b mb C	up to 25cm (10in)	white
Papaver H/A b mb C	up to 90cm (3ft)	red, mauve, pink and white
Pelargonium TP b t w C F Sc (some)	up to 75cm (30in) some trailing	red, pink and white, some scented foliage
Petunia HH/SP b t hb w C Sc (some)	25cm (10in)	all colours
Phacelia H/A b C	up to 50cm (20in)	blue, lavender and white
Phlox drummondii HH/A b (t) C	up to 45cm (18in)	purple, pale blue, pink and white
Portulaca HH/A b C	up to 20cm (8in)	most colours
Ricinus HH/A b F	up to 3m (10ft)	red, foliage red and bronze
Rudbeckia HH/A b mb C	up to 1m (3ft)	yellow, gold, orange-red and brown
Salpiglossis HH/A b t C	up to 60cm (2ft)	most colours
Salvia farinacea HH/SP b mb hb t w C	up to 38cm (15in)	scarlet, blue, pink and purple

Lunaria annua

Impatiens

Salvia splendens HH/SP b mb hb t w C	up to 38cm (15in)	scarlet, blue and pink
Salvia viridis HH/A b mb hb t w C	up to 38cm (15in)	scarlet, blue and purple
Sanvitalia H/A b t hb w C	up to 20cm (8in) creeping	yellow
Senecio cineraria (*S. maritima*) TS b t hb w F	up to 60cm (2ft)	flowers yellow, foliage silver
Silybum marianum H/B mb F	up to 75cm (30in)	flowers purple, white-veined leaves
Tagetes HH/A b t hb w C	up to 30cm (12in)	yellow and orange
Tithonia HH/A b mb C	up to 1.2m (4ft)	orange
Tropaeolum majus H/A b (t) C	up to 90cm (3ft) climber	orange, red and yellow
Verbascum H/B b mb S C F	up to 2m (7ft)	yellow
Verbena x *hybrida* TP b hb mb t w C	up to 30cm (12in)	red, purple, pink and white
Viola x *wittrockiana* H/SP b hb mb t w tolerates ps C	25cm (10in)	all colours

KEY TO SYMBOLS

Unless otherwise stated the plants all prefer a sunny position

H = Hardy
HH = Half-hardy
T = Tender
TS = Tender Shrub
A = Annual
B = Biennial
SP = Short-lived Perennial
TP = Tender Perennial
b = beds
e = edging
hb = hanging baskets
mb = mixed borders
t = tubs
(t) = mainly used in beds but some could be used in tubs, pots or similar containers
w = window boxes
ps = partial shade
sh = shade
Be = Grown to attract Bees
C = Grown for Colour
Cu = Grown for Cutting
F = Grown for Foliage
He = Grown as Herb
S = Grown for Shape
Sc = Grown for Scent
Sp = Grown for Seed Pods

Verbena

Tagetes

PERENNIALS

Planted on their own in the herbaceous border, or among structural shrubs in a mixed bed, perennials form part of the permanent planting. They provide flower and foliage interest from spring through to the end of autumn, when they die down for the winter. There are types to suit every garden condition, style and colour scheme, and a carefully planned planting will ensure interest and colour throughout the year.

Everlasting Perennials

PERENNIALS ARE REGAINING THEIR POPULARITY AT THE FOREFRONT OF GARDENING. WHILE SHRUBS PROVIDE THE BASIC STRUCTURE OF A BORDER AND ANNUALS TEMPORARY COLOUR, PERENNIALS FORM THE PERMANENT PLANTINGS THAT CREATE THE MAIN INTEREST.

WHAT IS A PERENNIAL?

In theory, perennials are plants that live more than one or two years. However, in gardening terms there are certain perennials that fit this definition but are not generally included in this category: woody plants, such as trees and shrubs, for example. Within this group some sub-shrubs, including *Dianthus* and *Perovskia*, are usually included as perennials. Alpines, most of which are perennials, are also often considered as a separate category. Bulbs are usually excluded as a group but individuals such as lilies are included. Many perennials are herbaceous plants in that they die back each year below ground and reappear in spring, but there are also those, some irises for example, that wholly or in part remain evergreen throughout the winter.

***Above:** Perennials are suitable for any garden style, such as this lush planting.*

WHY CHOOSE PERENNIALS?

Perennials form the backbone of a garden, adding a wealth of colour, shape and texture. They have the advantage over annuals in that they reappear every year, basically recreating the same border, so that you do not have to worry about the overall picture each year, just the detail. Their versatility is astonishing, as there are plants for every type of garden situation as well as for every style and type of border design. No matter whether you live in the countryside, by the sea or in the middle of town, you will find that there are ample perennials to suit all your needs.

How to Choose Perennials

As when choosing any other garden plants, it is important to consider the physical environment in which you live: the type of soil, whether it is moist or dry, whether it is in sun or shade or exposed to winds. Generally this will limit your choice of plants to some degree but there will still be plenty to choose from. The design is a much more personal matter: deciding which plants will create the look you want. It is important at this stage to consider the colour, shape and texture of not only the flowers but also the foliage and overall planting to obtain the most pleasing effect.

Above: *The contrasting shapes of perennials give the gardener plenty of scope for designing interesting and dynamic borders.*

Above: *This classic mixed border of spring-flowering perennials contains a wonderful mixture of fresh, bright colours.*

Selecting Healthy Plants

From the maintenance point of view it is important to select only plants that are healthy and strong. Some perennials are very tough, in terms of resisting both the weather and disease. These are not necessarily unattractive plants, many having come down to us through cottage gardens, and are always worth considering for a trouble-free garden. Many of the modern cultivars are more brightly coloured and have larger flowers but do not have the same resistance, so select your plants or seeds with care. It is always useful to look at other gardens in your area: plants that are obviously thriving in your neighbours' gardens are also likely to do well for you.

Above: *There are many perennials, such as these primroses, that are robust and will thrive in most garden conditions.*

Above: *This border has a distinctive layered effect, with winter aconites in front of* Helleborus foetidus.

The Importance of Form

The next aspect to consider is the look of the plant. There are innumerable permutations of colour, shape, texture and size, of both the flowers and the foliage, and all these aspects must be taken into consideration when combining plants together to form an attractive border. For example, however much you may like it, a tall red-flowered plant is no substitute where a short red one is required; you will either need to choose another plant, or change the design. It is always best to think about the design, and the function of the plants in the border, before you buy them. The texture and shape of the plant and its foliage are just as important as flower colour and size.

Above: The tall spikes of stately Lythrum salicaria *provide a mass of mauve flowers in the summer. Plant them where they will be noticed.*

A Plant for All Seasons

Another important thing to remember about perennials is their flowering periods. Many only have a relatively short time in flower. This must be co-ordinated with other plants. You will be disappointed if you have two pink plants that you hope will look stunning together, if one flowers in May and the other in September. Likewise, if you choose carefully the border can be full of colour throughout the growing season and often during the winter as well. Many plants also remain attractive when not in flower.

How to Use this Chapter

In this chapter you will find a comprehensive guide to using perennials in a variety of ways. *Perennials in the Garden* gives advice on designing gardens in different styles, taking account of the conditions in your garden, and suggests ways of using perennials to create the effect or garden style that you want. *Perennials for Different Conditions* will help you choose suitable plants for every part of your garden, whether wet or dry, sunny or shady. *Seasonal Splendour* shows you how to maintain interest in your garden throughout the year using shrubs that flower at different times of the year and colourful evergreen foliage. Finally, you will find useful charts listing perennials by colour, size and season of interest, to help you find the plants you need when creating your beds and borders.

Above: Snapdragons are quite short and should be placed near the front of a border for maximum effect.

Perennials in the Garden

THERE ARE COUNTLESS USES FOR PERENNIALS IN THE GARDEN. THEY CAN HELP TO CREATE A WIDE VARIETY OF STYLES, FROM THE FORMAL TO THE ROMANTIC. THEY ARE EQUALLY EFFECTIVE IN THE SMALL GARDEN OR IN THE WIDER SPACES OF A LARGE PLOT.

CONSIDERING YOUR SITE

As with most plants, it is best to grow perennials in sites where they will thrive rather than forcing them into situations where they will languish and probably die. This is not quite as serious as it may sound as most gardens provide areas that will grow a wide variety of plants. However, there are some things to think about. There is no point in growing sun-loving plants in the shade or shade-loving plants in the sun (some shade-loving plants will grow in the sun if the soil is moist enough). Some plants need a moist soil and will soon fade away in dry conditions, and vice versa.

So when considering the style of garden you want, do think about the conditions you can provide and how this will influence your choice. For example, very few silver foliage plants will grow in the shade. The best way to garden successfully is to work with nature and not against it. It may be possible to change the conditions – chop down a tree to let in more light or create a damp area in part of the garden, for example – but this will mean additional work.

***Above:** Using your own style and colour preferences will provide you with a garden that is uniquely yours and will be a source of inspiration for others.*

CHOOSING A STYLE

The style of the garden is largely a matter of personal taste, as perennials will lend themselves to most designs. However, there may be a few restrictions. The site has already been mentioned. It is also important to consider the use of the garden as a whole. For example, if children are regularly playing in the garden, it may be difficult to maintain a formal border – an informal planting will be much more suitable. Similarly, a natural wildflower planting can look very out of place in a formal setting. However, in both these

cases, it may be possible to succeed with such a border if it is isolated, perhaps in its own area of the garden.

The gardener's personality is also important. It is inadvisable to consider having a neat formal border if you are a naturally untidy person who will soon let the border deteriorate. Similarly if your lifestyle is frenetic, with little time to spare, avoid complicated borders that are very time-consuming and perhaps choose something formal where maintenance may be minimal. Frequently style is dictated by needs. If you want to attract wildlife to your garden, then an informal style with plants that bear seeds or nectar will be important, as birds, bees and other beneficial insects rely on them for food.

Above: *You will make a bold statement with a Mediterranean-style planting. There are plenty of plants to choose from and it can be very colourful.*

Above: Aquilegia *and* Meconopsis cambrica *are more suited to an informal or cottage style garden where little maintenance is required. They will tolerate sun or light shade.*

Herbaceous Borders

These are the traditional ways of growing perennial plants. They consist of borders containing nothing other than herbaceous plants. They are usually planted in drifts, generally with the taller specimens at the back and shorter ones at the front. The colours are carefully planned so as to present a harmonious whole. The traditional colour scheme is hot, strong colours in the centre with cooler, softer ones at the ends. Some attractive herbaceous borders can be made by restricting the flowers to one colour, such as red, or perhaps two, such as white and gold or yellow and blue.

Perennials mostly look their best when they are set off against a green background, either shrubs or, better still, a yew hedge. Traditional herbaceous borders were long and often consisted of two parallel beds with a broad path between them. However, they can be of any shape you like to fit in either with your own designs or with the shape of your garden. Herbaceous borders can be quite labour-intensive but if you combine mulching with a "little and often" approach to maintenance, they are surprisingly easy to look after and are very rewarding. A wide range of plants, running to many thousands, are suitable.

Above: *A herbaceous border on a grand scale, with two parallel beds separated by a wide path. With a careful choice of plants it can be kept attractive from spring to autumn.*

Above: A mixed border of perennials and shrubs in early summer, planned to have plenty of colour later in the season.

Above: Island beds can be very effective in a larger garden. Create a path around them with grass, gravel or chipped bark.

Mixed Borders

Nowadays very few gardeners have herbaceous borders in the strictest sense. Most mix in a few other types of plants, such as roses and perhaps a few annuals. There is very little point in being a purist and sticking to one type of plant when the whole object is to create an attractive border. It makes sense to use whatever is available. A few shrubs will add a permanent structure to the border. The foliage of the shrubs can be used to set off the flowers of the plants in front of them. They can also provide a little shade for those plants that need it. In gardening terms there is very little difference between a mixed border and a herbaceous one. The shapes and design can be the same and apart from using other plants, aesthetically the two borders are likely to look very similar in style.

Island Beds

These are exactly the same as herbaceous and mixed beds except that they can be seen from all sides rather than from one or two. The main problem is that there is no background for the plants, so it makes sense to put taller plants in the middle, enabling the others to be seen against them. Shrubs or trees often make a good centre feature as they prevent the eye running straight over the bed to what lies beyond.

PERENNIALS FOR HERBACEOUS, MIXED AND ISLAND BEDS

Achillea
Aster
Campanula
Delphinium
Geranium
Heliopsis
Nepeta
Paeonia
Rudbeckia
Solidago

Cottage Style

Traditional cottage gardens can be very attractive but they can also be a lot of work. Essentially they are borders with a profusion of old-fashioned flowers growing in them. Originally they had little structure with everything just planted where there were spaces, creating a joyous mixture of colour, shapes and sizes. Nowadays it is often more organized, with tall plants at the back and shorter ones at the front, and the colours planted a little more harmoniously. However well-organized, it should still represent a riot of colour. Self-sowing annuals are usually included with the perennials.

COTTAGE GARDEN PERENNIALS

Alcea rosea
Aquilegia vulgaris
Aster
Astrantia major
Campanula persicifolia
Dianthus 'Mrs Sinkins'
Doronicum
Geum rivale
Lathyrus latifolius
Lupinus Russell hybrids
Primula vulgaris
Salvia officinalis

Informal Style

Many gardeners prefer an informal style, especially if there are children who play in the garden. Here the perennials are used along with shrubs

Above: *A cottage garden, with a mixture of various types of flowers and plants spilling out in profusion over the path, gives an informal impression.*

and perhaps bulbs to create a colourful, comfortable background for family life. Small borders with tough plants that will stand a little neglect or the occasional football are what is required. Foliage plants are a good, as they have a long season and need little maintenance, along with cranesbills (hardy geraniums) and flowering herbs.

Formal Style

Creating a formal garden involves a layout with clean lines, often straight or with regular curves, such as circles. The planting is also regular, frequently using plants with clear lines and shapes, such as cordylines or yuccas, with their fountains of strap-shaped leaves. Edges may be tightly clipped box, lavender, or small, neat flowers. Repetition and symmetry are important. Small gardens are often ideal, especially if they are mostly paved.

Wildflower Gardens

An increasing number of gardeners are growing wildflowers to compensate for their loss in the countryside.

PERENNIALS FOR A FORMAL GARDEN

Cordyline australis
Euphorbia characias
Iris
Miscanthus sinensis
Phormium tenax
Santolina pinnata subsp. *neapolitana*
Yucca gloriosa

Below: *A formal garden with repeated rhythms moving away from the house. The predominance of white and pink flowers helps to unify the garden.*

This sounds simple, but can be as difficult as other types of garden. Wildflowers are best grown in a meadow or overgrown lawn, which should be mown regularly to avoid getting coarse grasses that will overpower the flowers. To start with, grow the flowers in pots and plant them into the meadow. These will establish more easily than if sown into the grass. Only grow wild plants that are appropriate to your area and soil.

Perennials for Different Conditions

ALL GARDENS HAVE A VARIETY OF DIFFERENT CONDITIONS IN WHICH TO GROW PLANTS. THERE ARE USUALLY AREAS OF SUN AND OTHERS OF SHADE. MANY GARDENS HAVE PONDS AND WITH THEM PATCHES OF RELATIVELY MOIST GROUND.

SUNNY AREAS

Most, but not all gardens have sun for at least part of the day. The majority of herbaceous plants will tolerate full sun. However, there are a number that will not and some that can only be grown in sun under special circumstances. Some plants that prefer shade, such as hostas, will grow in the sun if the soil is kept moist, but once it dries out they start to wilt. Others will grow in the sun but they should be protected from the really hot midday sun, violas being a good example. Some plants, especially those from Mediterranean climates, really thrive in hot, sunny conditions and are ideal for hot dry areas. These are particularly useful in areas that are close to house walls and receive little rain, or in gardens with light, dry soil. Most plants that need sunny conditions will not grow well in the shade.

Above: *Silver foliage plants need to grow in a sunny position. In the shade they will languish and eventually die. Here silver* Stachys byzantina *is mixed with a sun-loving* Nepeta.

Left: *Grasses need a sunny position – very few of them will grow successfully in shade. When planted together they can make an interesting semi-formal planting.*

Shady Areas

When planting in shady areas, the choice is slightly more limited than for sun, particularly with flowers, but so long as the soil is moist there are still a large number of suitable plants. Most of the flowering woodland plants flower in the spring, before the leaves appear on the trees – lily-of-the-valley and pulmonaria are good examples. However, there are still plenty of foliage and some flowering plants that will create a good display in the summer and into the autumn. If the area is dry, particularly under a large tree that takes a lot of moisture and nutrients from the soil, the choice is much more restricted. Some bulbous plants, such as anemones and cyclamen, are able to survive because they become dormant before the dryness of summer really sets in. Those plants that will tolerate dry shade, such as *Euphorbia amygdaloides* var. *robbiae* should be planted in drifts so that you will get maximum benefit from them.

Above: Geranium macrorrhizum *is one of the best shade plants, seen profusely flowering here in spite of being in quite dense shade. It will happily spread and form excellent ground cover.*

Creating Shade

If your garden is always sunny it is worth creating some shade just to enable you to grow a greater variety of plants. This can be achieved by planting trees or even large shrubs. Remove some of the lower branches so that light but not midday sun reaches the ground. A trellis screen covered with climbers, or perhaps a pergola or arch, will also provide some shade as well as creating an attractive feature. Keen gardeners often create shade beds by suspending netting on a framework above the bed. This is not very elegant but does allow you to extend your range of plants and also gives you time to establish a tree.

FLOWERING PERENNIALS FOR SHADE

Anemone nemorosa
Brunnera macrophylla
Convallaria majalis
Eranthis hyemalis
Euphorbia amygdaloides var. *robbiae*
Helleborus viridis
Lamium galeobdolon
Lathyrus vernus
Liriope muscari
Polygonatum
Sanguinaria canadensis
Smilacina
Trillium

Waterside Areas

There are a large number of perennials that will grow in water or in the mud surrounding it. These tend to be specialist plants that will only grow in these conditions. Waterside planting can add another dimension to the garden. Because they have a plentiful supply of water, the plants' foliage tends to stay fresh for most of the year, often creating an oasis in an otherwise dry garden. The colours are predominantly yellow and blue, but most other colours can be found, allowing an attractive planting scheme to be developed. The main problem with water plants is that many of them can be invasive. These will need to be reduced every so often, or planted in bottomless pots in the ground, to allow the more delicate plants to survive.

PERENNIAL WATERSIDE PLANTS

Aruncus dioicus
Astilbe x *arendsii*
Caltha palustris
Cardamine pratensis
Gunnera manicata
Iris ensata
Lobelia cardinalis
Lythrum salicaria
Onoclea sensibilis
Persicaria bistorta
Primula japonica
Rodgersia pinnata

Moist Areas

Many people with ponds also have a damp area next to them in which to grow the wide range of plants that like a moist but not waterlogged situation. Other gardeners deliberately create such an area as they want to grow moisture-loving plants but cannot have a pond for safety reasons. Such areas, often called bog gardens,

Above: *Primulas and many irises are ideal plants for a streamside position.*

Above: *The arum lily can be planted either in shallow water or in marshy margins. It can also be used in a bog garden.*

can be a very attractive feature. Many of the plants are colourful and some, such as gunnera, can grow very large, creating eye-catching features.

Dry Areas

Areas with light, free-draining soil can become very dry in summer, particularly when they also receive a lot of sun. Mediterranean-type plants love these conditions. However, many gardens with light soil will still become very wet in the winter, because of higher rainfall than occurs in the Mediterranean climate, which can be a problem for these plants. There are still many plants that can tolerate these conditions, but it is a good idea to increase the moisture-retentiveness by adding plenty of organic material to the soil, and also mulching. This will enable you to grow a wider range of plants.

Mediterranean Beds

In recent times Mediterranean-style beds have become very popular. A lot of gravel is added to the borders, so that they drain very quickly, preventing the plants becoming waterlogged in winter. This type of bed is ideal for very dry climates. A wide range of plants can be grown, and the beds can look very attractive and require little maintenance.

PLANTS FOR A DRY GARDEN

Allium hollandicum
Cistus purpurea
Cordyline australis
Euphorbia characias subsp. *wulfenii*
Lavandula angustifolia
Ophiopogon planiscapus 'Nigrescens'
Papaver somniferum
Rosmarinus
Salvia nemorosa 'Superba'
Sedum
Stachys byzantina
Verbascum

Above: *A small, sunny courtyard can be an ideal site for Mediterranean garden plants that tolerate dry conditions.*

Choosing Perennials with Special Qualities

WITH SUCH A LARGE RANGE OF PERENNIALS AVAILABLE TO THE GARDENER IT IS NOT SURPRISING THAT MANY HAVE INTERESTING FEATURES THAT CAN BE USED IN A VARIETY OF DIFFERENT WAYS, EITHER INDIVIDUALLY OR MIXED WITH OTHER PLANTS.

FRAGRANT PERENNIALS

Many perennials have a smell of one kind or another. Some are delightfully sweet, such as dianthus, others are rank and foetid; *Dracunculus vulgaris,* for example. As always there is an in-between group, represented by such plants as *Phuopsis stylosa,* the smell of which some people find attractive and others repulsive. One tends to think

***Above:** Elegant, fragrant white flowers of Lily-of-the-valley* (Convallaria majalis).

Above: Phlox *has an intoxicating fragrance from mid- to late summer. It is ideal for the back of a border.*

of fragrance in terms of flowers, but many plants have fragrant foliage and this can be an important element in the garden. However, it is the flowers that most people love the best, particularly those that fill the whole area around them with fragrance. Lily-of-the-valley *(Convallaria majalis)* is one such plant, and it will rapidly spread to form large drifts, producing an intoxicating scent.

Aromatic Foliage

Most aromatic foliage needs to be crushed or at least brushed before it issues its scent. One of the best scents is that of monarda, which releases a wonderful fragrance at the slightest touch. If possible plant them near a path where they can be touched or brushed against.

Scent for Different Times

Fortunately, not all flowers are scented at the same time. Surprisingly, a large number of winter-flowering plants – *Iris unguicularis*, for example – are highly scented, probably because they need to attract pollinating insects and there are not many around in winter. Spring is also good, but it is the height of summer when the warm weather brings out the greatest number of perfumes. Plants also vary in their scents during the course of the day, many reserving their smell for the evening to attract the night-flying moths. *Cestrum parqui* is a curiosity as it has a savoury smell during the day, probably to attract flies, and a sweet scent in the evening to attract moths.

Using Scents

While a scented garden provides a great deal of pleasure and sensuous stimulation, mixing too many scents together is self-defeating, as you end up smelling none of them. It is better to spread the scents out so that you come on them one at a time. Areas where you sit and relax are good places for scented flowers. Beds near the house where fragrance can waft through open windows can also be delightful.

Above: Nepeta *has the advantage of scented leaves and attractive flowers.*

SCENTED PERENNIALS

FLOWERS

Alyssum maritinum
Cestrum parqui
Convallaria majalis
Cosmos atrosanguineus
Dianthus
Erysimum cheiri
Filipondula ulmaria
Iris
Mirabilis jalapa
Phlox
Viola odorata

FOLIAGE

Agastache foeniculum
Anthemis punctata subsp. *cupaniana*
Melittis melissophylum
Monarda
Morina longifolia
Nepeta
Salvia

Climbing Perennials

There are a small number of climbing perennials that add variety to the range of plants when you are planning your border. However, with the exception of golden hop, *Humulus lupulus* 'Aureus', they are generally not as vigorous as many of their shrubby counterparts. They are relatively short growing but this can make them ideal for inclusion in the herbaceous or mixed borders. Climbing perennials are treated in exactly the same way as ordinary perennials. Some are self-clinging or twining and will even attach themselves to their supports, but others will need to be tied in.

Supporting Climbers

Some perennials, such as a selection of the violas and geraniums, are scrambling plants rather than true climbing

Above: *The golden hop is a perfect plant for growing over an arch or pergola.*

Above: *This viola and thrift are growing through a rose providing an extended period of colour and interest.*

plants and are extremely useful for growing through the base of low bushes. Others, and here many of the geraniums such as 'Ann Folkard' or 'Salome' are perfect, will happily scramble across other plants, often providing colour when their host plant has finished flowering. If you choose carefully you can extend the flowering period considerably.

The true climbers can also be draped over other plants, but they are best supported in some other way. The majority, being relatively low growing, can be used in the border supported by wigwams of twiggy sticks to create attractive mounds of colour. The golden hop, being vigorous, may be used in a more conventional climbing way. It can be trained to grow over pergolas or arches, or up poles.

Herbaceous Clematis

Most clematis are shrubby but there are just a few that are herbaceous in character and die back each autumn. These tend not to be tall climbers but are well worth considering both for foliage colour (*Clematis recta* 'Purpurea') and for their flowers (*C. durandii*). Again, twiggy sticks form the best kind of support.

> PERENNIAL CLIMBERS
>
> *Clematis erecta*
> *Eccremocarpus scaber*
> *Humulus lupulus* 'Aureus'
> *Lathyrus*
> *Solanum dulcamara* 'Variegatum'
> *Tropaeolum speciosum*
> *Vinca major*

Ground Cover

There are generally two main reasons for using ground-cover plants: either to suppress weeds, or to provide a low-maintenance covering for an area where not many types of plants will thrive, such as a shady area or a bank. In the latter case the ground cover may also help prevent soil erosion. Either way, perennials are perfect. Virtually any perennial, if planted close enough together, will form ground cover, the basic requirement for weed suppression being that the foliage prevents light reaching the soil. Some make better cover than others as their foliage is dense or large, creating shade. Hostas are a prime example.

Suppressing Weeds

If the plants are covering the ground effectively, any weed seeds that germinate will quickly die from lack of light. However, ground cover will not suppress perennial weeds if their roots are already in the soil. For this reason it is vital to remove all perennial weeds before planting the ground cover. Otherwise, they can be difficult to eradicate without digging up the whole bed.

Above: Persicaria affinis *makes a dense carpet of foliage that is the perfect weed-suppressing ground cover.*

> PERENNIALS FOR GROUND COVER
>
> *Acaena*
> *Anthemis punctata cupaniana*
> *Bergenia*
> *Epimedium*
> *Geranium macrorrhizum*
> *Hosta*
> *Pulmonaria*
> *Stachys byzantina*
> *Vinca minor*

Foliage Perennials

Among the perennials are some truly delightful foliage plants. Some are used purely as foliage plants, either not producing flowers or having all the flowers removed as these spoil the effect. Others are ordinary flowering plants but they also have very good foliage. This attribute is rather useful when the plant is flowering as well as before and after flowering. *Alchemilla mollis* is a good example.

***Above:** Silver foliage has a softening effect in a border. Two popular species are* Stachys *and* Artemisia.

The Qualities of Foliage

Foliage is attractive for several different reasons. Although the majority of perennials have green foliage there is also a wide range of other colours, including variegation where more than one colour is present. Then there are the size and shape, which can vary from thin strap-like leaves to huge rounded ones. The texture is also important. Shiny leaves, for example, are useful

***Above:** These rodgersias have a wonderful ribbed texture that contrasts well with the smoothness of the water. The fans of leaves also complement the foliage of the iris.*

FOLIAGE AND ARCHITECTURAL PERENNIALS

FOLIAGE
Canna
Cordyline
Cynara
Grasses
Gunnera manicata
Hosta
Rheum
Rodgersia
Stachys byzantina

ARCHITECTURAL
Acanthus spinosus
Angelica archangelica
Cortaderia selloana
Cynara cardunculus
Gunnera manicata
Phormium tenax
Rheum
Stipa gigantea

for illuminating dark areas. Light and shade play an important part in the use of foliage. Foliage plants can simply be used as a foil for other plants, or they can be decorative in their own right, either among flowering plants or in a purely foliage border. Mixing foliage with contrasting characteristics always creates interesting designs. It can also be used as a break between two plants with flower colours that do not quite go together visually, so that they do not jar on the eye.

ARCHITECTURAL PLANTS

There are some plants with a striking, statuesque shape that immediately draws the eye, foliage generally being the most important element. *Gunnera manicata*, for example, has large eye-catching leaves, while cordyline has narrow leaves arranged in such a beautiful way that they cannot but attract attention. These plants will act as focal points in the garden, and this should be remembered when planning the design. They may be used at the end of a straight path or at a bend in a curved one. The feature may be away in the distance at the end of a lawn or on the boundary of the garden. Often this attraction accentuates the length of a path or of a garden, making it look bigger than it is. Architectural plants can also be effective in a border, perhaps in the middle or at regular intervals to set up a rhythm, which is particularly useful in a formal setting.

Above: Gunnera manicata *has some of the largest leaves of any garden perennial. A clump of these certainly creates an imposing sight.*

Seasonal Splendour

MANY PERENNIALS FLOWER FOR RELATIVELY SHORT PERIODS, AND THOUGH THIS CAN SOMETIMES SEEM A DRAWBACK, IT DOES GUARANTEE A CONSTANTLY CHANGING PICTURE. BY CAREFULLY PLANNING YOUR PLANTING, YOU CAN ENSURE INTEREST THROUGHOUT THE YEAR.

SPRING

This is the season of birth and renewal. It is the time when barren earth suddenly springs into life in a myriad of colours, each with its own kind of freshness. The predominant colours are yellow and blue, but all the other colours are also present. It is not only the flowers that are exciting and new; it is also the foliage, which appears in a seemingly limitless number of shades of green.

Planting for Spring

A good way to plan your spring planting is to choose those colours that represent the freshness and vitality of the season, such as yellow primroses, blue anemones and red pulmonarias. The silver-spotted foliage of the pulmonarias will continue to look attractive for a long time, but most of the spring-flowering perennials add little to the scene once they have finished flowering.

***Above:** Spring is a wonderful time of year with many old favourites, such as primulas, aquilegias and forget-me-nots, coming into flower.*

SPRING PERENNIALS
Aubrieta deltoidea
Bergenia cordifolia
Caltha palustris
Doronicum 'Miss Mason'
Euphorbia polychroma
Helleborus orientalis
Primula vulgaris
Pulmonaria angustifolia
Sanguinaria canadensis
Smilacina racemosa
Trollius europaeus
Viola odorata

***Above:** An important perennial in any spring garden is* Euphorbia polychroma, *which forms a perfect dome of gold up to 75cm (30in) high.*

Indeed many, such as the anemones, die back below ground and are not visible. Plant these types of flowers towards the back of the border or between other plants where they will show up in spring when the shoots are only just beginning to appear, but will be hidden when the later plants are fully grown.

No special maintenance is required for spring perennials except to remove any dead foliage as it appears. Try to weed and mulch the borders before too much growth has been made to avoid damaging the plants.

Woodland Plants

Many spring plants are of woodland origin, and appear, flower, seed and die back before the trees come into leaf. This allows them to make full use of the available light and moisture. Anemones and celandines are of this type. In the garden, they can be planted under deciduous shrubs and trees, where later-flowering plants would not thrive because of the shade created by the foliage. Some perennials that keep their foliage, such as primroses, hellebores and pulmonarias, can also be used in such places.

***Above:** The soft greyish pink of this dicentra is unusual in spring.*

Early Summer

At this time, the spring-like quality of freshness is still in evidence in the garden, and yet the multitude of colours and abundance of lush vegetation give a decidedly summery feel. As yet the sun is usually not too strong and so the colours have a brightness and intensity that they lose as summer progresses. Spring is colourful, but this colour is mainly seen against bare earth. By early summer the foliage has nearly all developed and the flowers are viewed against a wide range of foliage colours and shapes, which enhances them considerably.

***Above:** Early summer would not be complete without the towering spires of blue produced by delphiniums.*

Planting for Early Summer

The plants for early summer seem to be quite distinct from those later in the summer. In a late season many are left over from spring and the two periods can merge, with dicentras lasting into summer and *Geranium pratense* starting in spring. Although it is a good idea to try to co-ordinate the colours in the border, do not place all the early-flowering plants together or there will be gaps later in the year when they die; try to spread them among the later-flowering plants.

Long-lasting Plantings

Some plants have modern hybrids that flower for longer than the older varieties. For example, old-fashioned pinks tend to flower only once, in early summer, whereas many of the modern pinks, although not so attractive to many people and often less fragrant, do flower throughout the whole summer and well into autumn. Some plants that start to flower in early summer, such as the Mexican daisy, *Erigeron karvinskianus,* or *Erodium manescaui* continue to flower profusely throughout the whole summer and often until the first frosts appear. Some plants that do not flower for very long can be used as foliage plants for the later part of the summer. Either cut them back to the ground and let them regenerate, as you can with alchemilla, or remove the flowering heads, for example with lupins. Some

Above: There are many perennial wallflowers, which are valuable for their cheerful colours in the early summer.

plants, such as *Alchemilla mollis* and delphiniums, may well flower again later in the year if cut back.

Early Summer Maintenance

In the initial part of early summer, while the plants are still putting on lots of growth, be certain to stake them. If this is done now, the plants will hide the staking under the new foliage. Deadhead as plants go over. If the borders have been properly mulched there should be no need to water, but if there is a prolonged dry spell it may become necessary.

Above: Alchemilla mollis *often flower twice if cut back in mid-season.*

EARLY-SUMMER PERENNIALS

Alchemilla mollis
Baptisia australis
Campanula persicifolia
Centaurea montana
Delphinium
Dianthus 'Mrs Sinkins'
Geranium pratense
Hemerocallis
Lupinus Russell hybrids
Papaver orientale

High Summer

The borders in high summer can be drenched in sunshine. Some of the brighter colours, such as the reds, still stand out but many of the others have lost the freshness of early summer and are subdued into a haze. It can be one of the best times in the garden, but so often things begin to flag and steps should be taken to overcome this.

Summer Colours

To create a border that retains its colour at this time of year, it is best to use hot reds or oranges, such as some of the kniphofias and heleniums. White also holds up well in this light, especially if seen against green. Most of the soft pastel colours are bleached even paler by the bright light, but with hazy, romantic borders the effect can be enhanced – perfect for lazy summer days.

Flagging Foliage

Much of the foliage has been around since spring and it is beginning to look tired and ragged. Try to offset this by cutting back plants that have finished flowering earlier in the year, so that they produce fresh leaves to brighten up the borders. Regular deadheading will also help to keep the borders looking neat. Mulching should have helped to keep the moisture in the soil, but in a hot summer reserves may be used up and it may be necessary to water copiously until the ground is again fully saturated and the plants are revived.

Above: Helenium *'Indian Summer' brings an orange glow with its sun-loving flowers.*

***Above:** Lilies are always popular for their attractive blooms and range of colours.*

Beside the Water

By midsummer the water in the ponds has warmed up and the water plants are in full growth. This is one of the fresher-looking parts of the garden, both in the water and along its margins. Water lilies and irises are at their best and the colours are still vibrant. In dry gardens, where this time of year may be a problem, it is worth creating a water feature to provide an oasis of fresh greenery and colourful flowers.

The Importance of Planning

In the spring and early summer enthusiasm for gardening is high, and along with this the tendency to buy and plant out new plants. However, one's eye is often caught by plants that are in flower rather than ones yet to flower. This can easily upset the balance of plants in the garden with a preponderance of plants for spring and early summer and far less for high summer. Try to be forward-looking and plan for this period too.

FLOWERS FOR HIGH SUMMER

Acanthus
Astilbe
Campanula
Dianthus
Eryngium
Geranium
Helenium
Hemerocallis
Kniphofia
Lilium
Phlox
Veronica

***Above:** Different yellows with soft pink astilbes make a lovely summer border.*

Autumn

As autumn sets in, nature begins to wind down, but with good planning this can be one of the most colourful times of the year in the garden. By now, many plants are usually looking decidedly the worse for wear, but with judicious cutting back it should be possible to remove the more unsightly plants and dead flowers so that the autumn colours have a chance to shine through. A lot of the end-of-season look that many gardens have during this time of year can be avoided simply by cutting out spent material.

Above: Michaelmas daisies are among the stars of the autumn garden. They come in a wide variety of colours.

Autumn Colours

This season is a time of warm and hot colours with many yellow daisies, such as helianthus and rudbeckias, as well as fiery autumn foliage. However, there are still plenty of other colours. The Michaelmas daisies, in particular, produce a wide range of colours including blues, pinks and whites. Vernonias also have some wonderfully rich purples as well as whites.

Above: Rich gold is one of the prime colours of the autumn scene and long-flowering rudbeckias provide it.

Moving Plants

One of the problems with perennial gardening is to manage to accommodate enough plants in a border to maintain a continuous supply of colour from flowers and foliage. By mid-autumn many of the plants have finished, leaving large gaps in the arrangements. This is not so much a problem at other times of the year as there are always plants in leaf, although they may not yet be in flower. One solution is to move some plants. This works well with shallow-rooted plants, of which Michaelmas

AUTUMN-FLOWERING PERENNIALS

Anemone x *hybrida*
Aster
Boltonia
Chelone
Chrysanthemum
Helianthus
Kirengeshoma
Liriope
Nerine
Ophiopogon
Rudbeckia
Schizostylis
Sedum
Solidago
Tricyrtis

daisies are the prime candidates. Surprisingly these can be moved in full flower without any detrimental effect. Grow them in a spare bit of ground or the back of the border. Soak them well as they come into flower. Dig up the clump with a good rootball of soil still attached, replant it in a gap in the border and then water again. This is real instant gardening.

Wildlife

Autumn is a wonderful time for butterflies, moths and bees in the garden. Fortunately there are plenty of plants, such as the sedums and the Michaelmas daisies, that provide food for these visitors. It is worth making certain that you grow several attractant plants, as the sight of these creatures adds another dimension to the garden. If you want to provide winter food and shelter for birds and insects then you should leave some areas of herbaceous material such as seed heads for them to feed on during the winter, although this may mean that the garden looks less neat and tidy than it would otherwise.

Above: *A number of sedums flower in the autumn and these are not only valuable for their colour but also for the way that they attract butterflies and bees.*

Above: *The dainty flowers of* Schizostylis *appear in the autumn. They come in a range of reds and pinks.*

Winter

This is the most difficult time of year in the garden. And yet in some ways it can be the most interesting as it certainly is a challenge. The weather can vary dramatically from region to region and in some areas there may be total snow cover throughout the darkest months, in which case the main interest in the garden will be trees and shrubs. On the other hand there are mild areas that can support a surprisingly large range of material. In the middle are those that have a mildish winter with a few cold snaps here and there. Where the ground can be seen, as long as it is not frozen or waterlogged, there are always a number of plants to be grown.

Above: Iris reticulata *gives a warming splash of colour in late winter.*

Winter Flowers

There are only a handful of perennials that flower in the winter but combined with other plants, such as bulbs and shrubs, they can make up a good display. Some of the most popular winter plants are the hellebores. There are a number of species and an ever-increasing number of cultivars in a wide range of colours. The foliage of many species is very attractive and the plants are worth growing for this alone. Another worthwhile winter perennial is the winter iris, *I. unguicularis*. This flowers over a long period, throughout most of the dullest months. It has wonderful soft blue or mauve flowers that have a delightful scent. It has one other advantage in that it can be grown in the poorest of soils. Indeed an ideal spot is in a dry, rubble-filled soil next to a wall.

Surprise Appearances

If you are not in too much of a hurry to cut everything to the ground in autumn, it is surprising how many plants can continue to flower if the weather is mild, right into the middle of winter and beyond. Penstemons are good examples of this long- and late-flowering ability. Similarly in a mild winter many of the spring flowers will flower early. Sweet violets, *Viola odorata*, are usually flowering in winter, as are a number of primroses and ground-covering pulmonarias.

Where to Plant

Because winter flowers are generally not very interesting for the rest of the gardening year, they can be planted towards the back of the border or under deciduous shrubs where they will clearly show up in the winter but be covered by other plants when they are not looking at their best. If you have a large garden and can afford the space you might create a special winter garden, which you only visit at this time of the year.

***Above:** The appearance of winter aconites is a welcome sign as it shows that winter will soon be over.*

All-year-round Plants

Some perennials have all-year-round qualities that make them especially useful if you have limited space. Although pulmonarias have their flowers in late winter and spring, they can be used as a foliage plant for the rest of the year. If all the foliage is cut back after flowering, new leaves will quickly regrow and will retain their freshness. Bergenias have spikes of pink, red or white flowers in spring, but, again, retain their attractive leaves for the rest of the year.

***Above:** The unusual, delicate pale green flowers of these hellebores brighten up the garden in the winter.*

WINTER FLOWERING PERENNIALS

Eranthis hyemalis
Euphorbia rigida
Galanthus
Helleborus niger
Helleborus orientalis
Helleborus purpurascens
Iris ungicularis
Primula vulgaris
Pulmonaria rubra
Viola odorata

Perennials for Colour

Of all the qualities of perennials, colour is probably the most important. It is the first thing most people notice about a plant and it generally makes the most impact.

RED PERENNIALS

Alcea rosea (various)
Astilbe 'Fanal'
Astrantia major 'Ruby Wedding'
Canna (various)
Centranthus ruber
Cosmos atrosanguineus
Dahlia (various)
Dianthus 'Brympton Red'
Geum 'Mrs Bradshaw'
Hemerocallis 'Stafford'
Lobelia 'Cherry ripe'
Lupinus 'Inverewe Red'
Lychnis chalcedonica
Monarda didyma 'Cambridge Scarlet'
Paeonia (various)
Papaver orientale (various)
Penstemon 'Cherry Ripe'
Persicaria amplexicaulis
Potentilla 'Gibson's Scarlet'
Zinnia (various)

ORANGE PERENNIALS

Canna 'Orange Perfection'
Crocosmia (various)
Dahlia (various)
Gazania (various)
Geum 'Borisii'
Helenium (various)
Kniphofia (various)
Potentilla 'William Rollison'

YELLOW PERENNIALS

Achillea
Anthemis tinctoria
Asphodeline lutea
Helenium
Helianthus
Hemerocallis
Lysimachia punctata
Oenothera
Primula veris
Primula vulgaris
Sedum (various)
Trollius
Verbascum

BLUE AND VIOLET PERENNIALS

Agapanthus
Ajuga reptans
Aquilegia flabellata
Baptisia australis
Campanula
Delphinium (various)
Echinops ritro
Eryngium
Gentiana
Iris (various)
Limonium platyphyllum
Nepeta
Perovskia atriplicifolia
Scabiosa
Tradescantia Andersoniana Group (various)
Veronica

PURPLE PERENNIALS

Aster (various)
Echinacea purpurea
Erigeron 'Dunkelste Aller'
Erysimum 'Bowles Mauve'
Geranium (various)
Lythrum

Osteospermum jucundum
Penstemon 'Burgundy'
Phlox 'Le Mahdi'
Primula denticulata
Senecio pulcher
Tradescantia Andersoniana Group (various)
Verbena bonariensis

PINK PERENNIALS

Anemone x *hybrida*
Aster (various)
Astilbe (various)
Bergenia cordifolia
Dianthus (various)
Diascia
Dicentra
Erodium manescaui
Geranium (various)
Helleborus (various)
Lamium roseum
Linaria purpurea 'Canon Went'
Malva moschata
Monarda didyma 'Croftway Pink'
Papaver orientale 'Cedric Morris'
Penstemon 'Hidcote Pink'
Persicaria (various)
Phlox (various)
Phuopsis stylosa
Primula (various)
Sedum (various)
Sidalcea

WHITE PERENNIALS

Achillea ptarmica 'The Pearl'
Anemone x *hybrida* 'Honorine Jobert'
Anthemis punctata subsp. *cupaniana*
Campanula lactiflora alba
Convallaria majalis
Crambe cordifolia
Dicentra spectabilis 'Alba'
Geranium (various)
Gypsophila
Helleborus (various)
Penstemon (various)
Phlox (various)
Polygonatum hybridum
Silene uniflora
Trillium grandiflorum
Zantedeschia aethiopica

CREAM PERENNIALS

Anemone lipsiensis
Aruncus dioicus
Kniphofia 'Little Maid'
Rodgersia (various)
Sisyrinchium striatum
Smilacina racemosa
Trollius 'Alabaster'

MIXED

Aquilegia
Chrysanthemum
Dianthus
Gazania
Hemerocallis
Lupinus
Penstemon
Phlox
Primula
Zinnia

FOLIAGE

Alchemilla mollis
Bergenia
Canna
Hosta
Pulmonaria
Sempervivum

Best Perennials for Your Garden

USE THIS QUICK REFERENCE CHART TO SELECT THE PLANTS MOST SUITABLE FOR YOUR DESIGN AND GARDEN CONDITIONS. UNLESS OTHERWISE STATED, ALL PLANTS SHOULD BE SOWN OR PLANTED OUT IN THE SPRING (OR AUTUMN IN MILDER AREAS).

Plant Name	Height/Spread	Colour/Period of Interest	Method of Propagation
Acanthus	150cm (5ft)	white and purple/summer	seed
Achillea	120cm (4ft)	yellow, white, pink/summer	division
Actaea	180cm (6ft)	white/summer and autumn	seed or division
Agapanthus	90cm (3ft)	blue, white/summer	division
Alchemilla	38cm (15in)	yellowish green/summer	seed
Allium B	90cm (3ft)	all colours/summer	seed or division
Alstroemeria	90cm (3ft)	all colours/summer	division
Anemone	90cm (3ft)	white, blue, pink, yellow/spring	autumn division
Anthemis	75cm (30in)	white, yellow/summer	cuttings or division
Aquilegia	60cm (2ft)	all colours/spring, early summer	seed
Artemisia	120cm (4ft)	yellow, brown/silver foliage/summer	cuttings or division
Aruncus	2m (7ft)	cream/summer	division
Aster	2m (7ft)	all colours/summer and autumn	division
Astilbe	120cm (4ft)	white, pink, red/summer	division
Astrantia ps	60cm (2ft)	greenish, pink, red/late spring, summer	division
Bergenia s or ps	45cm (18in)	pink/evergreen foliage/spring	division
Caltha ms	45cm (18in)	yellow/summer	seed or division
Campanula	120cm (4ft)	blue, white/summer	seed or division
Canna	150cm (5ft)	Red, pink, yellow/summer and autumn	division
Cardiocrinum fs B	3m (10ft)	white/summer	seed or division
Catananche	45cm (18in)	blue/summer	seed
Centaurea	120cm (4ft)	purple, red, pink, yellow/summer	seed or division
Centranthus	75cm (30in)	reddish pink, white/summer	seed
Cephalaria	2m (7ft)	yellow/summer	seed
Chelone	90cm (3ft)	pink/autumn	division
Chrysanthemum	180cm (6ft)	various colours/autumn	cuttings or division
Clematis	180cm (6ft)	blue, white/summer	cuttings

Above: Crocosmia '*Lucifer*'

Above: Geranium sanguineum '*Album*'

Convallaria S	20cm (10in)	white/late spring	division
Coreopsis	75cm (30in)	yellow/summer into autumn	division
Cortaderia G	2.5m (8ft)	various colours/all year round	division
Cosmos S	45cm (18in)	mahogany/summer	cuttings or division
Crambe S	180cm (6ft)	white/early summer	division
Crinum B	120cm (4ft)	pink/late summer	seed or division
Crocosmia B	120cm (4ft)	orange, red, yellow/late summer	division
Cynara	2.5m (8ft)	purple/silver foliage/late summer	division
Dahlia T	120cm (4ft)	various colours/summer into autumn	division or cuttings
Delphinium	2m (7ft)	blue, pink, white/summer	cuttings, division or seed
Dianthus S	Up to 38cm (15in)	pink, white/summer	cuttings
Diascia	38cm (15in)	pink/summer into autumn	cuttings
Dicentra	75cm (30in)	pink, white/late spring into early summer	division
Dictamnus	90cm (3ft)	purple, white/summer	seed
Dierama	150cm (5ft)	pink/summer	seed or division
Digitalis	180cm (6ft)	purple, yellow, brown/summer	seed
Doronicum	90cm (3ft)	yellow/spring	division
Echinacea	150cm (5ft)	summer	division
Echinops	180cm (6ft)	blue, white/summer	seed
Epimedium ps	45cm (18in)	yellow, white, pink/late spring	division
Eremurus	2m (7ft)	pink, yellow/summer	seed or division
Erigeron	60cm (2ft)	purple, blue, pink, white/summer	division
Eryngium	2m (7ft)	blue, green/good foliage/summer	seed or division
Eupatorium	2m (7ft)	pink, white/summer and autumn	division
Euphorbia	150cm (5ft)	yellowish-green/spring into summer	seed or division
Filipendula S	120cm (4ft)	pink, white/summer	division
Foeniculum	2m (7ft)	yellow/good, fragrant foliage/summer	seed
Francoa	75cm (30in)	pink/summer	seed
Fritillaria B	90cm (3ft)	various colours/spring	seed or division
Gaura	90cm (3ft)	white/summer	seed
Gentiana	90cm (3ft)	blue, white, yellow/summer and autumn	seed or division
Geranium	90cm (3ft)	purple, pink, blue, white/spring into autumn	seed, cuttings or division
Geum	45cm (18in)	red, yellow, pink/spring into summer	division
Gladiolus B	120cm (4ft)	in various colours/summer	division
Gunnera	2.5m (8ft)	green/large foliage/summer	division
Gypsophila	120cm (4ft)	white, pink/summer	seed or cuttings
Helenium	150cm (5ft)	yellow, orange, brown/summer	division

Above: Anemome ranunculoides

Above: Gypsophila paniculata

Helianthus	2.5m (8ft)	yellow/summer into autumn	division
Heliopsis	150cm (5ft)	yellow/summer into autumn	division
Helleborus	60cm (2ft)	various colours/winter into spring	seed or division
Hemerocallis	120cm (4ft)	yellow, orange, red, pink/summer	division
Heuchera	90cm (3ft)	white, pink/good foliage/summer	division
Hosta	60cm (2ft)	blue, white/good foliage/summer	division
Humulus C	6m (20ft)	green/good foliage/summer	division
Inula	2.5m (8ft)	yellow/summer	seed or division
Iris	150cm (5ft)	various colours/summer, winter	division
Kirengeshoma ps	90cm (3ft)	yellow/autumn	seed or division
Knautia	75cm (30in)	crimson, pink/summer	division, cuttings or seed
Kniphofia	180cm (6ft)	red, orange, yellow/summer into autumn	division
Lamium	60cm (2ft)	pink, purple, white/good foliage/summer	cuttings or division
Lathyrus C	120cm (4ft)	various colours/spring into summer	seed or division
Ligularia	180cm (6ft)	yellow/summer into autumn	seed or division
Lilium some S	180cm (6ft)	various colours/summer	seed or division
Limonium	90cm (3ft)	blue/summer	seed or division
Linaria	180cm (6ft)	yellow, purple, pink/summer	seed
Linum	45cm (18in)	blue/summer	seed
Liriope	38cm (15in)	purple/autumn	division
Lobelia	150cm (5ft)	various colours/summer into autumn	cuttings, division or seed
Lupinus S	150cm (5ft)	various colours/early summer	seed or cuttings
Lychnis	75cm (30in)	red, cerise, pink, orange/summer	seed
Lysimachia	120cm (4ft)	yellow, white, red/summer	seed or division
Lythrum	120cm (4ft)	purple/summer	cuttings or division
Macleaya	2m (7ft)	pink, white/summer	root cuttings or division
Meconopsis	150cm (5ft)	blue, yellow, white, red/summer	seed or division
Miscanthus G	2.5m (8ft)	various/all year round	division
Monarda SF	150cm (5ft)	red, pink, purple, white/summer	division
Nepeta SF	150cm (5ft)	mauve, blue, white, and yellow/summer	cuttings or division
Nerine B	45cm (18in)	pink/autumn	division
Oenothera	150cm (5ft)	yellow, orange/summer into autumn	seed
Origanum SF H	45cm (18in)	purple/summer	seed or division
Osteospermum	Up to 38cm (15in)	purple, white/summer	cuttings
Paeonia	75cm (30in)	red, pink, white, yellow/ spring into summer	seed or division
Papaver	75cm (30in)	various colours/summer	seed or division
Pennisetum G	90cm (3ft)	various colours/all year round	seed or division

Above: Rheum

Above: Astrantia major

Penstemon	90cm (3ft)	various colours/summer	cuttings
Perovskia	120cm (4ft)	blue/summer	cuttings
Persicaria	120cm (4ft)	pink, white/summer	division
Phlox	120cm (4ft)	various colours/summer	cuttings or division
Phormium	180cm (6ft)	red, green/good foliage/summer	division
Physostegia	90cm (3ft)	pink, white/summer	seed or division
Polemonium	90cm (3ft)	blue, white, pink, yellow/summer	seed or division
Polygonatum ps	90cm (3ft)	white/spring into summer	division
Potentilla	60cm (2ft)	red, yellow/summer	division
Primula	60cm (2ft)	in various colours/winter/summer	seed or division
Pulmonaria ps	30cm (12in)	blue, red, white/some good foliage/ late winter into spring	division
Rodgersia	120cm (4ft)	pink, cream/good foliage/summer	division
Rudbeckia (cone)	2m (7ft)	yellow/summer into autumn	division
Salvia	150cm (5ft)	in various colours/summer into autumn	cuttings or division
Scabiosa	75cm (30in)	lilac, pink, yellow/summer	seed or division
Schizostylis B	60cm (2ft)	pink, crimson/autumn	division
Sedum	60cm (2ft)	pink, red, yellow/summer	cuttings
Sidalcea	120cm (4ft)	pink, white/summer	division
Silene	60cm (2ft)	pink, white/spring into summer	seed or division
Sisyrinchium	60cm (2ft)	yellow, blue, white, purple/summer	seed or division
Stachys	60cm (2ft)	purple, pink, yellow/silver foliage/summer	some division
Stipa G	2m (7ft)	various colours/all year round	division
Thalictrum	180cm (6ft)	various colours/summer	seed
Tradescantia	60cm (2ft)	blue, purple, white/summer	division
Trillium ps	45cm (18in)	various colours/spring	seed or division
Trollius ms	75cm (30in)	yellow, orange/spring into summer	seed or division
Veratrum	180cm (6ft)	green, red/summer	division
Verbascum	180cm (6ft)	yellow, pink, white/summer	seed
Verbena	180cm (6ft)	purple, blue/summer	seed or division
Veronica	120cm (4ft)	blue, pink, white/summer	division
Viola	30cm (12in)	various colours/summer	cuttings
Yucca	2m (7ft)	cream/summer into autumn	division
Zantedeschia ms	90cm (3ft)	white/summer	division

KEY TO ABBREVIATIONS

s = sun
ms = moist soil
ps = partial shade
fs = full shade
B = bulbous
C = climber
H = herb
G = grasses
S = scented
SF = scented foliage
T = tuberous

Above: Lathyrus latifolius

Above: Aquilegia

SCENT IN THE GARDEN

In addition to plenty of visual impact, a garden should be full of delicate scent, sensual perfume and intriguing aroma, by night and day. Not only do delightful smells lift the spirit and help us relax, but they also attract beneficial insects. Scented plants can be found for every style and for every time of the year, even in the depths of winter. The handy checklist at the end of this chapter will ensure your garden is never short on fragrance.

Delicate Aromas

SCENT IS OFTEN THE MOST MEMORABLE ELEMENT OF A GARDEN, EVEN MORE POTENT IN ITS IMPACT THAN FLOWER COLOUR OR THE HARMONY OF SHAPES AND TEXTURES. THE FAINTEST WHIFF OF FRAGRANCE CAN UNLOCK THE DOOR TO A HOST OF MEMORIES.

In the plant kingdom scent functions mainly to attract pollinators, but for the gardener it is the most elusive of all the senses and the hardest to define. Scents cannot be recorded and transmitted like sounds or images, nor is it always easy to put into words how we experience them. Moreover, our sense of smell is notoriously underdeveloped compared with that of the cats, dogs and other domestic animals we share our lives with.

There is even a variation of sensitivity within the human species itself. Some people seem to have a highly developed sense of smell while others have the misfortune to lose the faculty altogether. While women are said to have the keener sense of smell, according to Dr Alex Comfort, men are more responsive to it, so there is no battle of the sexes here.

Our reactions to scent tend to be individual, and it is not always easy to pinpoint a particular aroma. Although we might be able to distinguish between two or three different scents, if more are added the nose becomes anaesthetized, making distinctions difficult. Scent can, however, be used to produce

***Above:** The evening primrose* (Oenothera biennis) *releases its fragrance at night.*

Above: Hypericum *'Hidcote' is a useful plant for ground cover and has leaves that are aromatic when crushed.*

a sense of calm and wellbeing, or, conversely, to stimulate and invigorate, ensuring that your garden is a place of regeneration as well as tranquillity.

Types of Scent

Difficult to describe though they are, scents in the garden can be divided into several broad groups.

The commonest examples are usually defined as aromatic. They are generally sweetly spicy and always appealing: we seem never to tire of them. They are found in the almond-like fragrance of heliotropes and the clove essence of carnations and pinks. Violet scents are sharper and more transitory. As well as violets (*Viola*), mignonettes (*Reseda*) and *Iris reticulata* belong to this group.

Roses are usually fruity and spicy, pleasing both up close and at a distance. Some tulips also have this type of scent. Interestingly, many roses seem to belong to a further group, with citrus or lemon overtones. These fragrances are almost universally perceived as pleasant and exhilarating.

Citrus smells are light and refreshing, while herbal ones, such as thyme and lavender, tend to have a calming effect. Some herbal scents are more astringent, however, with notes of eucalyptus that not everyone finds pleasing, although many experience them as invigorating.

A musk-like odour can often be detected in honey-scented plants, and such fragrances seem warm and enduring. They are most commonly encountered among the orchids.

Some flower scents combine more than one note and seem to be "layered". We usually think of these as exotic, as they can be so rich and heady as to be almost cloying.

Above: Perovskia *smells of eucalyptus.*

*Above: Creeping thymes (*Thymus*) can be planted to be trodden gently underfoot.*

Benefits of Scented Plants

Apart from the pleasure they give to gardeners, scented plants are of inestimable value to the garden's ecology, given their appeal to pollinating insects. A diverse insect population is the best way of keeping down garden pests – whose attacks on plants also make them vulnerable to disease – since their predators are more likely to be present.

Brightly coloured plants are usually designed to attract birds, which have no sense of smell, so such flowers are often scentless. Many of the most fragrant plants have simple, cup-shaped flowers, for easy access to the pollen.

Night-scented plants have evolved to attract moths and other nocturnal insects. These plants include night-scented stock (*Matthiola longipetala* subsp. *bicornis*), tobacco plants (*Nicotiana*) and the exquisitely fragrant South American sub-shrub, willow-leaved jessamine (*Cestrum parqui*).

How to Recognize Scented Plants

Latin botanical names often provide good clues as to whether a plant is scented or not. Any genus name followed by the descriptive word *fragrantissima*, *odora* or *suaveolens* is bound to be fragrant. Sometimes the type of scent is indicated: *citriodora* means lemon-scented, and *moschata* is musky. But beware: *pungens* implies a strong (or pungent) scent that is not necessarily appealing.

Scent is not always betrayed by the name, however: *Magnolia grandiflora* refers only to the size of the flowers, not to their bewitching fragrance.

Above: The characteristic scent of Eucalyptus *is carried by its volatile oils.*

Parts of the Plant

Speak of scent in the garden and most people immediately think of flowers. While it is true that in most cases it is the flowers that provide the most intoxicating of garden fragrances, other parts of plants can be aromatic, even though they must sometimes be crushed, rubbed or bruised to release their attraction. This is the case with most herbs, but there are other well-known garden plants that have "secret" scents. *Hypericum* 'Hidcote' is widely grown for its yellow flowers and robust qualities, but its aromatic leaves give it a distinction of quite a different kind. *Perovskia*, a sub-shrub valued for its hardiness and late summer lavender-coloured flowers, has white-bloomed stems that smell of eucalyptus oil. Such scents are not always appealing, however: the crushed leaves of skimmias have a somewhat bitter note.

Anyone who has wandered through an apple orchard in autumn will recall the evocative, slightly alcoholic cider smell that arises from bruised windfalls. On a warm day you will see wasps buzzing drunkenly around, intoxicated by the fermenting juices.

Gum trees (*Eucalyptus*) have resinous bark, as do most conifers, so the many genera are not listed separately here. *Chimonanthus* has fragrant leaves, wood, flowers and seeds and is a delight in the winter garden.

Above: *'Constance Spry', one of the most richly scented of all roses, is superb when trained against a wall.*

PLANTS WITH AROMATIC WOOD, BARK OR LEAVES

Aloysia triphylla
Cercidiphyllum (fallen leaves)
Cistus
Eucalyptus
Helichrysum italicum
Hypericum 'Hidcote'
Laurus nobilis
Liquidambar styraciflua
Myrtus communis
Perovskia
Populus balsamifera
Rosmarinus officinalis
Ruta graveolens
Santolina
Skimmia
Thymus

Combining Plants

Devising a planting scheme that includes a large proportion of strongly scented plants can be even more difficult than planning a colour scheme, for which you can at least get some ideas by playing around with colour swatches. Trying to balance and harmonize the whole range of natural aromas and notes in a collection of plants is a more abstract process, since you cannot reproduce garden scents in the comfort of your sitting room.

On the whole, within a single bed scents are best in pairs or at a maximum of three. More confuse the nose and can seem to anaesthetize it, meaning that none of the scents makes its full impact. Rich, heavy smells are best combined with lighter, fresher scents: hence the value of underplanting roses with lavender. Alternatives would be old-fashioned, clove-infused carnations (*Dianthus*) – especially if you have alkaline soil – or sweet violets (*Viola*). Some scents are best appreciated on their own, and that applies especially to the powerfully scented *Magnolia grandiflora*, with its lemon-scented, waxy-textured flowers. It is often best to combine such plants with non-scented ones. For example, you could introduce a sweetly scented mock orange (*Philadelphus*) into a white garden if you are relying on 'Iceberg' as the main rose, since this has only a light fragrance. For scent later in the year add some lilies, such as *Lilium regale*, or plant the creamy white *Paeonia* 'White Wings'.

Above: *Bergamot (*Monarda*) is an aromatic that can be used in potpourri.*

Above: *Conifers such as* Thuja plicata, *with resinous bark, are highly scented.*

Siting Plants

Finding the right position in the garden for your scented plants can increase their impact considerably.

Where you site the plants will largely depend on how they distribute their scent. The mock orange, for example, a large shrub that wafts its scent far and wide, is ideal for the back of a large border, especially since it is rather dull when out of flower. But large plants whose flowers you want to bury your head in, such as *Rosa* 'Constance Spry', need to be sited for easy access, and they are ideally trained over a pergola spanning a walkway or against a house wall, close to where you sit in the evening. House walls are also ideal for other scented climbers, such as the vigorous jasmine (*Jasminum polyanthum*) and the deliciously fragrant star jasmine (*Trachelospermum jasminoides*).

A sheltered garden will seem to trap scent, making a veritable bower of fragrance. In a more open, windy site, locate the most sheltered areas (such as in the lee of a wall or a group of shrubs) and place your fragrant plants there, otherwise you will scarcely notice the scent because it will be borne away on the breeze.

Plants that need to be touched to release their fragrance, such as the herbs lavender (*Lavandula*) and rosemary (*Rosmarinus*), should be placed where you can rub their leaves as you pass. Some prostrate plants are tough enough to stand the occasional (light) footfall and can be planted in the

Above: *The leaves of* Skimmia japonica *have a curious, rather bitter aroma that is released when they are crushed.*

Above: Pelargonium triste *is an unusual member of this genus: its flowers emit a freesia-like scent at night.*

cracks in paving to make a scented carpet. The creeping thymes (*Thymus*) are ideal for this purpose, but you could try the slightly less robust camomile (*Chamaemelum nobile*), *Rosmarinus prostratus* or pennyroyal (*Mentha pulegium*), which are also ideal plants for the top of a retaining wall or the edge of a raised bed.

Many scented plants can be grown in containers and placed on a patio where you sit out in summer. Some are suitable for window boxes or hanging baskets that can be suspended from a pergola over a patio or near a barbecue area. A position near an open window will allow you to enjoy the fragrance from indoors.

Seasonal Factors

Aromatic plants, such as the conifers and woody herbs that originated in Mediterranean countries, give off most scent during hot weather, so you will be particularly aware of them in high summer. Other plants, however, seem to smell sweeter during mild, damp weather or after a shower of rain, when the moisture in the atmosphere holds the scent in some way. You will particularly notice the scent of the late-flowering climbing rose 'New Dawn' on a cool, damp morning in early autumn. Winter-flowering plants tend to be at their most fragrant on mild, sunny days, when their pollinators stir from their dormancy.

Above: Like most members of the pea family, laburnums produce sweetly scented flowers.

Above: The epiphytic orchid Oncidium *'Sharry Baby' has striking flowers that smell of chocolate.*

Night and Day

Unlike other attributes, such as colour, texture and shape, scent is not a constant. Flowers give off their scent when their pollinators are active. Often this is during the hottest part of the day, and there are few more evocative sights and sounds than those of bees, moving from flower to flower on a hot summer day, collecting pollen. Those that are most fragrant when dew is in the air will smell most strongly early in the day and at dusk.

NIGHT-SCENTED PLANTS

Brugmansia suaveolens
Cestrum parqui
Hemerocallis citrina
Matthiola longipetala subsp. *bicornis*
Mirabilis jalapa
Nicotiana alata
Oenothera biennis
Pelargonium triste
Reseda odorata

A few precious plants are scented at night because they are pollinated by night-flying insects. They are particularly appreciated by those who have daytime jobs and who look forward to the delights of a fragrant evening garden at the end of a stressful day.

How to Use This Chapter

This quick and easy guide to planning a scented garden begins with a section that covers all the main plant groups, giving recommendations for the best scented plants in each group. *Scent for All Seasons* explains how those plants can be used to give all-year-round fragrance. Finally, *Scent for Every Style* suggests ways in which gardens can be designed to include many favourite aromas.

Scented Plants in the Garden

EVERY GROUP OF GARDEN PLANTS INCLUDES DELICIOUSLY SCENTED SPECIES, FROM QUICK-TO-GROW ANNUALS TO EXOTIC FLOWERING TREES. THE FOLLOWING SELECTION INCLUDES IDEAS TO HELP YOU FILL A GARDEN WITH FRAGRANCE, WHATEVER ITS SIZE AND STYLE.

Above: Muscari armeniacum *is a diminutive plant with a delicate scent – good for planting* en masse *in the garden.*

BULBS AND CORMS

Valued primarily for their vivid bursts of colour, many of the flowers that grow from bulbs and corms also supply a rich fragrance that more than doubles their appeal. Try to mass them, where possible, to make the most of their brief but intoxicating moments of glory.

Bulbs and corms are among the most versatile plants in the garden, and most are easy to grow. Early bulbs, usually dwarf, are harbingers of spring, studding the bare earth with jewel-like colours, often at the coldest time of the year. Bulbs are also excellent in containers, and this is much the best way to appreciate the scent of low-growing species that you cannot get down low enough to sniff in the garden. Crocuses, dwarf narcissi, irises, tulips and grape hyacinths can all be grown in shallow pans of gritty compost (soil mix).

Some early bulbs are traditionally grown for enjoyment indoors, notably hyacinths (*Hyacinthus*) and *Narcissus papyraceus*. Remember that these are by no means hot-house plants. They are adapted to a hard life, so keep them outdoors in a cool, light but sheltered spot (perhaps against a house wall) and bring them indoors only when the flower buds start to show colour. After flowering they can be planted outside.

Freesias and *Hymenocallis*, which are not hardy in cold climates, can be grown in pots in an alpine house. Florists' cyclamen (usually unnamed varieties of *Cyclamen persicum*) are sold as winter-flowering houseplants. As they are always sold in flower you can be sure to choose the most fragrant. They enjoy a cool but light position. Store them dry in summer and water and feed in autumn to bring them back into growth.

Summer bulbs include the glorious lilies, though many garden forms are not scented. Look for the species *Lilium regale* and the later-flowering *L. speciosum*. The sumptuously fragrant Easter lily (*L. longiflorum*) is unfortunately not hardy, so must be grown under glass in cold districts. It is easily raised from seed. The bulb season ends with the dramatic South Africans: *Amaryllis belladonna* and *Crinum*, both with trumpet-like flowers.

BULBS WITH FRAGRANT FLOWERS

Amaryllis belladonna
Crinum
Crocus
Cyclamen persicum
Freesia
Galanthus
Galtonia candicans
Gladiolus tristis
Hyacinthus
Hymenocallis
Iris reticulata
Lilium (some)
Muscari
Narcissus
Tulipa clusiana
Tulipa sylvestris

Above: Lilium regale *is a strongly scented species lily for the summer border.*

Above: *Hyacinths have possibly the most distinctive scent of any bulbous plant.*

Annuals and Biennials

Annuals are generally used in the garden for instant impact, for the brilliance of the flowers and the ready way in which they are produced. Many have little or no scent, and most gardeners will want to grow them for their visual beauty alone, but there are also a number of wonderfully fragrant varieties which no scented garden should be without.

In addition to a description of the flowers, seed packets carry full instructions on germination and aftercare. If you do not have time to raise plants from seed, buy young plants from a garden centre in spring. However, you will have less choice.

Annuals are almost without exception flowers of high summer, needing warmth and light to perform at their best. Biennials, however, usually flower earlier, in late spring. It is also possible to make a late summer sowing of hardy annuals for overwintering. These will be the earliest to flower in the following season.

Above: *New cultivars are introduced regularly, so consult the latest catalogues to keep abreast of these.*

Above: *Annual nasturtiums have a light, peppery scent, and both the flowers and young leaves are edible. They are one of the easiest annuals to grow, and will self-seed year after year.*

Above: *Sweet peas (*Lathyrus odoratus*), which can be sown in autumn or spring, are an essential component of any scented garden. There are countless varieties, in many delicate colours.*

Above: Sweet-scented Heliotropium *'Marine' is actually a perennial, but it is usually treated as an annual in cold districts.*

Choosing Varieties for Scent

As a rule, scented annuals are less showy than those grown for splendid flowers, so it is a good idea to mix scented varieties with other strains. Night-scented stock (*Matthiola longipetala* subsp. *bicornis*) is a case in point: it is a spindly plant with modest little flowers of a bleached mauve. Scatter the seed among other plants, such as the showier gillyflower (*M. incana*), for the best of both worlds. Sweet peas (*Lathyrus odoratus*) are typical cottage garden plants. Despite the common name, not all cultivars are equally fragrant, so it is worth experimenting to find a variety that particularly pleases you, and many of the old-fashioned plants are among the most fragrant, if not the most colourful. Nasturtiums (*Tropaeolum*) have a fresh, peppery scent, reminiscent of the related watercress. Both flowers and leaves are edible, even if the taste is an acquired one.

ANNUALS AND BIENNIALS WITH SCENTED FLOWERS

Amberboa moschata
Erysimum cheiri
Exacum affine
Iberis
Lathyrus odoratus
Limnanthes douglasii
Lobularia maritima
Matthiola
Oenothera biennis
Reseda odorata
Tropaeolum

Shrubs and Perennials

These plants are the mainstay of the garden, flowering year after year and gradually increasing in size and importance. Nowadays, they are frequently used together to make low-maintenance mixed borders that provide interest over a long period.

Above: Dianthus *'Cobham Beauty' has a light, pleasing scent. Small fragrant pinks make ideal edging plants near a path.*

Aromatic Shrubs

Leaving aside the shrubby herbs, there are a number of shrubs with aromatic foliage, and those that are also evergreen will supply scent all year round.

Many conifers are dwarf and compact or so slow-growing that they can be treated as shrubs for a good few years. They are traditionally combined with heathers, but also work surprisingly well with grasses planted in island beds. But if conifers are not to your taste, try skimmias or Mexican orange blossom (*Choisya ternata*), although you will have to bruise the leaves to enjoy their aroma. The young leaves of the sweet briar (*Rosa eglanteria*) smell distinctly of apples after a shower of rain.

Above: Buddleja alternifolia *has honey-scented flowers in midsummer.*

Above: *The common myrtle (*Myrtus communis*) has an unmistakable aroma.*

Flowering Shrubs

As far as scent is concerned, there is almost a surfeit of shrubs. Mahonias have yellow flowers with a fragrance like lilies-of-the-valley, and some of the berberises, both deciduous and evergreen forms, are similar. *Viburnum* is also a genus richly endowed with flowering species. One of the best is the hybrid *V.* x *burkwoodii*, an elegant plant with heads of sweetly fragrant white flowers in spring.

The scent of lilacs (*Syringa*) seems to embody late spring, but some of the species have flowers with a fetid smell. The hybrids of *S. vulgaris* have the typical lilac scent.

Buddleias are indispensable for their honey-scented, mauve, white or purple flowers. The butterfly bush, *Buddleja davidii*, is almost too well known in some gardens, where it self-seeds with abandon. *B. alternifolia* has a more elegant form, particularly when it is trained as a standard.

SCENTED SHRUBS

Berberis sargentiana
Buddleja
Camellia sasanqua
Cestrum parqui
Choisya ternata
Citrus
Cytisus battandieri
Daphne
Deutzia
Elaeagnus x *ebbingei*
Erica arborea
Hamamelis mollis
Mahonia x *media*
Myrtus communis
Osmanthus decorus
Philadelphus
Skimmia japonica
Syringa vulgaris
Viburnum

Above: *The late summer-flowering* Buddleja davidii *'Black Knight' is dramatically coloured and richly scented.*

Fragrant Roses

If ever a group of plants was prized for its scent, it is the roses. Not all roses are scented, but it is a myth that only old varieties have fragrance. Some, such as 'Nevada', have a light scent, which seems to hang on the air some distance from the plant. Others bear their scent on their stamens, and this is usually a rich, heady fragrance that you have to drink in by burying your nose in the flower.

***Above:** Besides its unique colouring,* Rosa *'Escapade' has a delicious fragrance.*

Scented Perennials

This large and diverse group of plants contains some of the most exquisitely scented species.

The herbaceous clematis are less well known than the climbers, but they make excellent additions to the border, flowering in early summer. *Clematis recta* needs staking but produces a mass of starry, creamy-white flowers, held on stems up to 1.2m (4ft) tall. Herbaceous peonies also need staking, but few gardeners would

SCENTED ROSES

'Apricot Nectar'
'Blue Moon'
'Buff Beauty'
'Céleste'
'Constance Spry'
'Escapade'
'Fantin-Latour'
'Fragrant Cloud'
'Lady Hillingdon'
'Margaret Merril'
'Mme Hardy'
'Mme Isaac Pereire'
'Reine Victoria'
R. rugosa
'Sheila's Perfume'
'Whisky Mac'

Above: Cytisus battandieri *deserves its common name of pineapple broom. The flowers both look and smell like pineapples.*

think that a problem when confronted by their sumptuous flowers, many blessed with a rich, spicy fragrance unmatched in this group of plants. The pink 'Sarah Bernhardt' is an old but reliable cultivar, and 'Kelway's Supreme' has huge, bowl-shaped, satin-textured flowers, but all the cultivars are ravishing, and specialist nursery catalogues are usually temptingly illustrated. The single-flowered forms are more likely to be scented than those with double flowers.

The daylilies (*Hemerocallis*) now form a huge group. New cultivars have a longer flowering season, and some are night-flowering. Many are sweetly scented, but check the catalogues of the specialist breeders. Lily-of-the-valley (*Convallaria majalis*) is almost too familiar, but it has an unmistakable scent and is ideal for growing in a shady spot. It can be forced for winter flowering indoors if you pot up the "pips" in autumn and bring them into an unheated greenhouse or conservatory (sunroom). A little more warmth in midwinter will produce earlier flowers than appear outside. Give the plants a rest after flowering and return them to a position outdoors.

Carnations and pinks (*Dianthus*) make ideal edging plants, which are attractive when out of flower with their sheaves of steel-blue leaves. The clove-scented cultivars are particularly sought-after. Not all the newer forms are scented, although they have the advantage of a longer season.

One of the most intriguing of all plants is *Cosmos atrosanguineus*, whose blood-red flowers smell of melted chocolate. If you are a chocoholic, this is the plant for you.

SCENTED PERENNIALS

Clematis recta
Convallaria majalis
Cosmos atrosanguineus
Dianthus
Helleborus lividus
Hemerocallis
Hosta plantaginea
Iris unguicularis
Phlox
Primula
Smilacina racemosa
Verbena bonariensis

Above: *The delicate scent of primula flowers is best appreciated when they are grown in sizeable drifts in a mixed border.*

TREES WITH SCENT

A tree adds dignity and style to a garden, and several species are scented. Choose carefully, however, because not only will a tree often outlive the gardener, but many trees will also eventually outgrow their allotted space.

TREES WITH SCENTED FLOWERS

Acacia dealbata
Aesculus hippocastanum
Laburnum x *watereri* 'Vossii'
Magnolia delavayi
Magnolia kobus
Magnolia x *loebneri*
Malus floribunda
Malus hupehensis
Prunus 'Amonagawa'
Prunus x *yedoensis*
Styrax japonica
Tilia x *euchlora*
Tilia petiolaris

Flowering Trees

A scented tree in full flower will be one of the glories of the garden. In a mild climate, where frosts are unlikely, an airy acacia, such as *Acacia dealbata* or *A. baileyana*, will charm with its bobbly, duckling-yellow mimosa flowers in early spring. In a cold area, grow it against a warm wall or in a conservatory (sunroom). Acacias are among the few trees that positively thrive in a container. Hardier and rather grander are the magnolias, with sumptuous, chalice-like flowers, usually of a creamy ivory white, although pinks and purples also occur. In cold areas choose a position out of the morning sun, since the flowers can be blackened by a

***Above:** The pure white flowers of* Magnolia x loebneri *'Merrill' are delicately scented.*

Above: Acacia dealbata *produces masses of flowers from late winter to early spring – it makes a magnificent specimen in a sheltered garden.*

sudden rise in temperature after a clear, frosty night. Ornamental cherries (*Prunus*), usually prized for the wealth of their blossom, also include some scented cultivars among their number. The same is true of the crab apples (*Malus*). The musty scent of hawthorn blossoms (*Crataegus*), so evocative in the wild, is possibly best kept out of small gardens and its use restricted to boundary planting.

The evergreen Chinese privet would be an unusual choice. Normally used for hedging (in which case the flowers are generally sacrificed by the tight clipping necessary for a neat surface), this makes a surprisingly elegant specimen or back-of-the-border plant. A warning note must be struck, however: not everyone finds the scent of the creamy summer flowers appealing. Limes (*Tilia*) are too large for most gardens, but anyone who has one growing nearby (such as in a village square or as a pavement planting) will know the heady scent the flowers, though inconspicuous, release on warm evenings in early summer.

Bark, Stems and Leaves

Most conifers are scented, usually because of their sticky, resinous stems. You will especially notice this in a hot summer, when pines (*Pinus*) in particular give off a characteristic scent, but you will also be aware of it if you cut stems from your conifers for winter decoration indoors – do not be put off by the synthetic 'pine fragrance' used in household cleaning products. Eucalyptus scent is also familiar from cough medicines and other remedies.

The scent of the balsam poplar (*Populus balsamifera*) is unmistakable when the leaves unfurl in spring. At the other end of the growing season, one of the most appealing of all scented trees is *Cercidiphyllum*, whose leaves smell of burnt toffee when they fall to the ground in autumn.

TREES WITH AROMATIC BARK, WOOD OR LEAVES

Cercidiphyllum
Eucalyptus
Laurus nobilis
Liquidambar styraciflua
Populus balsamifera
Populus x *candicans*

Aromatic Herbs

Most herbs are not so much scented as aromatic, a quality that is often not immediately apparent but is released only when the leaves or stems are bruised or crushed. The many forms of mint (*Mentha*) are a good example. Most of the plants that are defined as herbs have scents that are refreshing and invigorating, but they are not always appealing. Sometimes a plant's aromatic qualities are a defence mechanism to deter browsing animals. In addition, herbs have been so widely used in medicines that they have acquired connotations beyond gardening. Nevertheless, in any scented garden, herbs will play a major role.

Most of the fragrant herbs have culinary uses, so they are doubly valuable in the garden. Fragrant sage (*Salvia*), rosemary (*Rosmarinus officinalis*) and thyme (*Thymus*) are as well known to cooks as they are to gardeners, but a scented garden will also have room for an aromatic evergreen bay (*Laurus nobilis*) and annual basil (*Ocimum basilicum*). Ornamental herbs, such as the attractive, ever-popular lavender (*Lavandula*) is also grown for its deliciously scented flowers, and cotton lavender (*Santolina chamaecyparissus*) for its aromatic foliage.

***Above:** Lemon balm (*Melissa officinalis*) is very easy to grow and smells strongly of citrus when crushed.*

HERBS WITH SCENTED LEAVES

Aloysia triphylla
Artemisia arborescens
Laurus nobilis
Lavandula
Mentha
Monarda didyma
Ocimum basilicum
Origanum vulgare
Rosmarinus officinalis
Salvia officinalis
Santolina
Thymus

Because most of the culinary herbs are native to countries around the Mediterranean, they need to be grown in well-drained soil in full sun. They are particularly well suited to growing in containers, which tend to be well drained and, if space in the garden is limited, can be moved to sunny positions as the plants come into flower. Bear in mind, however, that many of the cultivated forms with golden or variegated foliage will do better in light or dappled shade.

Take care when handling some of these plants, especially common rue (*Ruta graveolens*). People with sensitive skin may be allergic to the foliage, which can cause rashes.

Harvesting and Preserving

Many herbs can be used fresh in cooked dishes, added to salads or used to make refreshing tisanes. Such herbs should be grown close to the house to make harvesting easy. Many herbs can also be dried or frozen for use out of season, and drying can sometimes enhance the flavour.

Harvest in fine, sunny weather, picking the leaves and shoots early in the day, when the plants are at their freshest. If you intend to dry the plants, wait until the dew has evaporated before picking. Dry the leaves and stems on a metal rack in a warm, dry, well-ventilated place or in a very

Above: *All forms of lavender have that characteristic scent, but the Mediterranean* Lavandula stoechas *stands out.*

low oven. If necessary, the leaves can then be removed from the stems by rubbing. Once dried, herbs should be stored in airtight containers.

Above: *'Tricolor' is an ornamental variegated form of the culinary herb sage (*Salvia officinalis*).*

Climbing Plants

Most climbers are naturally big, rampant plants, and this is really part of their charm, since they will cast their scent far and wide.

Trained over pergolas, they can be used to create a delightful shaded place to sit and relax on a warm summer's day, or they can be planted to ramble through trees, which is logical when you consider that this is how they grow in the wild. They can also be grown over shrubs in the border to lengthen the period of interest, flowering either before or after the host plants (or simultaneously for a briefer but glorious display). Many can also be trained against house walls: a good way of growing plants that are not reliably hardy, since they will benefit from the reflected heat and extra shelter that the wall provides.

Above: Lonerica *has an intoxicating fragrance in the evening.*

Types of Climber

Climbing plants are usually categorized according to the way they cling (if they cling at all) to their support.

Twining climbers have stems that grow in a spiral, in the wild wrapping themselves around the stems of a host plant. The honeysuckles (*Lonicera*) are the most familiar example, but the group also includes the hop (*Humulus lupulus*) and wisteria. These plants are good for growing into trees or over trellis panels, either free-standing or attached to a wall.

Leaf stalk climbers, such as clematis, have specially adapted stalks that twist and grip the thin stems of a host plant. Some types of trellis are too coarse for these, so choose either a light trellis, pig wire or a framework of wires against a wall. They are also excellent rambling through shrubs.

Self-clinging climbers have special pads that adhere to the host, so no system of support is necessary. These are ideal for covering a wall.

Thorny plants, such as roses (*Rosa*), produce long, flexible stems that attach themselves to the bark of host plants by means of their sharp thorns. These usually need a little help in the garden. To train them into a tree, support the stems initially on long canes until the rose has a good grip. Against a wall, use a trellis or system of wires, and train the growing stems as near the horizontal as possible.

Above: 'Blairii No. 2', a sweetly scented Bourbon rose, is repeat-flowering and can make a spectacular climber.

Above: Free-flowering and prolific, this particular Clematis montana *will scent the air far and wide in late spring.*

A Scented Bower

For many, the scent of honeysuckle defines summer, and it can be enjoyed over a long period, since there are early- and late-flowering forms. Equally familiar is the common jasmine (*Jasminum officinale*). The sweet-scented *Jasminum polyanthum* bears large clusters of white flowers but is not hardy, so it must be grown in a conservatory (sunroom) in cold areas. Even more richly scented is the star jasmine (*Trachelospermum jasminoides*), an evergreen with curious white flowers from summer to autumn, that benefits from the protection of a warm wall.

Another plant that benefits from the support of a warm wall is wisteria, surely the most dramatic of all flowering climbers. In this case, the plant is fully hardy, but it needs a good roasting in summer to ensure that it flowers well the following year. Wisteria is also spectacular when it is grown more informally, through a large deciduous tree.

It is a pity that the large-flowered clematis are mostly unscented. For fragrance you need to look to the smaller flowered species. *Clematis montana* is a rampant plant, but not all cultivars are scented. Curiously, a montana can lose its scent from one year to the next for no apparent reason. The deliciously scented *Clematis flammula* and *C. rehderiana* are particularly valued for their late season – from late summer to autumn.

SCENTED CLIMBERS

Akebia quinata
Clematis (some)
Jasminum
Lonicera (some)
Rosa
Trachelospermum jasminoides
Wisteria

Ground-cover Plants

There are a few useful, stalwart plants that can provide scent as well as fulfilling the overriding need to cover large areas of otherwise bare ground or to create weed-suppressing mats of herbage.

Violets make excellent ground cover, especially in a woodland garden, where they revel in the cool, slightly damp conditions. Another valuable woodlander is lily-of-the-valley (*Convallaria majalis*), provided you can get it established. It is also attractive in a shady rock garden. In a more open site (but still with some shelter), primulas could be charming, but remember that not all species are fragrant.

For covering large tracts of rough ground, *Crambe cordifolia* can be magnificent, although it must be admitted that not everyone finds the scent of the clouds of white summer flowers appealing. Another perennial, *Geranium macrorrhizum*, has velvety-textured leaves that emit a resinous fragrance when bruised. They have the added distinction of turning red in autumn.

Many climbers can be used as ground cover, particularly over a bank. Peg down the stems to encourage rooting. Besides strengthening the plant, this will keep down weeds.

SCENTED GROUND-COVER PLANTS

Cistus
Convallaria majalis
Crambe cordifolia
Dianthus
Geranium macrorrhizum
Melissa
Mentha
Petasites
Thymus
Verbena

***Above:** Applemint, like all the mints, makes good aromatic ground cover – perhaps too good, as it can be invasive.*

Above: Houttuynia cordata *is a fine plant for ground cover or as a bog plant; the leaves smell of oranges when crushed.*

*Above: Many water lilies (*Nymphaea*) are described as fragrant. But how are you supposed to get close enough to tell?*

Water Plants

Many water lilies are scented, but in a large pool it can be difficult to get close enough to appreciate this. You are more likely to catch the fragrance of plants at the water's edge.

The sweet rush (*Acorus calamus*) has deliciously scented, handsome, sword-like leaves and can be grown either in wet soil or in shallow water as a marginal plant. The straight species is of scant ornamental value, and only the variegated form, 'Variegatus', is widely grown.

An intriguing bog plant, which can also be grown in borders provided the soil does not dry out, is *Houttuynia cordata*, which has attractive arrow-shaped leaves that look as though cast in bronze. Crush a leaf between your fingers, however, and you will find it smells distinctly of Seville (Temple) oranges. The cultivar 'Flore Pleno' has appealing double white flowers; 'Chameleon' has attractive leaves that are marbled with yellow and red. All forms make excellent ground cover.

All species of mint (*Mentha*) prefer reliably moist soil, but water mint (*M. aquatica*) actually likes to have its feet in water. A rather coarse plant, it can be invasive if given its head.

SCENTED BOG AND WATER PLANTS

Acorus calamus 'Variegatus'
Houttuynia cordata
Mentha aquatica
Nymphaea
Primula

Scent for All Seasons

IF YOU CHOOSE CAREFULLY FROM THE MANY SCENTED PLANTS AVAILABLE, YOU WILL BE ABLE TO ENJOY FRAGRANCE IN THE GARDEN THROUGHOUT THE YEAR. THE FOLLOWING PAGES DESCRIBE AND ILLUSTRATE A SELECTION OF PLANTS FOR EACH SEASON.

THE FRAGRANT GARDEN

A surprisingly large number of plants produce scent all year round. Conifers are always fragrant, though obviously you will be more aware of this during hot, dry weather in summer when the resin oozes from the branches. It is well worth passing your hands over the leaves in the dead of winter to remind yourself of their invigorating scent. All the woody evergreen herbs, such as bay (*Laurus nobilis*) and rosemary (*Rosmarinus*), retain their scent all year round, as do other evergreens, such as skimmias and choisyas.

Indoors, scented-leaf pelargoniums and citrus can be relied on to provide scent for all seasons.

***Above:** Aromatic bay (*Laurus nobilis*) is one of the most desirable of all evergreens.*

Planning for Scent

Achieving year-round scent in your garden will be a matter of trial and error. Plant catalogues and encyclopedias are often vague when it comes to flowering times – necessarily so, since this can vary with the weather from year to year and will also depend on the local conditions.

For scent in winter, look to those shrubs that flower intermittently during mild periods, such as *Viburnum* x *bodnantense*, which has intensely fragrant, deep pink flowers from late autumn to spring. Spring flowers begin with dwarf bulbs, then come the magnolias and shrubs, many divinely scented. Summer is the peak of the gardening year, when you can hardly count the different scents: this is the season of peonies, roses and all the many deliciously perfumed annuals.

Autumn is a quiet time in the garden, when everything in it is dying back – a season for taking stock of your successes and failures. This is a good time for planting to plug all those gaps in the succession of scent that you noticed throughout the year. But as you do so, you will also catch the scents of ripening fruits and seeds. And the deliciously sweet-scented ice plant (*Sedum spectabile*), beloved of bees, often flowers well into autumn.

Above: *Fragrant in all their parts, the various members of the* Citrus *genus provide year-round scent but need winter protection in cold areas.*

Above: *A scented-leaf pelargonium will provide fragrance when you touch the plant, perhaps most noticeably in warm, dry weather.*

SPRING

Many gardeners' favourite season, spring is the time when everything is fresh and full of promise. Most spring scents are appropriately fresh, light and airy.

Bulbs and Corms

Many spring bulbs produce scented flowers. Among the many daffodils and narcissi, those with short cups tend to have the sweetest fragrance, especially the Tazetta hybrids, such as 'Geranium' and 'Cragford'. *Iris reticulata* is delicious but unfortunately not reliably perennial. Dwarf bulbs that will multiply year after year include *Crocus tommasinianus* or forms of *C. chrysanthus*. Some of the more robust hybrids are strong enough to compete with grass and can be planted to create scented drifts in a lawn. Prolific to the extent of becoming weeds are the sweetly scented grape hyacinths (*Muscari*).

Queen of all the spring bulbs, at least so far as scent goes, is the hyacinth (*Hyacinthus*). In appearance flowers are stiff and uncompromising: they are best grown in formal beds *en masse* if you have the space; otherwise they are ideal in containers.

Few tulips are scented – they have been bred for flamboyance of flower – but you could try the dainty lady tulip, *Tulipa clusiana*. To add scent to a dramatic bed of hybrid tulips, combine them with biennial wallflowers (*Cheiranthus*), which have perhaps the spiciest, most evocative perfume of any of the spring flowers. Look for dwarf varieties in shades that will complement the tulips.

Above: Viburnum carlesii *'Diana' has one of the richest fragrances of any of the spring-flowering shrubs.*

Shrubs and Perennials

If you have acid soil, try some of the azaleas (*Rhododendron*). Not all cultivars are scented, but those that are often have a rich, lily-like fragrance entirely in keeping with their exotic-looking flowers.

Spring is the season of viburnums, such as *V.* x *burkwoodii* and *V. carlesii*, both richly perfumed and tolerant of any soil. There is rich scent to be found among the skimmias, which have a powerful lily-of-the-valley fragrance.

Skimmias are extremely versatile and make an elegant choice for containers and tubs near the front door with their squat, compact habit.

If you have light, acid soil, the tree heath (*Erica arborea*) will be a joy in this season with its honey-scented flowers. More tolerant of a range of soil types are the berberises and the handsome *Osmanthus decorus*.

Among perennials, do not overlook lily-of-the-valley (*Convallaria majalis*), a modest plant that is charming where allowed to push itself up through cracks in paving. It is one of the few scented plants that thrives in shade.

***Above:** The herbaceous* Clematis recta *is scented, unlike the large-flowered climbing hybrids.*

Climbers and Trees

There are not many climbers that flower in spring, and those that do tend to have no scent. However, two clematis are worth having for their scent. The evergreen C. *armandii* is handsome, with vanilla-scented flowers around mid-spring. More rampant is *C. montana*. Cultivars vary, but 'Elizabeth' (pale pink) and 'Alexander' (white) are sweetly scented.

Ornamental cherries and magnolias are generally chosen for their looks rather than their scent, but many will reliably perfume the air as well. Among magnolias, *M. denudata* is ravishing, with large flowers that open before the leaves unfurl. *M. salicifolia* has orange-blossom-scented flowers.

For later in the season, consider some of the crab apples (*Malus*), with their delicate blossoms, and lilacs (*Syringa*), which take the shrub season into summer with what is perhaps the most wonderfully potent scent in the entire garden.

SCENTED PLANTS FOR SPRING

Clematis armandii
Convallaria majalis
Crocus
Erica arborea
Erysimum cheiri
Hyacinthus
Magnolia (some)
Muscari armeniacum
Narcissus (some)
Primula (some)
Rhododendron (some)
Syringa
Viburnum

Summer

This is the peak of the gardening year, when the well-planned garden will be filled with an apparently unending succession of flowers. At this time of year, there is an abundance of choice to ensure that delicious scents greet you whenever you step outside on a sunny morning.

Shrubs and Perennials

The summer season is heralded by the peonies, stately plants with gorgeous flowers that are usually of an intoxicating spiciness matched by no other group of plants. Old-fashioned forms of clove-scented carnations and pinks (*Dianthus*) also have a part to play, provided you can supply the conditions that suit them – well-drained, alkaline soil in full sun. Some do best in a rock garden.

Summer is the season of roses, and no garden worthy of the name should be without them. All rose scents are appealing, but while some are light and fresh, others have deeper base notes that make them richer and more complex. One of the best is the climber 'New Dawn', which has a very pronounced, but not cloying, fruity scent that is at its best towards the end of the season as the nights become cooler and damper.

A group of roses known as hybrid musks includes the delightful 'Buff Beauty', with deliciously fragrant flowers of soft apricot-orange that

Above: *Roses vary surprisingly in the strength and character of their fragrance – always try them before buying, if possible.*

Above: *If you have acid soil, plant the heather* Erica vagans *'Summertime', which prefers such conditions.*

Above: Genista lydia, *which flowers in early summer, is a fine scented plant for a Mediterranean-style garden.*

fades to a creamy white in sun. The rambling rose 'Albertine' is virtually unsurpassed for scent, although the myrrh-like notes of 'Constance Spry' run it close. Among modern roses, the aptly named 'Fragrant Cloud' has a rich scent that hangs on the air. 'Margaret Merril' is also incomparable for a white garden. The bleached mauve of 'Blue Moon' does not appeal to all tastes, but the scent is full and lemony.

Mock oranges (*Philadelphus*) are richly, even cloyingly scented. The flowers are exclusively white. 'Virginal' is a good double, but eventually makes a large shrub up to 3m (10ft) in both directions. The cultivar 'Belle Etoile' has single flowers with appealing purple blotches at the centre. *P. coronarius* 'Aureus' has the added distinction of yellow-green leaves, but needs a sheltered position out of full sun to avoid scorching.

SCENTED PLANTS FOR SUMMER

Buddleja
Cestrum parqui
Clematis recta
Clematis rehderiana
Hesperis matronalis
Lilium regale
Lonicera (some)
Matthiola longipetala subsp. *bicornis*
Nicotiana
Philadelphus
Syringa
Wisteria

Trees

Scented summer-flowering trees are rare but delicious. In the past, limes (*Tilia*) were a popular choice for avenues leading up to stately homes, and now they are mature we can enjoy their fragrance. The pale yellow flowers, though they look insignificant, have an unforgettable scent.

In a small garden, the Mount Etna broom (*Genista aetnensis*) is a good choice. It is a light, airy tree that casts little shade but pours forth its fragrant yellow flowers at the height of summer. It needs a well-drained spot in full sun. Sophoras are equally desirable, but not all the species are hardy, and even those that are need long, hot summers to flower reliably.

Annuals and Biennials

Mignonette (*Reseda odorata*) is a charmingly old-fashioned flower with a sweet scent, ideal for a cottage garden. Stocks (*Matthiola*) are also fragrant, and there are many strains of varying colours. The spires of gillyflowers (*M. incana*) are in white and shades of pink, mauve, violet and purple. Sweet alyssum (*Lobularia maritima*), in white or purple, is low-growing and makes an excellent edging plant. Where happy, it will seed itself obligingly in paving cracks. Look out for new strains of another cottage garden favourite, sweet William (*Dianthus barbatus*), which will flower the same year as it is sown and make an invaluable addition to the border.

Above: Buddleja davidii *'Peace' is a white form of this highly fragrant species.*

Above: Paeonia *'Alice Harding', like nearly all the hybrid peonies, has spicily scented flowers.*

Night-scented Flowers

For flowers that are fragrant in the evening look to the aptly named night-scented stock (*Matthiola longipetala* subsp. *bicornis*) or to tobacco plants (*Nicotiana*). These hang their heads in the most pensive way during the heat of the day but revive as the temperature falls to release a potent, incense-like fragrance. *Hesperis matronalis* has the charming common names of dame's violet or sweet rocket. The flowers, which are mauve, purple or white, are carried in phlox-like heads.

Cestrum parqui, a sub-shrub of borderline hardiness, possesses panicles of curious, star-like, lime green flowers. You realize the point of the plant as night falls, when the flowers release a unique, bubble-gum fragrance to attract the night-flying moths that pollinate them. Position the plant in a warm corner of the garden where you relax in the evening.

Herbs

Most of the aromatic herbs are at their best in summer, when their essential oils are freely produced. On a really hot day, the curry plant (*Helichrysum italicum*) will give off its characteristic spicy odour without you having to bruise its leaves. The sweetly scented flowers of lavender (*Lavandula*) and thyme (*Thymus*) are a must, both for their unforgettable fragrance and their attraction for bees and other insects. Lavender can also be harvested and dried for scenting linen.

AUTUMN

Scents tend to be in short supply at this time of year, when most plants are busy setting seed and ripening their fruits. Many of the autumn-flowering plants have no scent at all, though it is worth keeping an eye on new dahlia hybrids: scented forms are being developed using a species that has not hitherto made its way into the garden.

Cheating Nature

Until such time as scented dahlias are widely available, we have to rely on a few tricks. For scent in the autumn garden, you can make a few late sowings of fragrant annuals to be planted out from midsummer. Tobacco plants (*Nicotiana*) will carry on flowering until the first frosts and will reward you with their deliciously scented flowers well into autumn. Pruning *Buddleja davidii* in late spring will delay its flowering season, and as long as the summer is not too hot, flowers should still be coming at this time of year. Ice plants (*Sedum spectabile*) will reliably produce their richly-scented pink flowers in autumn, too.

Many roses have an autumn display that matches the summer one. 'Buff Beauty' is, if anything, even better in autumn, since the flowers hold their distinctive soft orange colour for longer before they fade to white.

In a good year, you can expect the evergreen *Magnolia grandiflora* to push out a few more flowers in autumn. In a cold area train this against a warm wall or look for the

***Above:** Ice plants* (Sedum spectabile) *produce large, flat, flowerheads, composed of tiny fragrant flowers that are very attractive to butterflies.*

Above: Most crab apples not only bear fragrant spring flowers but also have aromatic fruits.

Above: The medlar (Mespilus germanica) *has edible fruits that develop a honeyed sweetness when softened by frost.*

cultivar 'Victoria', which is apparently impervious to the cold. There is no need to cheat nature in the case of *Elaeagnus* x *ebbingei*, as it actually flowers at this time of year. All its cultivars are evergreen and some are attractively variegated. The flowers are inconspicuous but exude a sweet, powerful scent even on chilly days.

Fruits and Foliage

Apples and pears are well known, but the queen of fruits so far as scent is concerned must be the quince (*Cydonia oblonga*). Pick a few and place them in a bowl in a warm room, where they will soon release their distinctive sweet and spicy aroma. They are not edible raw, but make a sublime addition to apple pies and crumbles. Quince jelly is a precious treat. The fruits of the little-grown medlar (*Mespilus germanica*) develop their fragrance as they begin to rot after the first frost; indeed, this is the point at which they become edible.

The leaves of walnuts (*Juglans*) and *Cercidiphyllum japonicum* are also unusually fragrant after they have fallen from the tree, bringing a special pleasure to an autumn stroll through any woodland or arboretum where they are planted.

SCENTED PLANTS FOR AUTUMN

Acidanthera bicolor
Amaryllis belladonna
Camellia sasanqua
Cercidiphyllum japonicum
Chaenomeles
Cydonia oblonga
Elaeagnus x *ebbingei*
Juglans
Magnolia grandiflora
Mespilus germanica
Sedum spectabile

WINTER

Far from being a dead time of year, winter is a season when the garden can be full of scent. Indeed, the fragrance of a winter garden seems to have an added poignancy when so much is lifeless and barren.

Winter Shrubs

One of the best shrubs is the witch hazel (*Hamamelis mollis*) which has spidery, ochre yellow flowers that are sweetly scented. It will do best in a sheltered spot and prefers acid to neutral soil. It is slow-growing, so it will be some years before you will feel happy about cutting branches for indoors. Another desirable plant is the

Above: Viburnum x bodnantense *'Dawn' is one of the most sweetly-scented of all winter-flowering shrubs.*

Above: *The winter flowers of* Sarcococca *have an almost overpowering scent and are quite happy to grow in shade.*

winter-sweet, *Chimonanthus praecox*, although this, too, is slow-growing. Rather faster are the excellent sarcococcas, low-growing evergreens with glossy, pointed leaves. They make excellent ground cover, even under trees. The scent of the inconspicuous white flowers is almost overpowering, and even a couple of branches brought into the warm indoors will scent the whole house.

Viburnum x *bodnantense* is excellent and reliable, flowering on and off throughout winter. Of even greater distinction is *Daphne bholua*, which benefits from a sheltered spot. Plant it near the front door so that you can appreciate its incomparable scent.

A number of shrubs are of small value when in leaf but earn their keep through the fragrance of their winter

Above: Daphne bholua *is a wonderful shrub for planting near the front door, where visitors will appreciate its scent.*

flowers. One such is the shrubby honeysuckle, *Lonicera fragrantissima*, a good plant for a wild garden.

On a warm wall, you could try *Acacia dealbata*, which produces fluffy yellow flowers towards the end of winter. In mild areas this makes an excellent specimen tree. Another plant that benefits from wall protection is *Abeliophyllum distichum*, with fragrant, white, forsythia-like flowers.

SCENTED PLANTS FOR WINTER

Abeliophyllum distichum
Acacia dealbata
Chimonanthus praecox
Daphne bholua
Hamamelis mollis
Iris unguicularis
Lonicera fragrantissima
Mahonia x *media*
Sarcococca
Viburnum x *bodnantense*

A Special Iris

The Algerian iris (*Iris unguicularis*) is unique. It produces its large flowers in the depths of winter. To appreciate them to the full, pull them from the plant while they are still in bud and watch them unfurl in a warm sitting-room, where they will release a delicious fragrance. The plant itself is tough and hardy, but, betraying its geographical origins, it needs a hot position (preferably at the base of a warm wall) in well-drained soil of low fertility. Once established, it should be left alone, and the flowering display will improve year on year, as long as the rhizome gets a good baking in the previous summer.

Above: The yellow flowers of Mahonia x media *bring the fragrance of lily-of-the-valley to the winter garden.*

Scent for Every Style

TELEVISION MAKEOVER PROGRAMMES AND STYLE MAGAZINES HAVE MADE DESIGNERS OF ALL OF US, AND NOW NEARLY ALL GARDENERS CONSIDER DESIGN AN ESSENTIAL ASPECT IF THE GARDEN IS TO BE MORE THAN JUST A COLLECTION OF PLANTS.

DEFINING STYLE

In gardening the word style is a convenient way of categorizing or of sorting plants into groups and arrangements that seem homogeneous, meaningful and aesthetically pleasing. When we design a garden or a section of a garden, we will choose plants that will help us create the effects we want to achieve, opting, for example, for those with a regular shape, such as many conifers or skimmias, or those that can be clipped and topiarized, such as box or privet, to create a formal garden. A cottage garden style implies a more relaxed approach to both planting and weed control, involving plants that are easy to cultivate and do not need endless trimming and pruning to look their best. If, in addition to achieving a particular visual style, we want to incorporate scented plants,

Above: *Aromatic herb gardens can be defined by formal, clipped hedges.*

***Above:** Terracotta containers are perfect for growing informal groupings of aromatic herbs.*

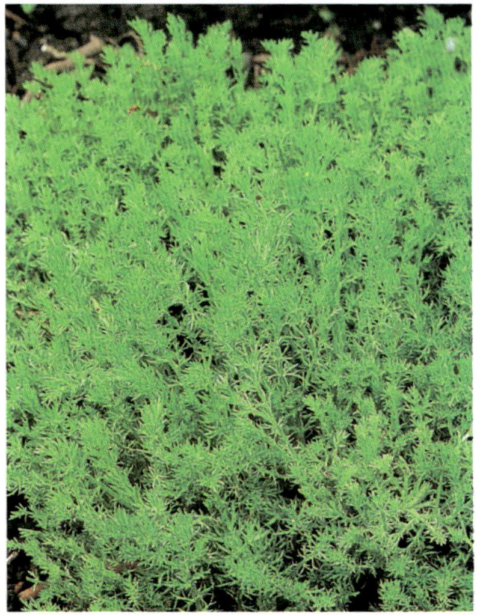

***Above:** Camomile can be used to create a fragrant lawn that needs no mowing and releases scent as you walk over it.*

our plans might need to be modified to varying degrees to accommodate this extra dimension.

Selecting a Style

The overall guideline that you should select a style for your garden that reflects your own personality and lifestyle is a truism, but it is nevertheless worth observing: there is no point opting for a garden that relies on summer bedding for scent, colour and definition if you do not have time to raise, plant out and then lift the spent plants at the end of the season. Given this caveat, however, there is a wide range of styles that can be adapted to include the many scented plants described in the previous section.

When scent is as important a factor in your garden design as colour or ease of maintenance, your plant selection should reflect this. It is well known that some roses, for example, are more fragrant than others, and this is true of several other plant groups. There are many more cultivars and strains available today than in the past, but even given this vast choice, there may be occasions when your wish to include a fragrant plant may have to override other design considerations, such as colour or form. Nevertheless, the gardener who longs for scent will find plants of almost every conceivable shape, colour and habit of growth to fit in with the most demanding of schemes.

Cottage Garden

The idealized picture of a cottage garden, with bees buzzing lazily above lavender and other sweetly scented flowers, is an appealing one, even if it exists more in the popular imagination than in reality. Contrary to what you might expect, planting a scented cottage garden requires the careful selection of fragrant cultivars and the exclusion of other, strongly growing but less aromatic varieties.

Choosing Plants

Typically, the cottage garden consists of simple plants that are easy to grow. The beds and borders should be overflowing with a profusion of plants.

Borders can be edged with box or lavender, both fragrant in different ways, which may be formally clipped or allowed to grow more freely. Roses are essential, but choose from the many scented varieties. Old roses are traditional, but many flower only once, and there is no reason to exclude modern roses that have a longer season.

***Above:** Scented roses in profusion are an essential part of cottage garden style.*

Above: Skimmia japonica *is a useful evergreen shrub with sweetly scented flowers in early spring.*

For climbers, think about the climbing roses ('Zéphirine Drouhin' is an old favourite, with magenta flowers over a long period), jasmine or honeysuckles. If these can be persuaded to frame the front door or sitting room window, so much the better. If you have a garden gate, it is a charming idea to train climbing plants over an archway spanning the path at the entrance to the garden.

Perennials include scented pinks (*Dianthus*); some have appealing names, such as 'Gran's Favourite', 'Sops in Wine' and 'Fair Folly'. Peonies, such as hybrids of *Paeonia officinalis* (often sold unnamed), are cottage garden

classics. All the perennial herbs belong in such a garden; traditionally they were used to provide potpourri and were often spread on the floor to cover damp smells, to say nothing of their value in the kitchen and as medicines. The Madonna lily (*Lilium candidum*), with white, scented flowers, is also a

Above: *Fragrant cottage garden pinks* (Dianthus) *have been grown for centuries.*

Above: *A cottage garden is a pleasing jumble of colourful and fragrant plants, at its best in high summer.*

typical cottage garden plant. For annuals, try dame's violet (*Hesperis matronalis*), old-fashioned tobacco plants (*Nicotiana*) and sweet peas (*Lathyrus odoratus*), which can also be incorporated in a vegetable plot to provide cut flowers for the house.

SCENTED COTTAGE GARDEN PLANTS

Convallaria majalis
Dianthus
Geranium macrorrhizum
Hesperis matronalis
Lathyrus odoratus
Lilium
Lobularia maritima
Matthiola
Nicotiana
Paeonia officinalis
Philadelphus
Reseda odorata
Rosa

Mediterranean Garden

In recent years, as climate change has made summers in much of the northern hemisphere drier and hotter, the Mediterranean-style garden has become increasingly popular. This popularity has been fuelled by an increased use of aromatic herbs in the kitchen and by the fact that many of these herbs are not only attractive but also easy to maintain.

The Best Conditions

The Mediterranean style implies a warm, sunny site and soil that is both free-draining and low in fertility. Lushness is the antithesis of this style. Basking in heat and starved of nutrients, Mediterranean plants develop a gaunt appearance that is an essential part of their appeal.

A sun-baked slope is ideal. Most Mediterranean plants do not mind wind, and some are coastal. White concrete terraces will help to reflect heat and light, as will a top-dressing of gravel, which will also improve drainage – vital for all these plants.

Choosing Plants

Height and structure should really be provided by pines, which exude their resinous sap as the temperature climbs in summer. There are plenty of dwarf varieties for the small garden. That also goes for junipers (*Juniperus*), though these are a little less "giving" of their fragrance. Another traditional conifer of the Mediterranean is the cypress (*Cupressus sempervirens*). Elegant, pencil-thin forms are the most desirable. For a cold climate, be

Above: *A beautiful herb garden of fennel, sage in flower, hyssop and oregano.*

Above: Citrus trees in pots are an essential feature of the Mediterranean garden.

Above: The distinctive scent of lavender is associated with the Mediterranean style.

sure to look out for the hardy forms that have been developed in recent years. Another excellent tree for this style of garden is the Mount Etna broom (*Genista aetnensis*) which produces a shower of yellow, scented pea blossom in summer but is so light and airy that it casts little shade.

Bulk out the borders with the excellent cistuses, grown mainly for their crinkled, papery summer flowers but of value here for their sticky, resinous stems and leaves. All the woody herbs suit this style of gardening.

Many favourite culinary herbs are indispensable additions to this type of garden and can be used to provide colour as well as scent. Lavender and rosemary are obvious candidates. Remember box (*Buxus sempervirens*), an excellent edging plant that can be clipped to shape or not, as the fancy takes you. Box borders have been discovered in excavations of Roman villas, so there is classical precedence for its use. It has a quite distinctive scent that is released during hot weather or after a shower and that most gardeners learn to love.

SCENTED PLANTS FOR A MEDITERRANEAN GARDEN

Artemisia
Buxus sempervirens
Cistus
Citrus
Cupressus sempervirens
Genista aetnensis
Helichrysum italicum
Juniperus
Laurus nobilis
Lavandula stoechas
Olea europea
Phlomis fruticosa
Pinus
Rosmarinus
Salvia officinalis

Formal Garden

The formal style is more a matter of design than the other garden types discussed in this book. The gardener who is attracted to formalism is more interested in the structure and shape of the garden – what might be referred to as the manipulation of an exterior space – than such incidentals as flowers. Nevertheless, scent need not be excluded from such a scheme.

Choosing Plants

While formality can be achieved through non-plant material, through the lie of paths, walls and formal pools, it would be almost a contradiction in terms to banish plants from the garden entirely. Plants that lend themselves to clipping obviously answer well the requirements of formalism. Unfortunately, extensive pruning – a gardening discipline in its own right – is often carried out at the expense of flowers. This is where plants with scented leaves come into their own. Box (*Buxus sempervirens*) is ideal for edging a planting area, in containers or clipped to shape.

Less versatile, but with an equally distinctive smell, are the curry plant (*Helichrysum italicum*) and lavender (*Lavandula*). A few tastefully positioned conifers, especially those that grow into a perfect shape without the intervention of the gardener, could complete a planting that would be low-key and subtle but would have the benefit of fragrance.

A specimen tree (possibly in a container) would make an excellent focal point. Bay (*Laurus nobilis*), with aromatic evergreen leaves, can be clipped to shape, though in some areas it needs some protection from cold, drying winds in winter (horticultural fleece would be adequate on a frosty night). An acacia (*Acacia dealbata*), citrus or olive (*Olea europea*), all with fragrant flowers, could also look extremely stylish, although none is reliably hardy.

If you cannot imagine life without flowers, consider the sculptural perfection of lilies. These can be grown in

***Above:** Bay* (Laurus nobilis) *leaves release a wonderful spicy scent when crushed.*

Above: In a formal garden, a raised bed is ideal for bringing scent close to the gardener.

SCENTED PLANTS FOR A FORMAL GARDEN

Buxus sempervirens
Citrus
Conifers
Laurus nobilis
Lavandula
Ligustrum lucidum
Myrtus communis
Rosmarinus
Santolina

pots and distributed around the garden in a formal arrangement. Earlier in the year, hyacinths planted in containers would have a comparable distinction, and their stiff, upright habit is entirely apposite in these surroundings. Annuals recommended for bedding are excellent when they are grown in formal blocks. Look for single colour strains of stocks (*Matthiola*), tobacco plants (*Nicotiana*) – 'Lime Green' is a sophisticated choice – and sweet alyssum (*Lobularia maritima*).

Above: This formal garden has been filled with a range of plants to appeal to the senses, including roses and lavender.

Modern Garden

The essence of the modern style is determined by a desire for simplicity. A contemporary garden is based on pure form and texture, creating an environment that is both stimulating and calming. The planting must be carefully considered and should include some well-chosen scented plants.

Choosing Plants

No plant is actually modern in the generally accepted sense of the term, but trends in gardening come and go. Plants fall in and out of favour, partly as a result of television programmes and partly as new cultivars are promoted. The beautifully scented *Lilium* 'Star Gazer' is an example of a bulb that is currently in vogue. Its deep, rose-red flowers, edged with white, is perfect for adding a splash of colour to a muted, contemporary scene. Other scented lilies that are suitable for a modern setting are *Lilium regale* with its large, trumpet-shaped white flowers and *Lilium candidum*, the Madonna lily.

Hostas can be grand and architectural, but they are usually grown for their leaves rather than their flowers. The exceptions are *H. plantaginea* and a hybrid derived from it, 'Honeybells'. Both of these have shining green

Above: *This sleek, black slate bench, with lilies planted close by, provides the perfect resting place to sit and enjoy the fragrances of the garden.*

Above: *Cotton lavender (*Santolina*) grows in a pleasing dome shape that lends itself to contemporary plantings.*

leaves and sweetly scented white flowers in the summer, and unlike most hostas, they are best in full sun. Both are excellent in containers.

One of the most architectural of all herbaceous perennials is *Angelica archangelica* (sometimes a biennial), which carries its large, dome-shaped heads of greenish-yellow summer flowers on stems up to 2m (6ft) tall. It is aromatic in all its parts.

A High-tech Garden

The modern garden uses a range of materials. Galvanized, beaten metal containers are part of the style, as is recycled glass, often moulded into "pebbles" in place of gravel (which is less acceptable these days, since it is not a renewable resource). Even old CDs can be recycled for use as a paving material. The traditional colours of stone and terracotta are less in keeping with the high-tech style.

Genetic modification will no doubt be used to introduce scent into previously unscented flowers, such as gladioli and chrysanthemums, but in the meantime, the modern gardener looks to such plants as *Yucca filamentosa*, a perennial with spiky, sword-like leaves and panicles of scented white flowers in late summer, *Mahonia* x *media*, a group of gaunt shrubs with richly fragrant, yellow flowers in winter above pointed, holly-like leaves, or the stiffly formal hyacinths (*Hyacinthus*), which flower in spring. All have the characteristic high-tech look that is appropriate to a garden designed in a contemporary style.

Above: *A bank of highly scented hyacinths add colour and form.*

Plants for Scent

MOST OF THE PLANTS LISTED BELOW ARE MORE FULLY DESCRIBED ELSEWHERE IN THIS CHAPTER, BUT THIS CHECKLIST IS PROVIDED AS A QUICK REFERENCE TO HELP YOU CHOOSE A RANGE OF SCENTED PLANTS FOR ALL SEASONS WHEN PLANNING YOUR GARDEN.

Plant name	Part of plant scented	Season	Day/night
Acacia t HH–FRH	flowers	winter–spring	day
Akebia quinata c FH	flowers	spring	day
Aloysia triphylla h FRH	leaves	spring–summer–autumn	day
Artemisia arborescens h FH	leaves	spring–summer–autumn	day
Berberis sargentiana h FH	flowers	spring	day
Buddleja s FH	flowers	summer–autumn	day
Camellia sasanqua s FH	flowers	autumn–winter	day
Cercidiphyllum t FH	fallen leaves	autumn	day
Cestrum parqui s FRH	flowers	summer–autumn	night
Choisya ternata s FH	flowers/leaves	spring	day
Cistus s FH	stems	summer	day
Citrus s/t FRH	flowers/leaves	all year	day
Clematis armandii c FH	flowers	spring	day
Clematis flammula c FH	flowers	summer–autumn	day
Clematis montana c FH	flowers	spring	day
Clematis recta p FH	flowers	spring–summer	day
Clematis rehderiana c FH	flowers	summer–autumn	day
Convallaria majalis p FH	flowers	spring	day
Cosmos atrosanguineus p FRH	flowers	summer	day
Crambe cordifolia p FH	flowers	summer	day
Crocus b FH	flowers	spring	day

Above: Crambe cordifolia

Above: Paeonia *'Bowl of Beauty'*

Cytisus battandieri s FRH	flowers	summer	day
Daphne s FH–FRH	flowers	winter/spring	day
Deutzia s FH	flowers	spring–summer	day
Dianthus p/a FH	flowers	spring–summer	day
Elaeagnus x *ebbingei* s FH	flowers	autumn	day
Erica s FH–FRH	flowers	all seasons	day
Erysimum cheiri p FH	flowers	spring	day
Eucalyptus t FH	stems	all year	day
Genista aetnensis s/t FH	flowers	summer	day
Genista lydia s FH	flowers	summer	day
Hamamelis mollis s FH	flowers	winter	day
Hebe cupressoides s FH	stems	all year	day
Helichrysum italicum h FH	leaves	all year	day
Heliotropium arborescens a FH	flowers	summer	day
Hemerocallis p FH	flowers	summer	day/night
Hesperis matronalis bi FH	flowers	spring–summer	night
Hosta 'Honeybells' p FH	flowers	summer	day
Hosta plantaginea p FH	flowers	summer	day
Hyacinthus orientalis b FH	flowers	winter–spring	day
Hypericum 'Hidcote' s FH	leaves	spring–summer	day
Iris p/b FH	flowers/bulb	winter/spring/ summer	day
Jasminum c FH–FRH	flowers	winter/summer	day
Laurus nobilis s/h FRH	leaves	all year	day
Lavandula h FH–HH	flowers/leaves	spring/summer– autumn	day
Lilium b FH–HH	flowers	summer	day/night
Liquidambar styraciflua t FH	leaves	spring–summer	day
Lobularia maritima a FH	flowers	summer–autumn	day
Lonicera c/s FH	flowers	summer/winter	day
Magnolia s/t FH	flowers	spring	day
Mahonia s FH	flowers	winter–spring	day
Matthiola a FH	flowers	summer	day/night

Above: Dianthus *'Louise's Choice'*

Above: Lonicera japonica *'Halliana'*

Melissa h FH	leaves	spring–summer–autumn	day
Mentha h FH	leaves	spring–summer–autumn	day
Muscari b FH	flowers	spring	day
Myrtus s FRH	flowers	summer	day
Narcissus b FH–HH	flowers	spring	day
Nicotiana a FRH–HH	flowers	summer–autumn	night
Nymphaea wp FH–FRH	flowers	summer	day
Osmanthus s FH	flowers	spring	day
Paeonia s/p FH	flowers	spring–summer	day
Pelargonium p FRH (scented-leaf)	leaves	all year	day
Perovskia s FH	stems	spring–summer–autumn	day
Petasites p FH	flowers	winter–spring	day
Petunia a HH	flowers	summer	day
Philadelphus s FH	flowers	summer	day/evening
Phlomis s FH–FRH	flowers	summer	day
Phlox p/al FH–HH	flowers	summer	day
Populus balsamifera t FH	leaves	spring	day
Primula p/al FH–FT	flowers	spring/summer	day
Reseda odorata a FH	flowers	spring–summer–autumn	day
Rhododendron s FH–FT	flowers	spring–summer	day
Rosa s/c FH	flowers	summer–autumn	day
Rosmarinus h FH–HH	leaves	all year	day
Ruta graveolens h FH	leaves	all year	day
Salix triandra s FH	flowers	winter–spring	day
Santolina s FH	leaves	all year	day
Sarcococca s FH	flowers	winter	day

Above: Pelargonium *'Little Gem'*

Above: Santolina chamaecyparissus

Skimmia s FH	flowers/leaves	winter–spring	day
Smilacina racemosa p FH	flowers	spring	day
Spartium junceum s FH	flowers	summer	day
Syringa s FH	flowers	spring	day
Thymus h FH	leaves	spring–summer	day
Trachelospermum c FRH *jasminoides*	flowers	summer	evening
Tulipa b FH	flowers	spring	day
Verbena p/a FH–FT	flowers	summer	day
Viburnum carlesii s FH	flowers	spring	day
Viburnum s FH x *bodnantense*	flowers	winter	day
Viola p/a FH	flowers	summer/winter	day
Wisteria c FH	flowers	summer	day

KEY TO ABBREVIATIONS

a = annual
al = alpine
b = bulb
bi = biennial

c = climber
h = herb
p = perennial
s = shrub

t = tree
wp = water plant

FT = frost tender = may be damaged by temperatures below 5°C (41°F)
HH = half hardy = can withstand temperatures down to 0°C (32°F)
FRH = frost hardy = can withstand temperatures down to –5°C (23°F)
FH = fully hardy = can withstand temperatures down to –15°C (5°F)

In the United States, throughout the Sun Belt states, from Florida, across the Gulf Coast, south Texas, southern deserts to Southern California and coastal regions, annuals are planted in the autumn, bloom in the winter and spring, and die at the beginning of summer.

Above: Rosa *'Ispahan'*

Above: Ruta graveolens *'Variegata'*

HANGING BASKETS

Whatever the time of year, there is nothing more welcoming than a prettily planted basket hanging on a wall or near the door. Even if you have no garden at all, you will almost certainly have somewhere for a basket or two. This chapter contains all the information you need, from choosing the right basket and the best plants to tips on regular maintenance for keeping the arrangement in tip-top condition.

Miniature Gardens

HANGING BASKETS ADD AN EXTRA DIMENSION TO GARDENING – POSITIONED JUST ABOVE EYE LEVEL, THEY INVITE YOU TO LIFT YOUR GAZE SKYWARDS. WHETHER YOU PLANT FOR SUBTLETY OR GO FOR A RIOT OF COLOUR, THEY MAKE FOR INSTANT APPEAL.

ENJOYING HANGING BASKETS

Hanging baskets are a form of gardening that is available to everyone, even those who have no garden. Fixed to house walls, they are an extension to the home, bringing pleasure every time you walk through the door. They are democratic: delightfully framing the doorway of an elegant town house, they are equally at home at the entrance to a country cottage. They can be fixed near a kitchen window – if you want to grow herbs, for instance. They can also be suspended on either side of a patio door and enjoyed from inside when it is too wet or cold to venture outdoors. They are also the ideal way for a city-dweller to experience something of the thrill of growing things.

Above: Extend a border vertically by using the same colours in an eye-level arrangement of plants.

DECIDING WHAT YOU WANT

A wealth of plants can be grown in baskets, not just the traditional lobelias, pelargoniums and fuchsias, splendid though these are. While they are generally associated with summer, you can plant baskets for spring, autumn or even winter interest, because many plants flower at these cooler times of year, even if the choice may not be as great.

Hanging baskets are also extremely versatile as they can be enjoyed in many ways. Most people think of them as vehicles for vibrant summer flowers, but they can be used not just for flower plantings, but also for plants with variegated or coloured leaves, herbs, and even fruit and vegetables. In a conservatory (sunroom), use them for trailing rainforest plants, such as cacti, ferns and orchids.

MAKING AN IMPACT

As with many other types of container, hanging baskets offer boundless opportunities to experiment. You can try out all kinds of colour combinations and be as subtle as you like or as ritzy as you dare. You can use an arbitrary mix of flowers that will certainly be cheerful if not elegant or you can adopt a more sophisticated approach and plan the effect from the outset. Hot vibrant colours, such as red, orange and yellow, will always make an impact, while soft blues, pinks, cream and white are more soothing. Purples are ambivalent, adding drama to an already brilliant planting but sounding deeper notes in a gentler pastel scheme.

Above: *This charming planting uses polyanthus, pansies and dwarf narcissi to brighten a gloomy corner in spring.*

Below: *This subtle arrangement makes effective use of the silky-textured, silver-leaved* Helichrysum petiolare.

Deciding on Style

Some of the best hanging baskets are to be found in municipal schemes and adorning the streets of towns, where they are often paid for by the shopkeeper. The baskets are usually planted for summer interest and often contain bright, eye-catching colours. You can, of course, copy these at home, but there is no reason you cannot add a personal touch. An informal mixture of plants suits a cottage garden, for instance, whereas an elegant, white-painted, stuccoed house needs a more tightly controlled look, perhaps involving no more than two colours. If you favour a very minimalist style, try a few hanging rat's-tail cacti with perhaps a spiky aloe for height. For a funky look, try using one of the more compact grasses, such as *Festuca glauca*.

Interest Through the Year

Hanging baskets are traditionally associated with summer, but they can also be enjoyed at other times of year. Spring baskets, possibly involving some dwarf bulbs, such as daffodils, irises or crocuses, with a few early bedding plants, are always a delight, but it is also possible to enjoy baskets in autumn with a combination of tender perennials – which seem to go on flowering for ever – with the addition of some late-sown annuals. Winter baskets offer less scope, but it is still possible to have some choice of colour. Choose robust, winter-flowering heathers and hardy pansies, and even dainty ivies, whether colourful variegated varieties or plain green, can be surprisingly interesting and attractive.

Above: *This glorious display uses pale pink nemesias to offset the rich purples of the verbenas and pansies.*

Sun or Shade

Once you have decided where your baskets are to go, the amount of sun or shade the position offers will influence your choice

Left: Coelogyne velutina *is a robust orchid with trailing flower stems, which, together with the upright leaves, create an unusual effect.*

of plants. Many of the summer flowers are sun worshippers, but remember that in a very sheltered spot against a warm wall, the heat on a hot summer's day will be intense. Reserve such a favoured spot for real exotics, such as South African osteospermums. Many plants will thrive in shade. Lobelias are shade tolerant, and begonias and busy Lizzies actually prefer it. Fuchsias usually do best if kept out of direct sun.

Size Matters

The size of the basket is an important consideration. Although large baskets are the most spectacular and can house the greatest number of plants, they will take up a lot of space when the plants are mature and will be heavy, particularly when wet. That can be an issue if you need to move the basket for any reason. However, a large basket would be first choice for growing fruit and vegetables, which normally need a good root run to develop properly. Smaller baskets create a daintier effect but perhaps offer less scope for exciting colour combinations.

How to Use This Chapter

You will find all the information you need for creating successful baskets on the following pages. *Getting Started* deals with such practical matters as choosing a suitable basket, selecting an appropriate potting mix, buying plants, planting the basket and maintaining it. Watering, feeding and dealing with pests and diseases are also covered. The subsequent sections are full of ideas, with *Baskets for All Seasons* illustrating a range of baskets planted for seasonal appeal, whether your taste is for subtle or brilliant or for dramatic foliage effect. Herb, fruit and vegetable baskets are also given due attention. In *Satisfying the Senses* you will find ideas for plants to smell and touch as well as stimulating the eye. Finally, there is a useful summary of seasonal tasks, followed by a list of recommended plants with information on plant type and size, season of interest, flower colour and cultivation tips.

Getting Started

ONCE YOU HAVE DECIDED WHAT YOU WANT YOUR HANGING BASKETS TO PROVIDE, YOU CAN BEGIN TO EXPLORE THE MANY TYPES THAT ARE AVAILABLE AND DECIDE WHICH BEST SUITS YOUR NEEDS AND THE STYLE OF PLANTING YOU HAVE IN MIND.

TYPES OF HANGING BASKETS

Hanging baskets come in all shapes and sizes, and when you come to shop for one you will be amazed at the range available. The traditional basket is half a sphere and is usually made of plastic-coated wire, with three chains to hang from. Wrought iron is also sometimes used, especially for hay baskets, which are meant to be fixed directly against a wall. More ornate antique baskets (and, increasingly, reproductions of these) can be found, but decorative as these are, they are usually less sturdy, so are less suitable for a very heavy planting. Decide whether it is the basket itself or the plants that you grow in it that will be the focus of interest.

Some baskets really are baskets and are made of wicker or bamboo or some other twiggy material. Many are beautiful to look at and are perhaps best with a simple planting. It is not always possible, or indeed desirable, to plant through the sides of such containers. Unless they have been treated with some kind of preservative, they

Above: Plastic-coated wire baskets.

Above: Wrought iron and galvanized wire baskets.

Above: Small hanging baskets often look most effective when a single flower colour is used.

will be vulnerable to changes in the weather and may dry out and split in hot sun. They may need to be replaced after a few seasons, while a metal basket is virtually indestructible and will last for many more years than those made of wicker or bamboo.

The ideal basket is strong but lightweight. It will be heavy enough once it is full of moist soil and all the plants have reached their optimum size so you do not want to start off with a heavy basket that is going to add substantially to the overall weight.

Some baskets are sold already lined with plastic, but remember to pierce this before use to allow for drainage.

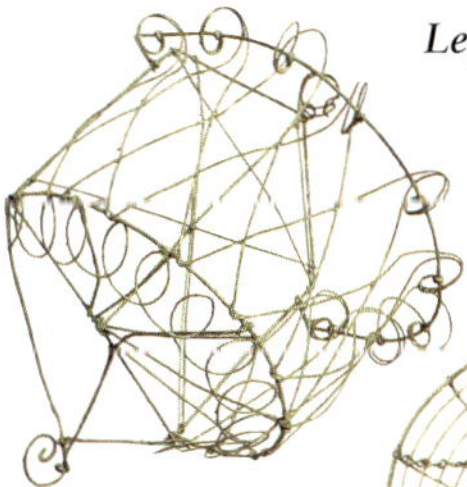

Left: Antique basket.

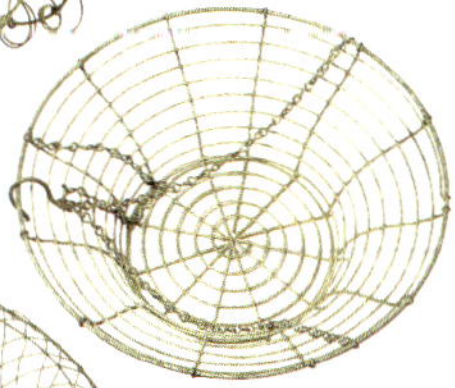

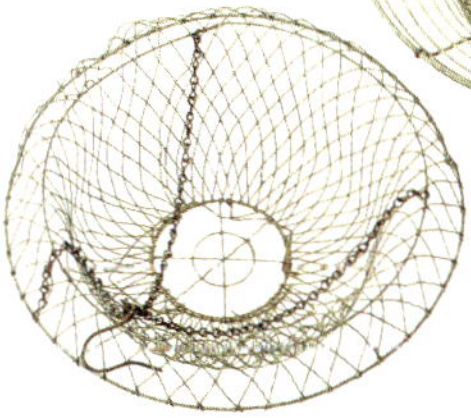

Above and left: Copies of antique baskets.

Brackets and Other Fixings

All hanging baskets have to be mounted, and usually some form of wall bracket is required. To determine the size of the bracket, you need to calculate how wide the basket will be once it is planted up and mature, then divide this figure by two. This is the minimum distance it will need to hang from the wall so that the plants can be displayed properly. Look for sturdy brackets that will not buckle under the weight of the basket and that are made from rust-proof material. Hanging baskets can also be suspended from hooks attached to the cross-beam of an archway or pergola or screwed to the ceiling of a conservatory (sunroom).

Above: This antique wicker bird cage is such a thing of beauty that it needs only the simplest planting.

Other Types of Container

Apart from the traditional hemispherical shape, other types of container are available. Your choice will often be determined by the type of plant you wish to grow.

Orchid baskets are shallow, usually square and made of wooden slats. They are designed to allow plant roots to grow through and grip the sides. Orchid potting mix is coarse enough not to slip through the openings. The baskets are usually designed for indoor use and are not robust enough to stand up to the weather. Similar baskets are available for other tropical plants that need air around their roots, such as some ferns and cacti.

Ideas for Improvising

If you like to experiment, keep a sharp eye out for objects that were intended for quite different purposes but that can be used as hanging baskets. Antique bird cages are very beautiful and make a witty statement hanging from the branches of a tree. For a cottage kitchen look, use an old metal colander. These are particularly effective and appropriate for culinary herbs or other edible crops. Look out for them in flea markets and junk shops. Car sales and second-hand stores are also a valuable source of unusual but usable hanging containers.

Above: Slatted baskets are ideal for orchids and other tree-dwelling plants.

Left: *Recycled cardboard is increasingly popular as a liner. Most have pre-cut holes that can be punched out.*

Different Linings

What you line your basket with is a matter of choice. The traditional material is moss, but, like peat, this is not a renewable resource, and many feel that alternatives are preferable. Some products, often based on recycled sisal, look remarkably natural. Coir lining is sometimes sold in rolls or ready cut to fit certain sizes of basket. Convenient pressed cardboard liners are pre-formed to fit various sizes of basket.

Remember that once the planting is mature, the liner will be all but invisible, so a material that at first glance looks a little unsympathetic will soon be hidden from view.This is especially the case with summer baskets.

Above: *This unusual edible hanging basket contains a profusion of decorative curled parsley. Sage or summer savory would look just as attractive as the parsley.*

Choosing a Compost

There are a number of different composts (soil mixes) on the market, some all-purpose, others tailored for specific needs. Loamless mixtures, which are light, are usually best.

Loam-based compost is based on soil. It is high in nutrients but also heavy. It can easily be lightened by adding perlite or vermiculite.

Lime-free (ericaceous) compost is specially formulated for those plants that will not grow in limy conditions, such as many of the heathers and azaleas.

All-purpose compost is cheap and light to handle, but many are based on peat, which is not a renewable resource, and most gardeners now prefer to look around for more ecologically acceptable peat-free alternatives.

Peat-free compost is also an all-purpose compost, but, for ecological reasons, is usually based on a renewable resource such as coir or bark.

Hanging basket compost is lightweight and often contains some water-retaining crystals and slow-release fertilizers, but it may be peat-based.

Above: *If the compost does not already contain water-retaining gel, you can mix some in before planting, pre-soaking if necessary so that it expands with water.*

***Above:** Pelleted fertilizers, which are very easy to use and can feed for a whole season, are a low-maintenance option.*

Orchids and cacti need specially formulated, free-draining, proprietary composts. Ordinary composts retain too much moisture and are not suitable for these plants.

Watering and Feeding

You can cut down on watering by adding water-retaining gel. Make sure the compost does not already contain any – an excessive amount will cause problems when it swells up. Most new composts contain some plant food, but this is usually exhausted after 6 weeks. To keep the plants flowering well, you should give a high-potash plant food. Tomato fertilizers are suitable, but you can also buy special hanging basket formulas. Pelleted fertilizers are easy to handle and feed the plant as they break down in the compost. One application will last for a whole season, but check, as individual products vary.

Liquid feeds are sold either as powders to be dissolved in water, as liquids to be diluted or as ready-mixed products. They are usually watered into the compost as a root drench at intervals, depending on the product. Some can be sprayed directly on to the foliage as a foliar feed, and these are especially good for giving your plants an instant boost if they have suffered a set-back, such as an unexpected cold spell or pest attack – but a certain amount of the product is inevitably lost.

***Above:** Using the right compost and feeding regularly will ensure that the plants in your hanging baskets flower for longer.*

Thinking Ahead

Hanging baskets have to be planned far in advance. Although it is possible to buy plants in flower for instant impact, this is an expensive option and the flowers are likely to be short-lived if they have been forced out of season. As a general rule, you need to plant up your baskets 6–10 weeks before the main season of interest. Spring-flowering bulbs, for instance, are sold in autumn and winter and should be planted at that time.

Buying Plants

The best advice when buying plants is to go to a reputable garden centre or nursery. Bedding plants are sold in strips, but larger plants such as ivies, pelargoniums and fuchsias are usually potted individually. "Plugs", basically young plantlets with well-developed root systems, are often sold via mail order by seed merchants; busy Lizzies, fuchsias, pelargoniums and begonias are often marketed this way.

If possible check the plant before purchase to make sure that it is not harbouring any pests or diseases. Bedding plants should have fresh, bright green foliage, with no hint of yellowing, and should be compact, not straggly. Potted plants should have a good root system. If possible, slide the plant from the pot. The roots should fill the pot nicely without being tightly coiled. Select plants that have plenty of healthy buds that are not yet open.

Bulbs are sold when dormant (usually in autumn and winter). Buy them from a reputable garden centre or nursery and look for firm, plump bulbs that show no signs of withering or fungal disease.

Left: Pansies can be relied on to provide a colourful display over a long period. They are available in a wide variety of shades, either singly coloured or in bold combinations such as this bright yellow and maroon pairing.

Planting

The aim when planting a hanging basket is to use as many plants as you can. The normal rules of carefully spacing plants to allow them to reach their full potential do not apply.

1 If you are using moss or an equivalent to improve water retention, place a circle of plastic, pierced to allow drainage, at the base of the basket.

2 Line the basket with the chosen liner, making holes in the liner with scissors or a sharp knife, if necessary.

3 Fill the basket about one-third of the way up with the appropriate compost (soil mix), tamping it down lightly with your fingers to remove any air pockets.

4 Push trailing plants through the side of the container, resting the rootballs on the surface of the compost.

5 Add more compost and plant the top of the basket. Angle the plants at the edge slightly so that they will trail outwards and cover the rim of the basket.

Hanging the Basket

You need good do-it-yourself skills to fix the brackets to the wall. Hanging baskets are heavy for their size when they are moist and full of mature plants and they can also be blown about in strong winds, so proper fixing is essential for safety. Use rawl plugs and long screws to hold them securely in position.

Routine Care

Hanging baskets need a certain amount of regular care and attention if they are going to give the display you want. Don't forget that you are asking the plants to outperform their garden counterparts, and, crammed into the basket, they are competing for water, light and nutrients.

Above: An automatic drip feed system can save time and effort and will be useful if you go away.

Watering

Even if you added water-retaining gels to the compost (soil mix), you will find that the compost in summer baskets quickly dries out. You will need to water the basket every day, and twice a day during the long hot days of summer. Morning or evening is the best time, because leaves can scorch if they get wet in the full heat of the sun. You may find that the compost is dry even after a rainy spell as dense leaf coverage makes it difficult for water to reach the compost.

Above: Use a watering can with a spout so that you wet the compost thoroughly.

Water with a can, making sure the tip of the spout reaches the compost. If you can lift only a small can, one canful may not be enough.

Watering winter and spring baskets is a matter of judgement. The plants are unlikely to be growing strongly and will need watering only when the compost is dry. Over-wet compost in cold weather can lead to root rot.

Feeding

To keep the plants growing strongly and flowering well you will need to feed them. Unless you added a slow-release fertilizer to the compost, apply a high-potash liquid feed every two to three weeks.

Above: Pinching out fuchsias and pelargoniums regularly will give a fuller plant with a better shape and more flowers.

Pinching Out

This involves removing the growing tips of young plants to make them bush out and thus produce more flowering stems. Use just your thumb and forefinger to remove the tips. If this is done regularly the plant will have a better, more even shape.

Deadheading

Removing faded flowers not only keeps the baskets looking good, but encourages the plants to produce further flowers rather than expending their energies on seed production. As the flowers begin to go over, either pinch back the stems or trim them off with secateurs (pruners) or scissors. If you want to propagate the plant from seed, to provide plants for the following year, allow a few flowers to go to seed at the end of the season when they can be collected and stored.

> GARDENER'S TIP
>
> Maintaining hanging baskets is a task that requires daily attention. If you go away for more than 2 days consider joining a local gardening club where the members look after the gardens of those who are away from home.

Pruning

Few hanging basket plants will need pruning, but you may find that woody-stemmed plants, such as fuchsias, will benefit from a trim if they start to become a bit leggy and overgrown. Trim them back as necessary, cutting just above a leaf joint. Ensure that you use sharp secateurs so that you achieve a clean cut.

Above: Deadheading flowers as they fade will encourage a succession of blooms.

Using Pesticides

Plants in hanging baskets are usually grown for one season before they are discarded, which means that they rarely succumb to diseases. They are, however, susceptible to attack by pests. Although keeping your plants healthy by feeding and watering them regularly will increase their resistance, you may find it necessary to use chemicals to keep pests under control.

There are two main types of pesticide. Contact pesticides are sprayed directly on to the pests and are usually instantly effective. Use specific formulations to avoid harming beneficial insects, such as ladybirds (ladybugs), hoverflies and bees. Systemic pesticides are watered into the compost and are absorbed by the plant so that insects that feed on the plant are killed. The effect is not immediate, but this is a good way of dealing with sap-sucking pests, such as aphids.

Aphids

These are one of the most common plant pests. These sap-sucking insects feed on the tender growing tips of plants and can transmit diseases. Green- and blackfly are most often seen, clustering on young shoots and the undersides of leaves. Pirimicarb is the best chemical spray as it is aphid-specific, and insecticidal soap is an effective organic alternative.

Mealy Bugs

Often affecting plants under glass, these look like spots of white mould. Biological or chemical controls are usually effective.

Caterpillars

The occasional caterpillar can simply be picked off the plant and disposed of, but a major infestation can strip a plant before your eyes. Contact insecticides are usually effective in these cases.

Red Spider Mite

The mites are prevalent in warm, dry conditions in the garden. The spider mite is barely visible to the naked eye, but infestation is indicated by fine webs and mottling of the plant's leaves. Keep plants misted, and remove the worst affected leaves. The mites are often resistant to pesticides, but some may be effective.

Vine Weevils

These white grubs are a serious problem for plants. The first sign of an infestation is the sudden collapse of the plant, which has died as a result of the weevil larvae eating its roots. Systemic insecticides or natural predators can be used as a preventative, but once a plant has been attacked it is usually too late to save it. You should never re-use the soil from an affected plant.

Snails

These will often travel up walls and hide behind baskets during the day, coming out at night to feed. Chemical controls are not recommended, since birds will be harmed by eating the poisoned snails, but you can easily catch them by shining a light on the basket at night.

Whitefly

These tiny white flies, often a problem under glass in dry conditions, can be deterred by growing French marigolds (*Tagetes patula*) in the greenhouse, or using biological or chemical controls.

Baskets for All Seasons

ALTHOUGH THEY ARE USUALLY ASSOCIATED WITH SUMMER, HANGING BASKETS CAN BE DESIGNED TO PROVIDE INTEREST THROUGHOUT THE YEAR. IF YOU PLAN CAREFULLY, YOU CAN HAVE FRESH, BRIGHT FOLIAGE AND COLOURFUL FLOWERS SEASON AFTER SEASON.

SPRING BASKETS

This is the season of dwarf bulbs, many of which can be grown with ease in baskets. However, they tend to be stiffly upright. Few flowering plants at this time of year are natural trailers, so to soften the edges of the basket, you will have to rely on the old stalwarts, ivy (*Hedera*) and periwinkle (*Vinca*).

Early dwarf bulbs include the indispensable snowdrops (*Galanthus*) and two irises, *Iris danfordiae* (yellow) and *Iris reticulata* (mostly in shades of blue and purple). Most bulbs need good drainage, so remember to choose a light, free-draining compost (soil mix). When they have finished flowering, plant the bulbs out in the garden.

PLANTS AT THEIR BEST IN SPRING

Crocus
Galanthus
Myosotis
Narcissus (dwarf cultivars)
Primula
Vinca minor
Viola

Your hanging baskets can be a last-minute inspiration, if you neglected to plan ahead. Simply dig up clumps from the garden and plant them up.

Planting Partners

Polyanthus (*Primula*), grown from seed sown the previous year, are delightful, low-growing plants with flowers in a range of jewel-like colours. Some have attractive markings in more than one colour. Use them on their own or to contrast with or complement dwarf narcissi, such as 'Tête-à-Tête', 'Jenny' or 'Jumblie'.

Left: *A classic spring combination, forget-me-nots, miniature narcissi and pansies always look delightful together.*

Above: Dwarf tulips, grape hyacinths and cheeky-faced violas make for a vibrant colour combination.

Easy-to-grow grape hyacinths (*Muscari armenaicum*) are more subtle, with deep purple-blue flowers like miniature bunches of grapes. They go well with the brighter blue of forget-me-nots (*Myosotis*). Crocuses are also a good bet, especially sturdier cultivars such as 'Snow Bunting' (white) and 'Dutch Yellow' (yellow).

Extending the Display

Most bulbs have brief seasons compared to other plants you might be using at this time of year. To extend the period of interest of the basket, plan for a succession of bulbs – for instance, early crocuses, followed by mid-season daffodils, then late dwarf tulips – and pot them up in containers, one type in each. As the buds of the earliest bulbs start to show colour, plunge the pot into the centre of the basket. When the flowers have faded, replace the pot with the one holding the later bulbs, and so on.

GARDENER'S TIP

Keep an eye on the weather: a sudden sharp frost can be the death of many a plant or can spoil the flowers even if the plant survives. If a cold spell is forecast, bring the basket into a frost-free place, such as a cool conservatory, greenhouse or garage.

Planning Ahead

Plant iris bulbs in autumn to winter when they become available in shops and garden centres. Snowdrops are best planted up as growing plants.

Above: Planting bulbs in pots means you can replace them after flowering.

Summer Baskets

No matter how much time and attention you lavish on your hanging baskets at other times of the year, summer is their peak season, as it is for the garden at large. At no other time of year will you have such a wide choice of plant material, offering you a wealth of colour, form and scent. This is the time when all your plans will pay off.

If it is properly cared for, a summer basket will provide pleasure for up to three months of the year, and possibly even longer. At the height of summer, the basket itself and the lining material should be invisible, covered by a mass of flowers.

Different Styles

Plant baskets the way you would plant any other area in your garden. If the cottage garden style appeals to you, use simple plants in a range of colours. Many cottage favourites, such as pinks (*Dianthus*) and nasturtiums, are ideal basket material if you stick to shorter cultivars. For a sophisticated look, team pastels with grey-leaved *Helichrysum petiolare*.

An Airborne Rose Garden

If you have a passion for roses, extend that towards some of the many miniatures and patio roses, which are ideal for containers of all kinds. Many of the so-called ground-cover roses

Above: *Fuchsias, petunias and lobelias are the epitome of summer plantings.*

Left: *Many miniature roses are dainty enough to be grown in a hanging basket.*

have long, flexible stems, which will trail over the edge of a hanging basket in a most appealing way, but watch out for thorns if you site it near a doorway or walkway.

The miniature roses are dainty, twiggy plants that are ideal as the centrepiece of a basket and can take the place of more familiar fuchsias and pelargoniums. These plants are often sold unnamed in many florists, sometimes out of season. In a mild spell in spring, autumn or even winter, you could use one as a temporary planting. If you want the basket to be permanent, protect the roots from frost in winter – they are more vulnerable than plants in the ground. Remember that, if you are intending to use a rose, you will have to watch out for the attendant problems. You may need to spray occasionally against troublesome blackspot and aphids. However, most modern varieties are robust despite their dainty appearance, and you should not experience any big problems

PLANTS AT THEIR BEST IN SUMMER

Begonia
Bidens
Dorotheanthus
Fuchsia
Impatiens
Lobelia
Pelargonium
Petunias

Fuchsias and Pelargoniums

These woody-based plants are the mainstay of many a summer hanging basket, and rightly so. Few plants can rival their ease of cultivation and length of flowering season. They both usefully have a number of different forms. Upright cultivars are perfect as the central plant of a large basket, while trailing forms are excellent cascading down the sides.

Tender Perennials

This group of plants is growing in popularity and nurseries and garden centres offer new species and cultivars every year. In addition to the marvellous osteospermums, there are bidens, felicia and argyranthemum, all of which produce their vivid flowers over a long period.

Annuals

Hardy and half-hardy annuals are the mainstay of the summer garden, and most are easily grown from seed. Alternatively, they can be obtained as plugs or plantlets, ready to be planted out in early summer.

Above: Pelargonium *'Eclipse' produces masses of pink flowers in large open heads.*

Above: *Yellow-leaved lysimachia is an excellent trailing plant and a good substitute for ivy in a predominantly yellow basket.*

Perhaps most familiar of all summer annuals are lobelias, trailing forms of which have been specially bred for containers. Colours include different shades of blue, as well as purple, with white and red. Equally noteworthy are the petunias, which can be found in a wide colour range, including white, yellow, cream, red and blue, with some bicolours. Double forms and those with ruffled petal edges are particularly appealing. Look out especially for the trailing types.

Foliage

At the height of summer a hanging basket can be virtually a ball of flowers, but don't underestimate the value of pure green to tone down a scheme. Ivies and periwinkles can be relied on to give a long-lasting performance, to which can be added the tender helichrysums, with felted leaves of grey or soft lime green, or the pick-a-back plant (*Tolmiea menziesii*), with its fresh green, toothed leaves.

GARDENER'S TIP

If the basket dries out, stand it on a bucket and give it a good soaking. Allow it to sit in the bucket until the compost (soil mix) is saturated. Adding a few drops of dishwashing detergent to the water will help water absorption.

Summer Problems

While summer is the time for sitting back and enjoying the fruits of your labours in the garden at large, you cannot just relax and let your hanging baskets get on with it. They need care and attention. Tender leaves can easily scorch with too much sun, and flowers will rapidly fade. This is the ideal time – from the plant's point of view – for setting seed. At this time you need to increase your watering, giving the basket a thorough soaking once or twice a day. If the weather is very hot, you might even need to move the basket to a more shady position. If you have baskets at the front and back of the house, swap them around every

Above: Yellow-flowered bidens is a tender perennial that is often treated as an annual. It produces dainty flowers on trailing stems all summer long.

few days, and turn them. Keep up the deadheading, or the flower display will be shortened. On the plus side, succulent plants, such as Livingstone daisies (*Dorotheanthus*), will positively revel in the heat and flower their hearts out, as will pelargoniums. Plants with aromatic leaves will release their oils now.

If you want your baskets to give pleasure throughout the season, look for plants that are in flower over a long period. Most floriferous of all are probably the pelargoniums, with flowers in shades of white, pink, salmon and red. The ivy-leaved varieties are trailing, so are ideal for the sides of a basket, with perhaps a more upright cultivar at the centre. Fuchsias also have a long period of interest, often surviving into late autumn, and there are trailing as well as more upright cultivars.

Above: *These osteospermums and diascias in subtle pastel colours are slightly tender but will carry on flowering until the first frosts appear.*

Make sure you include some foliage plants, such as ivies and helichrysum, which will provide a solid background throughout the season.

All plants will flower for longer if regularly deadheaded. This diverts the plant's energy away from seed production and encourages it to produce further flowers.

Left: *Nasturtiums are among the easiest annuals to grow. 'Alaska' has the added attraction of variegated leaves.*

Things to Watch Out For

In a very hot spell baskets can easily dry out and delicate plants will scorch. Remember that their roots are well above ground level and hence can easily bake, because there is little moist soil to keep them cool. The problem is made worse if the basket is next to a wall that reflects the heat. A wall that has been in the sun for most of the afternoon will continue to radiate heat well into the evening when the sun is no longer on it. If necessary, take the basket to a position where it will be shaded when the sun is at its scorching strongest.

GARDENER'S TIP

Pelargoniums and many tender perennials can be over-wintered in a cool, light, frost-free place, such as an unheated bedroom or a porch (sunroom).

Flowering plants run to seed faster in hot weather, so keep up your deadheading regime. But remember that plants with succulent leaves, such as Livingstone daisies, will thrive in baking conditions. Most of the grey-leaved plants, especially those with fine hairs covering the leaves, will also flourish in hot weather.

Above: This riotous mix of fuchsias, lobelia, petunias, scarlet pelargoniums, nemesias and verbena has been planned for maximum impact.

Autumn Baskets

A surprising number of plants are at their best in autumn. Shortening days bring cooler temperatures, and although there may not be as many flowers, they will last longer in the gentle autumn sun. Many annuals, particularly if sown late, will carry on until the first frosts, but others to enjoy later in the year include fruiting plants, such as bright red capsicums.

Annual capsicums, with their cheerful red, yellow or orange ball-like fruits, are appealing, as are the cultivars of *Gaulthesia mucronata*, the colourful fruits of which are beginning to ripen at this time of year to give additional interest to the basket.

Many members of the daisy family reach their peak at this time of year, and some dahlias and chrysanthemums make ideal basket plants. A dwarf chrysanthemum could be the central plant, surrounded by small ivies or possibly a late sowing of lobelias or helichrysum. This is also the season when the tuberous begonias are glorious, giving a show of colourful blooms. Look out especially for trailing cultivars such as 'Cascade Orange'.

Above: *Autumn is the season of the tuberous begonias, here partnered by pink diascias,* Helichrysum petiolare *and a fuchsia.*

Above: *The perennial bidens can be relied on to produce its starry yellow flowers well into autumn.*

Maintaining Interest

Autumn is an unpredictable season at the best of times. If the summer was cool and the autumn continues mild, many annuals will carry on flowering, provided they are deadheaded regularly. Many of the tender perennials, such as osteospermums, felicias and diascias, will also continue to flower. A late feed will give all such plants a boost, but they will not survive the first autumn frosts. This is the time to look to the true plants of autumn, such as chrysanthemums, which produce satisfying mounds of colour, and sedums. Winter-flowering heathers will even provide colour into the darker days of winter.

PLANTS AT THEIR BEST
IN AUTUMN

Calluna vulgaris
Capsicum annuum
Chrysanthemum
Fuchsia
Gaultheria mucronata
Impatiens
Sedum
Solenostemon

GARDENER'S TIP

After flowering, dry off the tubers of begonias and store them over winter in a cool, dry, frost-free place for planting out again the following year. When new buds appear, you could propagate them by cutting the tubers in sections and planting them like cuttings.

Above: *With its perfectly formed flowers and arching habit, 'Dark Eyes' is an ideal fuchsia for a hanging basket.*

Winter Baskets

It is possible to have colour and fragrance even in winter, but your choices are obviously more restricted then, since this is the time of year when most plants are resting. Winter-flowering pansies, invaluable though they are, will actually flower only during mild spells. For colour in the very depths of winter, you should look to the heathers (some of which have foliage that takes on attractive tints as the temperature dips) and dwarf berrying shrubs, such as gaultherias. The latter need lime-free (ericaceous) compost (soil mix), but winter heathers will tolerate lime.

PLANTS AT THEIR BEST IN WINTER

Buxus
Erica carnea
Galanthus
Hedera
Skimmia japonica
Viola (winter-flowering)

This is also the time that the ivies come into their own. They exhibit a quite astonishing range of leaf shape (some being attractively crinkled at the edges) and variegation. Some are tinged pink or bronze in cold weather. A basket planted with ivies alone can be more attractive than you might think. You could even try tiny dwarf conifers or a hebe for leaf contrast. Small varieties of skimmia are also a possibility. Choose either a berrying female or the compact male form, 'Rubella', which has red-edged leaves and pink flower buds, which develop in autumn and last throughout winter, finally opening in spring. Plant them out in your garden the following year or pass them on to friends.

Left: *Variegated ivies are an obvious choice for a winter basket, here livened up by yellow and bronze winter-flowering pansies.*

GARDENER'S TIP

Even hardy plants are vulnerable to cold when they are out of the ground in a hanging basket. During freezing weather, move the basket under cover at night-time or drape a length of horticultural fleece over it.

Above: A hanging basket planted solely with one or two cultivars of small-leaved ivies will be a real eye-catcher once the plants are mature.

Danger Zones

Not only is the weather at its harshest in winter, but there is usually precious little light or sun. Although many plants tolerate wet and even a light covering of snow, evergreens in particular hate cold, drying winds, which will seriously damage their foliage if they do not kill the plant outright. Make sure your baskets are not hanging in a wind funnel. At this time of year, it also makes sense to hang your baskets only in the most sheltered spots. If particularly severe weather is threatened, move your baskets under cover. Even the shelter of a porch or a covered car port should be sufficient to protect the plants and keep them in good health.

Above: *A miniature clipped* Buxus *will provide sculptured interest and colour.*

Above: Erica *comes in a range of colours that will brighten up a winter basket.*

Satisfying the Senses

PLANTS APPEAL TO OUR SENSES IN MORE THAN ONE WAY. WHILE WE ALL REJOICE IN THE COLOURS AND BEAUTY OF THEIR FLOWERS, WE SHOULD NEVER OVERLOOK THEIR MORE SUBTLE APPEAL TO OUR SENSES OF TOUCH, TASTE AND SMELL.

USING COLOUR

Colours make an immediate impact. Strong yellows, oranges and reds are known to increase the heartbeat slightly and are always considered exciting. Blues and pinks are more calming, and most restful and soothing to the eye of all is plain green.

Think of the position of the basket when you are choosing colours. Strong vibrant reds and yellows work best in hot sun, but creams, pinks and lavenders tend to bleach out and look white. Conversely, pale colours will glow in half-light or shade, while deep reds and purples will look almost black.

Above: *This riotous mix of sweet peas uses a range of colours together, harmonized by the abundance of fresh green leaves and stems.*

> GARDENER'S TIP
>
> When you choose a colour scheme remember that pale colours, such as pastel shades of blue, pink and yellow, tend to recede and appear further away, while strong oranges, reds and purples always seem to be nearer to the viewer and will dominate a display.

Combining Colours

Use combinations of different colours as a painter would. Complementary colours (red and green; blue and orange; purple and yellow) tend to fizz when they are placed next to each other, making some exciting effects. If you add some grey to such a combination, in the form of foliage plants, it can soften the impact. If you decide to base a planting scheme on complementaries, however, it is best to avoid adding white, which tends to flare out, preventing the eye from finding a resting place.

Different tones of the same colour always look pleasing together. Creams and apricots blend happily with oranges and reds, for instance, as do lavenders and mauves with purples. Clear red and blue seldom make good bedfellows, but a rich purple can be enlivened with the right shade of red. You will soon learn what works.

If you are using a combination of pinks, try not to mix those that tend towards blue with those that have some orange in them. Try the bluish pinks with warm mauve and purples, and the orange-pinks with red and yellow. Potential clashes can always be softened by the use of plain green or grey foliage.

Above: *The vivid colours of nasturtiums and French marigolds combine to create an eyecatching arrangement.*

Below: *The begonias and diascias used here could have clashed were it not for the presence of the ever-dependable* Helichrysum petiolare.

Dramatic Effects

Bearing in mind the effects the different colours have on the senses, the most dramatic plantings involve rich, deep, saturated colours, such as purple, orange, yellow and red. A typical planting might involve a richly coloured petunia or fuchsia – several cultivars have red or purple flowers – surrounded by dark blue, trailing lobelias with a few orange and red nasturtiums tucked in for added vibrancy. Purple on its own, or as the principal colour, would certainly be dramatic, but if you are mixing purples beware: red-purples and blue-purples make unhappy bedfellows. Play for safety and include plants with grey foliage or some ivies, which will bring a welcome calming note to the scheme.

STRIKINGLY COLOURED PLANTS

Antirrhinum
Fuchsia
Lobelia
Nasturtium
Pelargonium
Petunia
Verbena
Viola

Above: *Pink flowers are always enhanced by silver-grey foliage, and these warm pink pelargoniums and diascias make a beautifully subtle planting with* Helichrysum petiolare.

Above: *The combination of a virginal white pelargonium with purple daisies and verbenas is undeniably romantic.*

Above: *As well as the familiar strident colours, busy Lizzies come in some lovely soft shades.*

Soothing Schemes

For subtlety, choose pastels. Creams, pinks, blues and lavenders always work well together, though the results can be insipid unless you include a few deeper shades of those colours. In theory, white should be the most calming of all, and silver and white baskets are undeniably romantic, but again you have to be careful where you place them. In full sun, the flowers tend to bleach, and a subtle scheme might end up looking washed out. On the whole, white flowers are best used to highlight other pale colours.

A simple planting might surround a pale fuchsia (there is no clear white, but some of the pink varieties are very pale) or pelargonium with white lobelias and cream, lavender or white petunias. The ever-reliable grey-leaved *Helichrysum petiolare* could give the planting substance. You can warm up a cool scheme by using pinks with a touch of orange in them – a colour usually called salmon. Diascias are among the most desirable, many having flowers of a smoky apricot.

PLANTS WITH PALE FLOWERS

Diascia
Fuchsia
Lobelia
Nemesia
Osteospermum
Pelargonium
Petunia
Viola

Using Foliage

Although planting schemes are usually planned around the flowers, you could plant a basket for the appeal of foliage, either on its own, for a subtle look, or combined with flowering plants. A dramatic combination would be black lilyturf (*Ophiopogon nigrescens*) mixed with silver-leaved *Helichrysum petiolare*. Blue fescue (*Festuca glauca*) would be a more understated alternative. For richer, bolder effects, annual coleus (*Solenostemon*) would give as vivid a display as any combination of flowers and over a much longer period. Coleus seedlings vary and can never be accurately predicted, but colours include red, brown and gold. Foliage begonias (*Begonia rex*) have purple or silver leaves with a pronounced metallic sheen.

PLANTS WITH SILVER OR GREY FOLIAGE

Artemisia
Dianthus
Festuca glauca
Helianthemum 'The Bride'
Helichrysum petiolare
Nepeta
Santolina
Senecio
Stachys byzantina

Be careful where you place baskets planted for foliage effect, however. Most need some sun to enhance the colour, but the leaves can scorch in too hot a position – somewhere sheltered from the midday sun is usually best.

The ever-popular spider plant (*Chlorophytum comosum* 'Vittatum') is generally grown as a houseplant, but there is no reason not to allow it an excursion outdoors in the frost-free months. It is an ideal basket plant, with green-and-white striped, arching leaves, and new plants attractively hanging from the tips of long runners.

Left: *A sumptuous combination of purple heuchera, orange and brown pansies, mimulus and golden lysimachia. The purple foliage sets off the pansies.*

Above: The green foliage of Helichrysum petiolare *'Aureum' makes a striking partner to blue anagallis and pansies.*

Combining Foliage with Flowers

For the best of both worlds, try blending foliage plants with flowering ones. Alaska Series nasturtiums solve the problem in one, because the leaves, which are beautifully marbled with splashes of pink and cream, are almost as appealing as the orange, yellow and red flowers. Otherwise, try matching leaf colour with flower colour. An ivy with cream variegated foliage will echo any cream flowers you may have chosen, for instance. The yellow-leaved *Lysimachia nummularia* 'Aurea' works splendidly as a foil to red and orange flowers and is a dramatic complement to purple verbenas, but take care when combining it with other shades of yellow – you should experiment with different shades to find out what works best. Purple- and bronze-leaved plants are also striking when used in conjunction with red or yellow flowers. For a more sophisticated effect, try combining them with cream or white flowers.

If you like variegated plants it is probably best to stick to one variety only in each basket, combined with plain-leaved plants as a foil. If you include too much variegation there is a danger of creating a visually confusing look, whereas with a single, well-chosen variety you can ensure maximum effect.

PLANTS WITH COLOURED FOLIAGE

Begonia rex
Chlorophytum comosum 'Vittatum'
Festuca glauca
Fuchsia 'Autumnale'
Gynura
Hedera (variegated forms)
Helichrysum
Lysimachia nummularia 'Aurea'
Ophiopogon nigrescens
Solenostemon (annual)
Tradescantia fluminensis 'Albovittata'
Tropaeolum Alaska Series

Introducing Scent

The scent of plants is as important a part of their appeal as is the colour of their flowers, and you may wish to plant a few baskets with this as the principal theme. A minority of plants have a distinctly unpleasant smell, but many have a potent fragrance that promotes a sense of well-being.

Some flowers have a scent that is emitted only at certain times of the day – when their natural pollinators are active. Night-scented plants, such as *Nicotiana*, for instance, are usually pollinated by nocturnal moths. Scents can also vary in intensity at different times of day according to the moisture content of the atmosphere. Roses are often at their sweetest when the dew hangs in the air.

Above: Baskets filled with fragrant ground-cover roses make a summer focal point at the end of the pergola.

Types of Scent

Scent is the most elusive of the senses and not everybody reacts in the same way to particular fragrances. For some, they awake precious memories stored up from childhood, while others are completely indifferent to them. One gardener might find that a particular scent has strong and positive associations while another might be completely unmoved by it.

Citrus smells are light and refreshing, while herbal scents such as thyme and lavender tend to be calming and relaxing. Some herbal scents are more astringent and often have notes of eucalyptus that not everyone finds pleasing, although many people experience them as invigorating. Musky scents can be very provocative, though these essences are rare in the plant world. Some flower scents combine more than one note and often seem to be "layered". Such scents, which we usually think of as exotic, are so rich and heady as to be almost cloying, though undeniably intoxicating. The commonest scents in the garden are usually defined as aromatic. They are usually sweetly spicy and always appealing, and we seem never to tire of them. They are often found in the distinctly almond-like fragrance of heliotropes and the warm clove scent of old-fashioned carnations and pinks. Violet scents are sharper and more fatiguing but also more transitory. Mignonettes (*Reseda*) and *Iris reticulata* as well as violets have scents in this group.

Rose scents are usually fruity and spicy, pleasing both up close and at a distance. They are best in a sunny spot where the warmth brings out their fragrance. Some varieties of tulips as well as roses have these lovely scents. Interestingly, many of the roses have scents that seem to belong to a further group, the citrus or lemon group. These scents are almost universally perceived as pleasant and exhilarating rather than calming. Distinctive honey-scented tones are occasionally detected in plants and their fragrance is warm and enduring. They are most commonly found among the orchids.

Above: *Few pansies are scented, but orange forms are sometimes fragrant, recalling their link to sweet violets.*

Above: *White* Lobularia maritima *has a delicate, pleasing scent that gives this simple scheme an added appeal.*

Positioning Scented Plants

Bearing in mind the power of scent, you need to think carefully where you place hanging baskets containing scented plants. While it is a joy to fling open a window and breathe in a heady mix of roses and jasmine, you may find such smells too cloying if they are near a bedroom window that is open on hot, sultry nights. Nevertheless, a basket of predominantly night-scented plants can be a pleasing addition to a pergola over a paved area where you dine *al fresco* on balmy summer evenings.

Plants with aromatic leaves, such as most of the herbs, especially woody-stemmed ones like artemisia, lavender and rosemary, are richest in their essential oils at the height of summer, and these tend to be released only when they are crushed. Site these in full sun somewhere where you regularly pass by, perhaps near a doorway or suspended from a garden arch, so that you can reach up and rub a few leaves between your finger and thumb to release their fragrance. Hanging them near a barbecue area will allow you to

Above: *Include some late-flowering narcissi with* Anemone blanda *and ivy for a fragrant spring display. Make sure you hang the basket where you can appreciate the scent.*

Above: *Dwarf lavender has scented grey leaves as well as strongly fragrant flowers. It prefers a sunny site.*

Above: *Blue petunias, here planted against a sunny wall, often have a rich scent not found in the other colours.*

have material close at hand to garnish grilled steaks, lamb or fish or simply to fling on the flames to release their evocative aroma.

Heavy scents, of the kind found in such plants as jasmine and stephanotis, are rich and penetrating and are delicious when caught on the passing breeze. Within the confines of a greenhouse or conservatory, or in the house itself, they can be overpowering. For fragrance indoors, you could consider growing some of the *Dendrobium* or *Coelogyne* orchid hybrids or *Cyclamen persicum* hybrids, but note that not all of these are scented. Look for plants in flower and sniff out their potential before you make a purchase.

SCENTED PLANTS

Convallaria majalis
Crocus (some)
Cyclamen persicum
Dianthus
Iris (some)
Lathyrus odoratus
Lavandula
Lobularia maritima
Muscari armeniacum
Narcissus (some)
Nicotiana
Petunia (some)
Pelargonium (scented-leaved)
Phlox
Reseda odorata
Rosmarinus
Narcissus (some)
Primula (some)
Tulipa (some)
Verbena

Benefits of Scented Plants

Scented plants have the inestimable value of attracting beneficial insects, such as hoverflies and ladybirds (ladybugs), into the garden. A healthy ladybird population will help keep aphids at bay, since they feed on these pests. The poached egg plant (*Limnanthes douglasii*), with its saucer-shaped, yellow and white flowers, will be alive with bees throughout summer. Butterflies are an ornament to the garden in their own right.

Many plants are believed to have healing qualities, and they have been used in traditional medicines for centuries. A cup of mint tea helps settle the stomach after a meal, while an infusion of lemon balm can be very soothing. Feverfew is said to alleviate headaches and migraines, but no herb other than the familiar culinary ones should be taken in any form for its health benefits without consulting a medical practitioner.

Above: Lavandula stoechas *ssp.* pedunculata *is a form of lavender from Provence that is particularly attractive to bees.*

Citronella oil is widely used as a component of insect repellents. Growing citrus-scented plants, such as lemon balm (*Melissa officinalis*), in a basket near a favourite evening sitting place may help to deter mosquitoes and other unwelcome night-time insects provided you rub its leaves periodically to release the lemon scent.

Left: *The silver-leaved thyme is a strong feature of this basket and will be alive with bees when it is in flower.*

Combining Scented Plants

Placing two or three scented plants together can be detrimental to the effect of each and can confuse the nose. You will achieve the most pleasing results by restricting yourself to one scented plant in each basket, particularly if the scent is a heavy one. However, the aromatic herbs and scented-leaved plants, such as pelargoniums, which are fragrant only when bruised, can work well together, because you have some control over when the scent is actually released. In a mixed basket, a succession of scents is possible. The leaves of some nasturtiums (*Tropaeolum*), for instance, have a fresh, peppery scent when young, and this could be enjoyed before later, scented flowers – pansies or petunias, for example – appear. Alternatively, use these plants with herbs or pelargoniums that owe their scent to aromatic oils, which are at their richest when the weather is hottest – from mid- to late summer. Misting the plants will help to release their fragrance.

Above: *An elegant planting with an added dimension: the scent of the purple lobularias will attract a host of insects.*

PLANTS THAT ATTRACT BEES AND BUTTERFLIES

Aster (dwarf forms)
Aubrieta deltoides
Lavandula species
Limnanthes douglasii
Lobularia maritima
Sedum 'Vera Jameson'
Thymus species
Viola tricolor

Left: *In addition to the beauty of its abundant mauve flowers,* Pelargonium *'Little Gem' has the advantage of soft-textured, lobed leaves, which exude a warm, rose-lemon fragrance.*

Plants to Touch

Good gardeners love to handle their plants, some of which seem to grow just to be touched, especially those with furry or silky leaves and those with aromatic leaves that release their fragrance when bruised. This characteristic is, perhaps, the subtlest of pleasures that plants can give us, and appreciation of it is one to be encouraged. Some people believe that plants that are caressed regularly grow more vigorously and are more disease-resistant, although it is obviously difficult to demonstrate this scientifically. Touching may imitate the contact that plants would receive in the wild from passing animal life.

PLANTS WITH TEXTURAL LEAVES

Fuchsia (triphylla types)
Gynura
Helichrysum
Pelargonium (scented-leaved)
Rosmarinus
Stachys byzantina

Leaf Texture

Waxy and furry coatings to leaves developed as a response to climate, to protect the plants from hot sun by helping the leaf to retain moisture. Such textures are at their most pronounced, therefore, when the sun is at its hottest, so a basket featuring these is best sited in a sunny position that will encourage the plants to build up their protective coatings.

Plants with smooth, waxy leaves include, most obviously, succulent plants such as *Schlumbergera*. The nearest hardy equivalents are the sedums, with their fleshy, almost glassy leaves, which can assume a grape-like bloom as the temperature rises. Furry-textured leaves have an irrestistible appeal to children, who love to stroke the charmingly and aptly named lambs' ears (*Stachys byzantina*), which is usually used to edge a flower

***Above:** The leaves of the triphylla-type fuchsia 'Thalia' – at the centre of the basket and yet to bear its orange flowers – are velvety and eminently strokeable.*

Right: *The silver-grey foliage of* Convolvulus cneorum *is a delightful foil to the white flowers.*

border but also makes an excellent basket plant, particularly in one of its non-flowering forms such as 'Silver Carpet'. *Helichrysum petiolare* also has soft, velvety leaves, though they are firmer-textured and, being smaller, not quite so easy to stroke. An attractive alternative is *Convolvulus cneorum*, with its silky-textured, silver-grey leaves that are no less appealing than the glistening white, funnel-shaped flowers. This is actually a Mediterranean shrub, but its lax habit makes it perfect for a basket.

Leaves that are soft, thin and silky usually need some shelter from hot sun, and most will do best in shade. Triphylla-type fuchsias are outstanding here, with large, usually bronze-flushed leaves with a metallic sheen. *Gynura aurantiaca* 'Purple Passion' has purple hairy leaves that shine almost blue, making a strong appeal to our tactile sense. Popular as a houseplant, there is no reason this should not find its way into a hanging basket outdoors provided there are no great temperature fluctuations and it is sheltered from any strong winds. Another useful trailing foliage plant is wandering Jew (*Tradescantia*). Their leaves have a glittering crystallized appearance, almost as though they have been lightly sprinkled with sugar.

Above: *The yellow leaves of* Helichrysum petiolare *'Limelight' bring their distinctive texture to a colourful summer basket.*

Edible Pleasures

In an age when commercial crops are routinely sprayed against pests and diseases and fed with chemicals to increase crop size and extend shelf life, many gardeners are attracted to the idea of growing their own fruit and vegetables at home. You do not have to have a large area of flat ground, as you might imagine, and growing edible crops in hanging baskets is actually a very practical option if you have only limited space. This way you can be sure that they are always ready to hand to be picked. Moreover, home-grown crops are always tastier and fresher than their shop-bought equivalents.

Make sure that your edible baskets are positioned near to the kitchen so that you do not have too far to walk in wet weather. Remember, though, that all vegetables need an open, sunny site to grow properly, so if the area near your kitchen door is shady, you may need to hang your basket elsewhere for the best crops.

What to Grow

Look out for quick-maturing, dwarf, trailing forms that have been specially developed to meet the needs of gardeners with limited space. All edible crops are greedy plants so will need a lot of feeding to give you the results you want. Lettuces and other salad leaves are an ideal crop for growing in hanging baskets. 'Little Gem' is a reliable dwarf variety. The cut-and-come-again varieties, such as 'Frisby', are particularly useful, because you can simply snip off the leaves you need for a salad and the plant will carry on producing more, so you do not have to remove a whole plant at a time. Some are decorative in their own right, with red or crinkly-edged leaves.

***Above:** The pretty flowers of the trailing tomato plants, here combined with nasturtiums (also edible), give a hint of tasty crops to come.*

Cherry tomatoes are also an excellent choice and, of course, look

Left: This sumptuous basket combines perennial herbs with fragrant flowers.

extremely attractive as the cherry-like fruits ripen in late summer. 'Tumbler' is the cultivar generally recommended.

Beans have the advantage of pretty flowers before the beans form. Be sure to harvest the beans regularly while they are still small and sweet. Older beans will be tough and stringy. Sadly, root crops, such as carrots, parsnips and potatoes, are definitely not suitable for such a limited space. They need a deeper root run than it is possible to achieve in a hanging basket.

You could try adding some flowers to the planting, to create a basket that is truly beautiful to look at as well as a valued food source. Beware of overplanting the basket, however. If the vegetables have to compete for the water and nutrients, they may not produce the tasty crops you want.

GARDENER'S TIP

Seed merchants bring out new varieties every year, so check their catalogues for the latest additions. For success with edible crops, use baskets no less than 35cm/14in in diameter.

Maintaining the Basket

The demands of the majority of vegetables are much greater than those of flowering plants, which should be considered when deciding what to grow. They need a free-draining compost (soil mix), so choose a lightweight type that will not compact with the frequent watering. Because free-draining composts tend to be low in nutrients, and vegetables demand greater amounts of fertilizer, feed the baskets with a soluble variety. Tomato fertilizers are quite high in potassium, to promote good fruiting, but tend to encourage other leafy vegetables, such as lettuces, to bolt. For these, look for a high-nitrogen feed. If the idea of using chemicals to enhance an edible crop does not appeal, there are also organic equivalents, usually based on seaweed extract. Apply all fertilizers at the manufacturer's recommended rate. Overfeeding (and overwatering) can impair the flavour of the crop.

Growing Herbs

If you do not have a herb garden – or even if you do – you might like to grow some herbs in a basket that you can hang near the back door or kitchen window so that they are always within reach. Held aloft as they are, hanging baskets offer what most herbs need above all – good drainage. Unlike many other plants, herbs thrive in relatively poor soil, so feed less often than you would a flowering basket. However, you will need a very free-draining compost (soil mix), so be sure to add perlite or vermiculite so that there is no danger of waterlogging.

Some herbs are perennials, which means that the basket can be a year-round feature. You can also include herbs in mixed baskets – sage and parsley make particularly attractive additions to flower baskets. It would be a practical idea to grow basil with tomatoes, because the two flavours complement each other so nicely, and you would have the ingredients of a tasty salad growing together.

Nearly all the herbs that are suitable for hanging baskets are sun-lovers. Indeed, sun is often needed to enhance their aromatic properties. Most have tough leaves – sage, lavender

Below: *With its crops of parsley, sage and tarragon, this basket is every cook's dream. It will produce fresh leaves over a long period of time if trimmed regularly.*

Above: Chives have pretty flowers, but if you want to reserve your plants solely for culinary use it is best to nip them off before they are fully formed.

and rosemary – but those with more delicate leaves, such as basil and tarragon, may need some shelter from the midday sun during the hotter months. The exception is mint, which is not only shade-tolerant but demands reliably moist soil if it is to prosper. Make sure that you keep mint baskets well watered.

Maintaining a Supply

Herbs actually benefit from being harvested regularly. Not only does this keep the plants neat and compact, but it prevents them from flowering and setting seed and makes them put out fresh young leaves, always the most tender and tasty. Basil and parsley are annual herbs, which tend to become coarse if allowed to bolt and lose their characteristic flavour. If you pick from them regularly to provide garnishes, they are unlikely to run to seed, but if flowers should begin to form, nip them out with finger and thumb or scissors.

You might, however, allow herbs such as lavender, rosemary and thyme to flower. Not only are the flowers pretty in themselves, but they will provide a valuable nectar source for bees and other pollinating insects.

HERBS FOR A HANGING BASKET

Basil (annual)
Chives
Lavender
Parsley (annual)
Rosemary (prostrate varieties)
Sage

Above: Herbs can please the eye as much as the taste buds. This striking scheme combines mint, parsley, lavender and thymes with alpine pinks.

Growing Strawberries

Believe it or not, you can even grow strawberries in hanging baskets, and at least you can be sure you'll experience no problems with mice, the scourge of many a fruit garden. Pick and choose among the varieties. Alpine strawberries are the best, being naturally small and neat-growing, but you could also experiment with some of the larger fruited varieties. All strawberries have the additional attraction of white flowers in spring.

You can either raise plants from seed or buy plantlets, probably the better option if you are short of time. Look for compact cultivars. You will have most success with those that are recommended for container growing.

It is also worth checking when the cropping season is. Some fruit in early summer, others in midsummer, while a third group provides late crops. A few varieties produce relatively small crops but over a long period, and these may be the best choice for a busy town-dweller. Make sure that any variety you choose is self-fertile, unless there are other strawberry plants grown nearby.

Below: *Two types of strawberry are used here, the large-fruited 'Maxim' and smaller alpine plants. A crimson pelargonium adds a dash more colour.*

Above: This half basket uses attractive alpine strawberries almost as much for the appeal of their foliage as for their fruits. Red petunias and a variegated helichrysum sit above them.

Strawberries are susceptible to mildew, a common fungal infection encouraged by high humidity and fluctuating temperatures – the kind of conditions that often prevail in late summer and autumn. Spray at the first sign of disease, but make sure that any product you use will not taint the fruit or damage wildlife.

Even if you can't grow a large enough crop to make preserves, you can still have alpine strawberries to add to your breakfast cereal or cornflakes in the summer or to make tiny pots of compote for enjoying with scones (biscuits) and cream. Alpine strawberries are also traditionally eaten in France dropped in a glass of champagne – a custom certainly well worth importing.

RECOMMENDED STRAWBERRIES

'Calypso' (perpetual-fruiting)
'Mignonette' (alpine)
'Temptation' (perpetual-fruiting)

Planting Combinations

You need not restrict yourself to one strawberry cultivar, but two or three is probably the maximum you will manage in one basket. Allow an alpine strawberry to trail at the edges of the basket and place a larger fruited type in the centre.

Strawberries are such attractive fruits that they can be used in conjunction with flowers for a display that is as much for the eye as the taste buds. Small pelargoniums, petunias or nasturtiums are possibilities, and if you stick to shades of red you can be sure to have a vivid display. There are also a few white strawberry cultivars, which would look charming mixed with a few cream petunias.

GARDENER'S TIP

Most strawberries ripen best in an open, sunny site. Alpine strawberries, however, will ripen perfectly well in light shade, so if the only position available is shaded, restrict yourself to these varieties. As the fruits begin to ripen, protect strawberry baskets with a piece of netting, otherwise the birds may help themselves to the entire crop.

Edible Flowers

Some flowers are edible and make colourful additions to salads and drinks. A bowl of chilled punch at a summer party will be considerably enhanced by the presence of a few viola or borage flowers floating on the surface, and they can also be used to garnish desserts, either fresh from the plant or given a coating of egg white and sugar. Flowers for culinary use are best picked when they have just opened, but before they are fully open and beginning to fade.

The pink flowerheads of chives make a delicious addition to salads, but the flowering stems are tough and best not used.

GARDENER'S TIP

Pick flowers on a sunny day before noon for the strongest concentration of essential oils.

Borage flowers can also be frozen in ice cubes to add to drinks, allowing you to revisit in a modest way the pleasures of summer once the plants that produced the flowers are spent. Place individual flowers in each compartment of an ice tray and fill with water. Once frozen, release the cubes

Below: *Leaving aside the blue felicia, this chirpy planting provides parsley leaves as well as marigold flowers, both of which can be used in the kitchen.*

from the trays and bag them up separately for storing in the freezer.

Nasturtium flowers can be used as a last-minute garnish to salads and have a fresh, peppery taste. Pansy flowers have a less distinctive flavour, but they have a lovely velvety texture.

Rose or marigold petals can be used to flavour butters or to scent oils and vinegars, adding to the appeal of your salad dressings. Soften butter (preferably unsalted) first and gently mash the flowers into it. The idea is to release some of the oils into the butter while preserving the integrity of the flowers. Flavoured butters are best used fresh, before the flowers discolour, otherwise the butter turns rancid.

Oils and vinegars act as preservatives, so have a longer shelf life than butter. Choose a lightly flavoured oil, such as sunflower. Wine or cider vinegar should be gently warmed before adding the flowers. Steep for two weeks on a sunny windowsill, shaking occasionally, then strain the liquid.

The petals of pot marigolds (*Calendula*) can be used to colour rice in place of saffron but will not impart any flavour. To dry marigold petals, lay the individual flowers on sheets of

EDIBLE FLOWERS

Borago officinalis
Calendula
Rosa
Tropaeolum
Viola

Above: *Not only can nasturtium leaves and flowers be used in salads and cooked dishes, but the seeds can also be pickled.*

absorbent kitchen paper and allow them to dry naturally in a well-ventilated area. Once dry, pull the petals from the centre of the flower (which can then be discarded) and store them in an airtight screwtop jar.

To keep your plants producing new flowers, remove faded ones promptly.

Combining Plants

Using edible flowers in conjunction with other edible plants means that your useful baskets can be as attractive to look at as baskets planted for appearance alone. Try marigolds with nasturtiums, for instance, with a few added parsley plants for bulk. This type of planting also gives you more scope for variations in colour, flower and leaf shape and scent.

Seasonal Tasks

GOOD TIME-MANAGEMENT WILL HELP YOU SUCCEED WITH HANGING BASKETS. THE FOLLOWING CALENDAR PROVIDES A TIMETABLE THAT WILL ENABLE YOU TO KEEP PACE WITH TASKS AS THEY NEED TO BE DONE, AND TO MAINTAIN HEALTHY BASKETS ALL YEAR ROUND.

SPRING

Early spring

- plant up evergreens, such as herbs and ivies, for a permanent display
- tidy up permanent plantings and remove any dead leaves
- sow seed of vegetables under protection
- coax overwintered fuchsias, pelargoniums and chrysanthemums back into growth with bottom heat if necessary
- take cuttings of overwintered fuchsias and chrysanthemums as they come into growth

Mid-spring

- plant herbs and ivies for a permanent display
- sow seed of flowering annuals, such as nasturtiums and marigolds
- sow seed of annual herbs, such as basil and parsley
- bring dormant begonia tubers back into life
- prune woody plants such as roses
- lightly trim evergreen herbs

Late spring

- start feeding permanent plantings as they come back into growth
- buy bedding plants suitable for baskets from garden centres
- plant up baskets for summer interest
- pot up spent bulbs for use the following year or plant out in the garden

Above: *A cheery display for a spring basket.*

Above: *A glorious summer combination.*

Summer

Early summer
- make late sowings of annuals for autumn baskets
- start feeding summer baskets with a high-potash fertilizer
- order bulbs from bulb suppliers for planting in autumn

Midsummer
- begin harvesting cut-and-come-again crops
- begin harvesting dwarf beans
- begin harvesting strawberries
- begin harvesting annual herbs
- sow seed of winter pansies and keep the seedlings cool
- deadhead flowering plants to keep up the display

Late summer
- take cuttings of herbs and other woody plants for overwintering
- take cuttings of tender perennials for overwintering
- continue harvesting strawberries

Autumn

- sow seed of hardy annuals for early flowers the following season
- sow seed of biennials, such as *Myosotis*, for an early spring display in 18 months
- gradually dry off fuchsias and pelargoniums for overwintering
- dry off begonia tubers and store dry over winter
- plant up baskets of dwarf bulbs

Winter

- order seed of annuals and vegetables from seed catalogues
- order strawberry plants from commercial suppliers
- protect permanent plantings from heavy frosts
- continue to care for baskets indoors, watering to keep them just moist

Above: *Fuchsias provide colour in autumn.*

Above: *An evergreen basket for winter.*

Best Hanging Basket Plants

THIS QUICK REFERENCE CHART CAN BE USED TO SELECT THE MOST SUITABLE PLANTS FOR YOUR HANGING BASKETS IN TERMS OF THEIR REQUIREMENTS AND SEASON OF INTEREST. NOTE PARTICULARLY THE PLANTS' PREFERENCES FOR SUN OR SHADE.

Plant name	Height	Flower colour	Season of interest
Allium schoenoprasum FS	25cm/10in	herb	spring/summer
Anagallis Tr FS	10cm/4in	blue, red, pink	spring/summer
Antirrhinum hh FS	30cm/12in	pink, red, purple, yellow, bronze, orange, white	summer
Argyranthemum fh FS	30cm/12in	white, pink	summer/autumn
Asarina Tr FS	5cm/2in	purple	summer
Aster FS	25cm/10in	white, pink, violet, purple, red	summer/autumn
Begonia t Tr PS (tuberous and semperflorens)	20–60cm/ 8–24in	white, yellow, orange, red	summer/autumn
Bellis perennis FS	15cm/6in	white, pink, red	spring
Bidens fh Tr FS	25cm/10in	yellow	summer
Buxus FS/S	15cm/6in	foliage	all year
Calendula officinalis FS	25cm/10in	cream, yellow, orange	summer
Calluna FS	15cm/6in	white, pink, purple, crimson	summer/autumn
Chamaemelum FS	10cm/4in	foliage	all year

Plant name	Height	Flower colour	Season of interest
Chlorophytum comosum t Tr PS	25cm/10in	foliage	all year
Convallaria majalis Sh	20cm/8in	white	spring
Crocus FS	10cm/4in	white, yellow, purple, lilac	late winter/spring
Diascia FS Tr	30cm/12in	pink, lilac, apricot	summer
Dwarf beans FS	30cm/12in	vegetable	summer
Erica FS	30cm/12in	white, pink, purple	winter/spring
Eschscholzia FS	30cm/12in	cream, pink, orange, white, red, yellow	summer
Felicia t FS Tr	25cm/10in	blue	summer
Fuchsia hh PS Tr (some)	25cm/10in	pink, red, purple	summer/autumn
Galanthus officinalis PS	15cm/6in	white	late winter
Glechoma hederacea 'Variegata' FS/PS Tr	15cm/6in	foliage	all year
Gynura aurantiaca t PS Tr	30cm/12in	foliage	all year
Gypsophila FS Tr	30cm/12in	white	summer
Hedera (small-leaved) FS/Sh Tr	15cm/6in	foliage	all year
Helichrysum petiolare hh FS Tr	15cm/6in	foliage	all year
Impatiens t PS/Sh Tr (some)	15cm/6in	white, pink, red	summer/autumn
Lathyrus odoratus FS Tr	25cm/10in	white, pink, red, violet	summer
Lavandula FS	45cm/18in	blue, purple	all year

Best Hanging Basket Plants

Plant name	Height	Flower colour	Season of interest
Lobelia hh S/PS/Sh Tr (some)	10cm/4in	white, blue, purple, red	summer
Lobularia maritima FS	10cm/4in	white, purple	summer
Lysimachia nummularia 'Aurea' PS Tr	5cm/2in	foliage	all year
Mentha Sh	45cm/18in	herb	spring/summer/autumn
Mimulus PS Tr (some)	15cm/6in	yellow, orange, red, pink	summer
Muscari armeniacum FS	12cm/5in	purple, white	spring
Myosotis FS	30cm/12in	blue	spring
Narcissus FS	15–30cm/ 6–12in	white, cream, yellow	spring
Nemesia hh FS	20cm/8in	cream, orange, pink, blue, purple, yellow	summer
Ocimum basilicum hh FS	25cm/10in	herb	summer
Orchids t Sh Tr (some)	30cm/12in	all colours	any time of year
Pelargonium t FS/PS Tr (some)	30cm/12in	white, pink, red	summer
Petunia hh FS Tr	20cm/8in	white, purple, blue, red	summer
Primula PS	15cm/6in	white, pink, yellow, red, orange, purple	spring
Rosa (miniature and ground-cover) FS	25cm/10in	white, pink, yellow, red, orange	summer/autumn
Rosmarinus officinalis FS Tr (some)	30cm/12in	herb	all year

Plant name	Height	Flower colour	Season of interest
Salpiglossis hh FS	45cm/18in	yellow, orange, red, purple, blue	summer
Salvia officinalis FS	30cm/12in	herb	all year
Schlumbergera t PS Tr	20cm/8in	red, pink, white	winter
Solenostemon hh PS	30cm/12in	foliage	spring/summer/autumn
Strawberries FS Tr	12cm/5in	fruit	summer
Tanacetum parthenium FS	45cm/18in	white	summer
Thymus vulgaris FS	12cm/5in	herb	all year
Tomatoes hh FS Tr (some)	15cm/6in	fruiting vegetable	summer
Tradescantia t PS	20cm/8in	foliage	all year
Tropaeolum FS Tr (some)	20cm/8in	yellow, orange, red	summer
Verbena hh FS Tr	25cm/10in	red, pink, blue, mauve, white	summer
Vinca PS/Sh Tr	15cm/6in	white, blue, purple	foliage all year
Viola FS/PS	20cm/8in	white, violet, yellow, orange, maroon, black	spring/summer/autumn/winter

KEY TO ABBREVIATIONS

t = tender (needs minimum 5°C/41°F)

hh = half hardy
(survives lows of 0°C/32°F)

fh = frost hardy
(survives lows of -5°C/23°F)

Unmarked plants are fully hardy
(down to -15°C/5°F)

FS = full sun

PS = partial shade
(i.e. best protected from hot sun)

Sh = shade

Tr = trailing

WINDOW BOXES

Chosen to complement the style of a house, window boxes can add the perfect external finishing touch and offer considerable scope for year-round planting schemes. On a kitchen windowsill they can be filled with herbs or even planted as mini-vegetable gardens. This chapter gives you all the information you need to create beautiful displays, from choosing the best boxes and plants to caring for them and keeping them looking good all year round.

Dressing up Windows

AN EMPTY WINDOWSILL IS A MISSED OPPORTUNITY, AND FOR ANYONE WHO LOVES PLANTS A WINDOW BOX CRAMMED WITH COLOUR WILL BE PURE DELIGHT. THE CHALLENGE IS KNOWING JUST HOW TO TRANSFORM THAT EMPTY SPACE INTO SOMETHING MAGICAL.

Left: *This window box, bursting with petunias,* Brachyscome *daisies and* Convolvulus, *brightens the window from outside and within the house.*

There are so many wonderful plants to use and so many ways to use them, that creating the right window box for your home can be tricky. But once you know the basic principles involved in planting containers and window boxes, you can display your creative skills.

THE PLEASURE OF WINDOW BOXES

For many apartment dwellers, window boxes provide their only view of garden plants and flowers, and are like a breath of fresh air. For garden owners they can be important as exterior decoration, adding colour and design to the façades of their homes and forming a link with their gardens.

Above: *A window box planted with soft pale pink petunias and deeper-hued verbenas provides a link between house and garden.*

DECIDING WHAT YOU WANT

Before you buy containers and plants, you need to decide exactly what you want a window box to do for you and your home. You can make it blend with the decorative style, or create a contrast. Alternatively, you might want to continue the theme of your garden, extending the planting right up to your windows.

You may choose a country style of planting, or opt for a classic, modern or Mediterranean look. Perhaps a mass of colour appeals to you or just one or two accents, or you might prefer a subtle blend of foliage, scent for open windows or doorways, or the window box to be of culinary use.

Making an Impact

How you use colour will affect the success of your window box. You can throw together a mix and end up with a cheerful bunch of flowers, or you can colour co-ordinate for a more sophisticated approach, and to complement the external decoration of your home. Hot colours are loud and exciting, cool or pastel colours calm and relaxing.

The height and shape of the plants you choose also contribute to the overall effect. Clipped topiary and the erect, compact outlines of dwarf conifers suggest classic design, while wispy stems create a romantic image. Large leaves make bold statements, whereas fronds soften an arrangement. Flowering or colourfully leafed trailing plants are invaluable for window boxes for their ability to drop curtains of colour from the sill. This adds depth to a planting and softens the outline. Trailing lobelias and *Helichrysum petiolare* are especially valuable; they team well with many plants and can completely camouflage a dull container or soften a plain wall.

Above: *A bold black wooden window box is softened by the delicate cascades of foliage and flower.*

Creative Containers

For maximum impact the window box or container itself should fit comfortably with the style of the house and garden and complement the planting it contains. Material, shape and colour all contribute to the final effect. If you cannot find exactly what you need, you can often improvise by decorating or customizing a box or even adapting some other type of container. Pots, bowls, cans, even old boots can be employed.

Left: *This stylish box planted with* Heuchera, Senecio, *lavender and* Brachyscome *daisies would be more suitable for an elegant town house than a country cottage.*

Left: A hot and exotic style planting of succulents in a terracotta window box will enjoy a sunny position.

Interest Through the Year

The traditional approach to planting window boxes is a splash of fresh colour for the spring, usually supplied with bulbs and a few early bedding plants, followed by an exuberant show of summer bedding plants. But you can do much better than that.

Colourful plants are available at all times of the year and containers can be planted to make the best of each season. They can be replanted as one season gives way to the next, either in the same style or differently.

Alternatively, you can plant a window box to provide interest for the whole year. Use evergreen plants with colourful and interesting foliage for the permanent structure, and seasonal plants to add a succession of colour.

Decorative Styles

You can of course plant your window box in any way you wish, but a few identifiable styles are worth considering. Country style reflects a relaxed attitude to planting, with mixed colours and loose outlines. A classic style is altogether more restrained and formal, with tighter control over colour. A modern style involves the use of plants with interesting structure and foliage in unorthodox arrangements. A hot and exotic style uses sun-loving plants, many of which come in vibrant colours, combined with soft grey foliage and often includes spiky cacti and other succulents.

Right: Osteospermum *daisies keep their petals furled in cloudy weather so require a sunny position. Here O. 'Buttermilk' combines delightfully with yellow violas and white* Bacopa.

Planning Ahead

To ensure good results at all times with your window boxes, you need to plan ahead. Although you can buy plants when you are planting up your containers, you will not always find exactly what you want in the right colour when you want it. To avoid problems you can sow your own seed and grow the plants on until they are the right size for your container. Find a spare corner in the garden to act as a nursery for growing plants, as well as those that are resting at the end of their season of interest. You can even plant up containers ahead of time, to put on to a windowsill when they are looking their best, but large boxes are best planted in situ, since they will be too heavy to move once planted up.

Sun and Shade

When planning your containers, consider how much light your windowsills receive and try to plant accordingly. Sun-loving plants will look sick and lose colour if they are kept in perpetual shade, and those preferring dark, moist conditions may die in hot sun.

How to Use This Chapter

You will find all the information you need to create delightful window boxes on the following pages. The beginning of the chapter describes the types of containers and compost (soil mix) you can use as well as providing planting information. *Seasonal Splendour* explains how you can achieve interest during the entire year, and *Satisfying the Senses* tells you how to plant for colour and scent, and how to grow edible produce in containers. To help you with your window box planning there is a calendar of *Seasonal Tasks*. Finally, a quick-reference list gives useful information on cultivation requirements and season of interest for a selection of recommended plants.

Above: Mesembryanthemum *need a hot sunny position.*

Above: *Ferns are ideal for a dark, damp and shady spot.*

Getting Started

TO GET THE BEST FROM YOUR WINDOW BOXES YOU WILL NEED TO SELECT THE RIGHT CONTAINERS TO SUIT THE STYLE OF YOUR HOUSE. IT IS ALSO IMPORTANT THAT YOU KNOW HOW TO PLANT THEM UP CORRECTLY TO GIVE THE PLANTS A GOOD START.

TYPES OF WINDOW BOX

You can buy a wide range of attractive window boxes to blend in with your setting or planting design. There is something to suit every taste and budget, from modern lightweight materials and simple rustic boxes through stylish terracotta to the grandest stone trough. They are available plain or decorated and in many colours. Some containers have a built-in reservoir, which is useful if you are unable to water daily during a hot, dry summer. These are usually made of plastic or fibreglass.

Window boxes with a removable liner enable the contents to be lifted out at the end of a season.

Plastic

These boxes are often plain, but are lightweight and practical, needing less watering than boxes made of porous materials. However, they are often less attractive.

Above: *A simple galvanized tin window box is a perfect foil for the showy contents.*

Wood

There are styles of wooden container to suit every taste. Protect with wood preservative to ensure they age attractively.

Terracotta

Available in a range of sizes and styles, terracotta looks good and improves with age. However, it is heavy and susceptible to frost damage.

Plastic

Wood

Terracotta

Lightweight fibre

These boxes are a practical alternative to plastic, although they will not last as long. They are useful for lining baskets or rustic twig containers.

Bark

These are lightweight containers that have a rustic appeal, ideal for a country-garden setting.

Galvanized tin

Once only a utilitarian material, tin now makes a fashionable and smart window box that will make an eyecatching display when planted.

Fibreglass

Lightweight and durable, fibreglass planters are often moulded and finished to give the appearance of metal or terracotta.

Above: *A trug planted with pot marigolds and herbs has informal appeal. Culinary herbs can be grown near to the kitchen window for convenience.*

Making the Right Choice

When choosing a window box, decide first whether you want it to blend in with the setting of either the house or the garden. Choose with care: a rustic planter will be in keeping with a cottage but may look out of place in front of an elegant town house. Bear proportion in mind, too, and look for a window box that fits comfortably on the sill or bracket without crowding the space or looking lost in front of a very large window.

If you cannot find exactly the style or colour you want, you could make your own or adapt another container to make a window box. Alternatively, you could decorate a bought one.

Galvanized tin

Bark

Lightweight fibre

Fibreglass

Improvising with Unusual Containers

Many containers not normally associated with planting can be adapted for use as window boxes, to give striking visual effects. These can include small metal buckets or watering cans, unusual pots, copper kettles and old wooden boxes.

Large cans, perhaps painted in dramatic colours, can look good lined up on a windowsill. Baskets can also be used as window boxes, provided they are generously lined with moss or plastic before planting up. The only considerations are that the container is not so tall as to obscure the view from the window and that it fits on to the sill. It must also be possible to fix it safely on the windowsill without danger of it falling off or being blown over by the wind. It will also be necessary to add drainage holes. These can be simply made using a drill with the appropriate bit for the material of the container.

Above: *A small oval old metal bucket has been converted into an attractive container for lily-of-the-valley.*

Above: *Vivid red geraniums dominate this rustic, home-made window box, which is an ideal choice to complement an unpainted window frame.*

Customizing Window Boxes and Other Containers

If a container is not exactly what you want, you can paint or decorate it to suit your requirements.

Wooden, terracotta and plastic containers can be painted to tone in with your house or to complement a planting theme for maximum impact. You can even change the paint colour seasonally to suit different plantings. The paint can be applied as flat colour, in bold designs or with special effects such as marbling or crackle glaze.

Above: *These brightly painted pots look stunning in a sunny spot, filled with vibrant geraniums and herbs.*

As most window boxes are flat-fronted, they are easy to decorate with different materials, such as sea shells, using self-hardening clay or a glue gun. For a mosaic effect, pieces of coloured china, broken tile or mirror can be applied to create a pattern, using water-resistant tile adhesive and grout. Sketch out your design on paper before you start, to avoid mistakes.

Above: *Mussel shells on a small terracotta window box prettily complement this colour-themed planting of lavender and violas.*

Composts

There are several types of compost (soil mix) available for using in containers, and it is worth thinking about which is best suited to the plants you want to grow. The most commonly used is "multi-purpose", and this is indeed suitable for many purposes. It is usually peat-based, but peat-free versions are available, which are preferable because of the environmental damage caused by peat removal. Both versions have similar properties: they are light and can be difficult to moisten if they are allowed to dry out completely, and their nutrient content will be rapidly used up, so the plants will need regular feeding. Special container composts are available which are largely similar, but often have water-retentive granules added. (Make sure you don't add more water-retentive granules, if this is the case.)

For long-term plantings, or for growing fruit or vegetables in window boxes, a loam-based compost is preferable. It is heavier than multi-purpose, but contains more trace elements and will not run out of nutrients so quickly. Plants will still need feeding, however, and permanent plantings will also benefit from yearly top-dressing – removing the top layer of soil, taking care not to damage the roots, and replacing it with fresh.

Ericaceous compost is the best choice if you are growing lime-hating plants, such as many of the summer-flowering heathers (most of the winter ones are fine in standard compost). Herbs will also tolerate standard compost, but will grow best in a loam-based type with sharp grit added to make it really free-draining.

Below: *Window boxes are high-maintenance, but can be spectacular.*

Mulches

A layer of protective material placed over the compost or soil helps to retain moisture, conserve warmth, suppress weeds and prevent soil splash on foliage and flowers. It should also provide an attractive backdrop for plants before they have filled out and completely covered the surface.

Composted bark

Coarse bark is an effective mulch, as weeds that have germinated are easily removed. As it rots down, it also conditions the soil. It works best when spread in a layer at least 7.5cm (3in) thick, and is therefore not ideal for small containers.

Stones

Smooth stones can be used as decorative mulch for large plants grown in containers. You can save stones dug out of the garden or buy them from garden centres. Try to find colours that will complement your buildings.

Gravel

This makes a decorative mulch for container plants and provides the correct environment for plants such as alpines. It is available in a variety of sizes and colours, which can be matched to the scale and colours of the plants used.

Water-retaining Gel

You can reduce the frequency of watering needed by adding water-retaining gels to the compost. Sachets of gel are available from garden centres. You mix it with the compost at the recommended rate, though some types may need soaking in water first. Ensure you don't add it to special container composts that already contain a water-retaining gel, as large amounts can froth up out of the compost.

Above: *Water-retentive gel holds many times its weight of water and is useful for containers.*

Planting Up Window Boxes

Most solid window boxes are easy to plant, but need some initial preparation to ensure best results.

1 It is essential to provide all types of window boxes with some form of drainage material in the base. In small window boxes this can be broken pieces of pot – known as crocks – or gravel, which is available in various sizes from garden centres.

2 When planting up large window boxes, it is more economical to recycle polystyrene plant trays as drainage material. Lumps of polystyrene are excellent for this purpose, and, as they retain warmth, they are an additional benefit to the plants.

GARDENER'S TIP

Some plants that have been grown in small pots for a length of time can become "pot-bound". When replanting gently tease out the roots around the bottom and edges to encourage the roots to grow down into the container.

3 Partly fill the container with compost (soil mix) and arrange the plants. Adjust the level of the compost to ensure the tops of all the rootballs are at the same height, about 2.5cm (1in) below the rim of the container. Fill up around the plants with compost, adding slow-release plant food granules at the same time, and gently press it down. Water thoroughly.

Above: *A variegated periwinkle,* Vinca minor *'Aureovariegata', blue-leaved hostas and summer-flowering busy Lizzies* (Impatiens) *will brighten a gloomy corner for many months. The periwinkle will bear blue flowers in the spring.*

Planting Wicker Baskets

If you use an open container such as a wooden container with a slatted bottom or a basket, you may need to line it to prevent the compost falling out.

Above: *A wicker basket will be able to retain moisture if it is lined with moss.*

Plastic Boxes

When buying plastic window boxes, check that the drainage holes are open. Some manufacturers mark the holes, but leave it to the customer to punch or drill them out as required. Make sure there are enough holes, and that they are large enough to prevent any danger of waterlogging.

Above: *With plastic window boxes the drainage holes sometimes need to be drilled before you can begin planting.*

Plant Supports

Most window boxes are planted with fairly low-growing plants, so as not to cut out too much light from the window, but sometimes height may be required, and this can be achieved by training climbers up canes or a small trellis. Ivies work well for a year-round box, or for a riot of colour in summer, try dwarf sweet peas, which will provide a gorgeous scent as well as colour, nasturtiums or morning glories.

Above: *Climbing plants may simply be allowed to trail, but you can grow them up plastic or wooden trellising.*

Seasonal Splendour

WINDOW BOXES CAN LOOK MAGNIFICENT DURING EVERY SEASON OF THE YEAR, WHETHER YOU DECIDE TO CREATE A DIFFERENT SCHEME EVERY FEW MONTHS WITH FLORAL COMBINATIONS, OR A DISPLAY THAT LASTS FOR THE WHOLE YEAR.

Left: Different varieties and shades of yellow and white daffodils and pansies herald the arrival of spring.

SPRING WINDOW BOXES

After the gloomy winter months, spring boxes need to be bright and cheerful. Bulbs are plentiful, and their crisp, exquisite colours, with plenty of white and yellow, work extremely well with fresh green foliage. Many species have dwarf varieties, which are ideal for small containers or window boxes.

> **GARDENER'S TIP**
> To save bulbs for next year allow the leaves to die right back and then dig up and store in a cool, dry place.

Hyacinths, available in an enormous number of delicate and intense shades, provide a heady scent. Spring bedding in jewel colours, such as pansies, auriculas and polyanthus, provide more joy. As the season progresses the strong colours seem to give way to softer ones, with blues and pinks leading into summer.

Evergreen plants such as ivies and periwinkle *(Vinca minor)* make valuable contributions to early spring boxes when foliage can be sparse.

Above: Potted daffodils, pansies and tulips provide a cheerful display.

Planting Partners

Early bulbs look good massed together in pots, but you can fill the gaps around less tightly packed ones with vividly coloured bedding plants. Double-flowered daisies make excellent backdrops for yellow daffodils and the variously coloured tulips.

Blue and yellow is a common spring combination, starting with early blue-flowered bulbs accompanying daffodils, and later yellow tulips with blue and yellow hyacinths, blue pansies and forget-me-nots. Blue also makes a striking combination with red; try red tulips with forget-me-nots.

Maintaining Interest

Plant up a spring window box so that its interest increases from winter to summer. Follow late crocuses, daffodils, narcissi and pansies with hyacinths, tulips, forget-me-nots, bluebells and wallflowers.

PLANTS AT THEIR BEST IN SPRING

Bellis perennis
Crocus
Erisymum cheiri
Hyacinthoides
Hyacinthus
Muscari armeniacum
Myosotis
Narcissus
Primula
Primula auricula hybrids
Primula Polyanthus Group
Tulipa
Viola

If you did not plant up your spring boxes in the autumn, you can create an instant spring arrangement by using pots of plants already in flower. Simply arrange them in a window box and fill around the pots with bark to hide them. As soon as a plant is past its best, replace it with something new. Old pots of bulbs will flower again next year.

Above: *An old strawberry box carrier makes an attractive and unusual spring window box for a group of beautifully marked auricula primulas, planted in old-style terracotta pots.*

Summer Window Boxes

Window boxes need flowering and foliage plants that are going to look good throughout the summer months. Use plenty of bushy, but not very tall bedding plants, such as pansies and petunias, dwarf snapdragons, flowering tobaccos *(Nicotiana)* and compact pot marigolds. Many border perennials are also useful for creating a variety of different heights.

Over the years, plant breeders have produced myriad varieties of summer bedding in every colour imaginable, so it is unlikely you will be unable to find the exact colour you want to fit into any scheme. There is such an abundance of colour that care needs to be taken to avoid ending up with a garish mix.

Above: *White tobacco flowers and pale pink geraniums make a lovely summer display, with variegated ground ivy trailing attractively over the sides of the box.*

Below: *Scented petunias, delicate white marguerites and star-flowered* Isotoma *make a stunning layered arrangement.*

Planting Partners

With so many varieties of summer bedding you can create just the right colour scheme to suit you. Compact and trailing fuchsias are stunning and you can use them to conjure up pretty combinations in whites, pinks and purples. Try them with sweet alyssum, violas, *Impatiens*, tobaccos and lobelias. Blue *Felicia amelloides* will combine well with *Osteospermum*, petunias and verbenas.

Use brightly flowered *Impatiens* with colourful trailing plants, including ivies, lobelias and *Tradescantia*, and with attractive foliage plants such as long-lasting begonias and coleus. They can also be teamed with architectural hostas, bergenias and ferns for a shady windowsill.

Above: *White osteospermums make a good background, accentuating bolder colour choices.*

Lobelias combine well with many summer bedding plants, such as dwarf snapdragons, nemesias and *Tagetes*, as well as with foliage plants like begonias and *Chlorophytum*.

The silvery *Helichrysum petiolare* sets off summer's bright colours, especially blues, mauves and pinks.

Above: *Alaska nasturtiums, with cream-splattered leaves, are planted with yellow snapdragons,* Gazania *and* Brachyscome *daisies to make an extended summer display.*

Maintaining Interest

To extend the season, plant a window box so that there is a succession of interest, with new flowers replacing plants that are past their best. For example, a container of pink geraniums *(Pelargonium)* such as 'Tomcat', *Lavandula pinnata*, salvias and alyssums, with blue *Brachyscome* daisies and *Convolvulus sabatius* will only improve as the season progresses. By the end of summer, the pinks, reds and purples of the geraniums, salvias and lavenders will be at their most prolific. Many plants will continue flowering well into autumn, if they are properly maintained with regular watering, feeding and deadheading.

If you are using individual pots in a window box, now is the time to include annuals or exotic bulbs such as *Tigridia* as they come into flower. Perhaps intersperse the arrangement with some foliage plants or trailing ivies.

Left: *The bold blooms of* Pelargonium, *ranging from pinks to reds, will provide a long-lasting summer display.*

Below: *All the plants in this pink arrangement are still in their pots. As soon as one is past its best, a new pink plant can easily replace it.*

Above: The plants in this shallow planter require little depth for their roots, but they will need watering and feeding often.

To ensure window boxes look their best, remember to deadhead regularly. Once a plant begins to set seed flowering will reduce. With some prolific plants deadheading may be necessary on an almost daily basis.

Watering is another important task that must not be overlooked. During summer, containers dry out very quickly and require watering daily. If this is neglected, the plants will soon suffer stress, lose their leaves and become vulnerable to disease. If the weather is very hot, you may even need to water twice a day, in the morning and in the evening. If you do water in the morning, avoid wetting the leaves, otherwise the sun can scorch them, causing them to turn brown and die off, and spoiling the display.

PLANTS AT THEIR BEST IN SUMMER

Ageratum
Antirrhinum
Argyranthemum
Calendula
Dianthus
Fuchsia
Gazania
Impatiens
Lobelia
Lobularia maritima
Nasturtium
Nemesia
Nicotiana
Osteospermum
Petunia
Salvia
Tagetes
Verbena
Viola

Autumn Window Boxes

As summer fades into autumn, the low sun casts its spell on the autumnal hues as bright summer colours mellow into russets, golds and purples. Golden rudbeckias bloom well into autumn. Chrysanthemums are prolific, with masses of rust, maroon, orange, gold and red flowers that last for weeks; the dwarf varieties are ideal choices for window boxes. Michaelmas daisies and autumn heathers come into their own with pink to purple flowers; the heathers often have interesting foliage shades, too. Depending on the variety, all these bushy plants will supply flowers throughout the season. In addition, blue gentians and bulbs, such as *Colchicum* and the pink *Amaryllis belladonna*, will provide some unexpectedly bright highlights with their wide range of colours.

Above: *Dwarf chrysanthemums provide colour over a long period.*

Planting Partners

Red-tinged foliage works especially well in autumn light. Choose red or rust coleus, and bronze or purple heuchera to complement the season's flowers. If you have space for it, a container-grown Japanese maple will appear to burn with glorious colour outside your window.

Above: *A bark window box provides a sympathetically rustic container for autumn-flowering heathers.*

Maintaining Interest

Many of the long-flowering summer plants will continue well into autumn, providing plenty of colour. Asters and kaffir lilies *(Schizostylis)* bridge the gap from summer into autumn. As these start to fade, introduce ice plants *(Sedum spectabile)*, heathers and autumn-flowering bulbs such as nerines and sternbergias for the middle of the season. Chrysanthemums will continue to show until the cold of winter finally arrives. Autumn crocuses can flower right through the season.

Michaelmas daisies and chrysanthemums are prone to grey mould *(Botrytis)* and powdery mildew, which can disfigure the plant. Remove and destroy affected areas but if the problem persists spray with a fungicide.

Berries are attractive to birds, which rely on them for an autumn feast. While you may resent their gluttony, view it as a spectacle to enjoy from inside your window. The more berry plants you have, the longer brightly coloured fruits will last for both you and the birds to appreciate. For larger containers, low, spreading cotoneasters can be a real boon with their fiery-red berries.

PLANTS AT THEIR BEST IN AUTUMN

Amaryllis belladonna
Aster novae-angliae
Aster novi-belgii
Calluna vulgaris
Colchicum
Cyclamen
Fuchsia
Impatiens
Nerine
Rudbeckia
Schizostylis
Sedum

Above: *Autumn-flowering crocuses* (Colchicum) *provide a beautiful and delicate colour that is best appreciated at close quarters.*

Winter Window Boxes

To dispel midwinter gloom you need robust plants with plenty of colour and interesting foliage in your window boxes. Evergreen plants come into their own at this time of year, providing permanence of structure and colour that lasts, no matter what the weather does. There are many shades of green, with blue, silver-grey and golden hues as well as creamy and yellow variegations; colours that become almost magical in the crisp winter light.

***Above:** Pot-grown dwarf conifers, variegated ivies and red polyanthus provide instant winter cheer.*

Planting Partners

Box (*Buxus*) can be trimmed into interesting shapes to form miniature topiary, which can be combined with dwarf conifers (including cultivars of *Chamaecyparis* and *Thuja*).

Some berried plants can be included in winter boxes. Although it is fast growing, wintergreen *(Gaultheria procumbens)* can be contained for a couple of years, before it needs to be replanted in the garden. It has big red aromatic berries and its glossy leaves are red when young, and would combine well with *Juniperus squamata* 'Blue Carpet'. In mild areas, the green, orange and scarlet berries of winter cherry *(Solanum pseudocapsicum)* make a contribution.

Another seasonal partnership is a combination of white variegated ivy, cheerful *Euonymus fortunei* 'Emerald 'n' Gold' and a silver-leaved senecio such as 'Sunshine'.

Foliage plants such as bergenia, heuchera and ivies, especially variegated ones, make important contributions to winter containers. Combine them with multi-coloured winter-flowering pansies, pink cyclamen and, for late winter, white snowdrops to bring precious cheer to window boxes.

***Above:** The copper leaves of* Cordyline *work well with the softer texture of a dwarf conifer and miniature hebe for interest in the winter.*

Maintaining Interest

Winter-flowering pansies often bloom stoically through the cold of winter. Varieties of *Cyclamen persicum* also bloom throughout winter, while *C. coum* continues into spring. Others that flower at the end of the season are multi-coloured polyanthus, yellow winter aconites, snowdrops, iris, and *Erica carnea*, in shades of pink and white.

If you are using individual pots in your window boxes, they can be planted up with winter-flowering pansies, which are available in a bright array of bold colours, polyanthus or *Cyclamen coum* in shades of red, pink or white. You can also plant hellebores – *Helleborus niger* (the Christmas rose) and *H. orientalis* produce their delicate white, pink or purple flowers in winter or early spring. When they have finished flowering, you could remove the pots and plant them out in the garden.

Danger Zones

Cold, wind and rain are the combined perils of winter. Any terracotta containers you have must be frost-proof if you live in a frost zone, otherwise they will absorb moisture, which will freeze during frost and result in cracking. Self-watering containers should be drained before winter to prevent frost damage. If strong wind is expected you may need to protect taller plants.

PLANTS AT THEIR BEST IN WINTER

Bergenia
Buxus sempervirens
Cyclamen
Dwarf conifers
Erica carnea
Euonymus fortunei
Galanthus
Hedera
Heuchera
Primula Polyanthus
Viola

Above: *Winter pansies are wonderfully resilient and will often bloom bravely throughout the winter as long as they are regularly deadheaded to promote new buds. They make a dramatic and cheerful display, especially in an old wooden trug, as here.*

Year-round Window Boxes

In the same way that a garden has certain plants that provide structure throughout the year, evergreens can provide the backbone of a year-round window box. Evergreen plants come in many shapes, sizes and shades and should be carefully selected to supply height and depth to the planting. Before you start planting, plan the positions of the plants so that the colours and shapes look well balanced. Plant the structure plants first, then add the colour plants. Extra colour can be introduced each season by including smaller flowering plants.

Above: Choosing foliage plants with differently shaped leaves creates a structured planting scheme for year-round interest.

Topiary shrubs and dwarf conifers are important structural plants for the year-round display, and can be supplemented with evergreen trailers to add depth and soften outlines. Choose variegated varieties of evergreen plants such as ivies (*Hedera*) and periwinkle (*Vinca minor*) to add further interest.

Above: *Evergreen* Skimmia reevesiana *'Rubella' and* Arundinaria pygmaea *provide height while trailing* Cotoneaster conspicuus *and variegated periwinkle soften the edges of this year-round window box. Heathers supply winter colour.*

Planting Partners

Evergreen plants have a surprising range of foliage colours and textures, and many colourful combinations are possible. *Cordyline* has dramatic, spear-shaped leaves and many varieties are red or purple. Planted with golden dwarf conifers or tufts of golden grass, the effect can be stunning. Adding more colour, such as a blue-green hosta with broad leaves or a bright green, tiny-leaved hebe, would only heighten the interest. Grasses always add grace and movement to a planting, no matter what their colour.

Tiny topiary plants, clipped in several different shapes, would make an intriguing group for a container. Be creative with your shapes for an eye-catching display. Box (*Buxus*) is the most suitable plant for this treatment.

> GARDENER'S TIP
>
> If the leaves of permanently planted glossy foliage plants begin to lose their sheen and colour, it is a sign that the plants need a feed. Sprinkle a long-term plant feed on the surface of the potting soil and boost with a liquid feed.

A collection of pretty alpines arranged in a small trough would make a charming permanent planting. Try compact species and cultivars of armeria, aubrieta, campanula, dianthus, phlox, sempervivum and saxifrage together with tiny hebes.

A mulch of gravel for such plants is both attractive and practical as it prevents soil splashing on to the leaves of the plants. A trough like this should last a number of years before it needs replanting.

Above: *A selection of easy-to-grow alpine plants have been grouped together in this basket-weave stone planter to create a miniature garden.*

Maintaining Interest

You can ring the changes in a permanently planted box by including some seasonal highlights in the planting. Bulbs can be part of the permanent planting, emerging when their flowering time is due. There are bulbs for almost every season – snowdrops, spring and autumn crocuses, narcissus and daffodils, hyacinths, tulips, crocosmia, lilies, nerines, cyclamen and many more. If you include some perennials for spring and summer interest, you will hardly need to disturb the planting.

Below: *Hyacinths add a welcome burst of colour and a glorious scent to the early spring window box.*

Above: *Winter-flowering pansies progress through to spring to add brilliance to* Narcissus *as they bloom.*

Adding Bedding Plants for Variety

A permanent planting of foliage can start to look a bit lifeless after a couple of seasons. It can be given seasonal highlights by adding a succession of bright bedding plants, replacing plants as they fade.

By rotating winter- and summer-flowering pansies you can sustain the appearance of the window box through the year. But by planting any of the spring and summer bedding plants you will change the overall effect. Choose plants with long flowering periods.

Such a window box might include creeping Jenny *(Lysimachia nummularia)*, *Arabis caucasia*, rock cress *(Aubrieta deltoidea)* and bellflowers *(Campanula)* as constant residents. These provide beautiful edging and trailers and may need to be divided or cut back every couple of years.

Above: Lysimachia nummularia, *heather and* Lobelia *would combine well.*

The scheme could include deep maroon heathers in winter followed by hyacinths and crocuses for spring. Trailing lobelia and *Pelargonium* (geranium) could supply both summer and autumn colour.

EVERGREEN PLANTS FOR WINDOW BOXES

Buxus
Cordyline
Chamaecyparis pisifera
Cotoneaster conspicuus
Dwarf conifers
Euonymus fortunei
Grasses
Hebe
Hedera helix
Vinca minor

Right: *Topiaried* Buxus *in a window box makes a stylish year-round statement. In spring, the dainty, white flowers of* Bacopa *enhance the effect.*

Satisfying the Senses

WINDOW BOXES APPEAL TO OUR SENSES IN MORE THAN ONE WAY. THEY SHOULD ALWAYS BE VISUAL FEASTS, BUT CAN ALSO BE USED TO SATISFY OUR SENSE OF TOUCH, TASTE AND SMELL BY INCLUDING TEXTURED, SCENTED AND EVEN EDIBLE PLANTS.

USING COLOUR

How you use colour in a window box will depend on what you want to achieve. You can create a carefully co-ordinated planting or make a brash statement. You can plant in a single colour or use several together to create a witty image.

Your use of colour will influence the mood of the planting. Hot colours introduce excitement into a planting. Intense blues will cool things down. White imparts a sense of purity and tranquillity. Pastels introduce a romantic tone.

When planning your window boxes remember that light affects colours. Strong, hot colours, especially red, work better in strong light, as does variegated foliage. Pastels become bleached out in strong light and respond better to shade.

Above: Make a bold statement with flame-coloured flowers in an area with plenty of light.

Left: A well-filled container of large white geraniums (Pelargonium), *verbenas, marguerites* (Argyranthemum) *and white-flowered* Bacopa, *with silver-leaved* Senecio, *is a joy to the eye as well as deliciously fragrant.*

GARDENER'S TIP

Try to position blue flowers where they can be seen at dusk, when their colours become far more intense and are a treat not to be missed.

Colour Combinations

Not all colours mix well and it is usually best to place plant colours that harmonize next to each other. White and blue seem to work with almost any other colour, and pastels are easy to arrange together. The ones to be careful of are brilliant oranges with strong magenta.

Above: *White-flowering tobaccos* (Nicotiana), *pink* Impatiens *and tumbling, white, variegated geranium* (Pelargonium) *and lobelia have been planted to create a visually satisfying linear effect.*

Above: *Shocking pink petunias and verbenas dominate this container, which also features softer pink marguerites to delight the eye. The silver-leaved* Stachys byzantina *are a perfect colour foil as well as being delightful to touch.*

Using Foliage for Visual Impact

With its variety of shapes and colours, foliage is an essential element of garden design, whether in the garden flower beds or in a window box. Foliage comes in a vast number of colours and shades, including white, cream, gold, silver, red and purple. It is possible to create window boxes using only foliage plants, either with contrasting colours or within a narrow range. For example, you could use only foliage with yellow or golden tinges, but with plenty of variation in shape, and perhaps set off by a plant with darker green leaves. Also leaf colours change through the year. Variegated hosta leaves can deepen in colour as the year progresses.

COLOURFUL FOLIAGE

Begonia rex
(red, black or silver variegations)
Coleus blumei
(multi-coloured leaves)
Hedera helix (variegated)
Helichrysum petiolare (silver)
Ophiopogon (black)
Pelargonium (variegated)
Senecio (silver)

Blending Foliage with Flowers

More commonly, though, foliage is regarded as a part of a planting that features flowers, and the type of foliage can be chosen specifically for its ability to work well with certain flower colours. Dark green works well with strong hot colours. Soft greens and silver suit cool blues and pinks.

Above: *The intense purple of this heliotrope is teamed with a purple-leaved dahlia with dark red flowers and purple- and red-flowered trailing verbenas.*

Maintaining Colour

To sustain a colourful display over a whole season, use evergreen foliage plants for the basis of the planting. You can team them with plants that have a long flowering season, or keep a colour scheme going by replacing fading plants with different ones in the similar colours.

For spring, a succession of bulbs with polyanthus and pansies provide good value. For summer, annuals and bedding plants provide the bulk of bright colour; ageratum, sweet alyssum, antirrhinums, flowering begonias, marigolds, and *Impatiens* are all excellent. Geraniums (*Pelargonium*) also give some spectacular displays. The many varieties of compact and trailing fuchsias produce their elegant flowers over a long period, and combine well with petunias and lobelias, also reliable performers. Remember to deadhead flowers regularly to maintain a constant supply of fresh buds.

Above: *The blue-green leaves of the nasturtium contrast dramatically with the bronze leaves of* Fuchsia fulgens *'Thalia'.*

Above: *Fuchsia has a long flowering period and is used here to striking effect with vibrant crimson and purple petunias.*

Scent

Fragrant flowers or aromatic herbs in a window box will scent the air as it wafts in through an open window. Choose the type of fragrance to complement the use of the room. A bedroom window box will allow you to wake up to sweet-smelling flowers on summer mornings, but take care as anything too heady can be overpowering and even interrupt sleep. For a kitchen window the aroma of fresh herbs would be more suitable.

> GARDENER'S TIP
>
> During the summer, pick and dry the leaves of scented geraniums for use in pot-pourri or in muslin bags to scent linen.

Plants with fragrant foliage release their scents more readily when they are bruised. Site these where they will be brushed against. Scented geraniums *(Pelargonium)* have an incredible diversity of scents: lemon, spice and peppermint. They need to be overwintered in a greenhouse in frost areas.

***Above:** A selection of scented geraniums* (Pelargonium fragrans) *will release their delicious fragrance when you brush against their leaves.*

Additional Benefits

Many plants have healing qualities and, while they should not be used to treat a health condition without first checking with your medical practitioner, some have provided successful country remedies for centuries. Lavender soothes headaches and rosemary is a general pick-me-up. Camomile is used in herbal teas and feverfew is said to alleviate migraines. If you have a problem that can be relieved by a simple remedy, why not grow the herb on a windowsill for a ready supply?

Some herbs can be used to repel insects. Pennyroyal rubbed around an area will deter ants, and black basil keeps flies at bay. Conversely, some sweet-smelling flowers are irresistible to butterflies, especially ice plants, which flower in autumn.

Above: *The leaves of lemon verbena, a deciduous shrub, have a powerful scent. Here they are combined with scented geranium* (Pelargonium).

Left: *The scented flowers of many herbs, including marjoram and thyme, are irresistible to butterflies.*

SCENTED PLANTS

AROMATIC
Calendula
Mentha x gracilis 'Variegata'
Nasturtium
Origanum onites
Origanum vulgare
Pelargonium, scented
Thymus

SWEET
Lavandula
Pelargonium, scented
Petunia
Verbena

TASTE

Nothing tastes as good as freshly picked vegetables, fruit or herbs, and window boxes can be used for growing many of these as well as edible flowers. Containers are perfect for anyone who likes the taste of home-grown food but does not have a garden to grow it in.

Decide on your priorities and how practical it will be to grow the crops you are interested in. A sunny position is best for vegetables, fruit and herbs; choose a sill sheltered from wind for vegetables. You will be limited to vegetables with fibrous or shallow roots, but it makes sense to grow items that cost a lot in the supermarket or taste many times better when they are freshly picked. Or perhaps you are interested in growing something that is difficult to buy. If you want to include flowers in your cooking, it's far more convenient to grow your own, and you can be sure they will not have been sprayed with chemicals.

If you place your edible window box at a kitchen window, it will be convenient to harvest your crops as and when you need them. And you will be able to inspect them daily, which will allow you to take action against any pests or diseases that may attack.

If you sow seed directly into a container on a sill, you may need to give protection to tender seedlings.

Below: *An old fruit box filled with herbs is both pretty and useful. It has been colour-washed to tone with the herbs.*

Maintaining a Supply of Edible Plants

Once you have decided which food, herbs or flowers you want to grow, you can start sowing seed or buying small plants. Make sure you buy and sow the seeds in good time. With salad crops, such as lettuces, radishes and spring onions, you can sow every few weeks to ensure a regular supply. Vegetables can also be started in pots so that as you harvest one plant another strongly growing one will be ready to replace it in the window box. If you want to grow herbs, make sure you have plenty of those you use often so that you do not run out.

Above: Fresh herbs cram a terracotta window box. Regular cutting of the plants will encourage plenty of new growth.

Make your food or herb window box attractive; there is no reason why the container should not be prettily planted, and, to make it perfect, it can include some fragrant flowers.

Below: You may be surprised to find how many different vegetables can be grown in a small space.

Herb Window Box

Fresh herbs make a huge difference to the taste of food, so it is always useful to have plenty growing close to hand, and a kitchen windowsill is especially convenient. You can grow virtually any herb in a container, but some do grow rather bushy and they will need to be cut frequently to keep them compact. Concentrate on growing those herbs that you tend to use most of in your cooking. There is no reason, however, why you should not also grow some others simply for the pleasure of their fragrance and appearance.

GARDENER'S TIP

Herbs are at their most flavoursome and aromatic before they flower, so as soon as the plants are well established you can start picking them for use in the kitchen.

Some herbs are available in attractively coloured varieties. Sage, mint and thyme all have variegated versions, and sage can also be purple.

Herbs can also be grown in individual pots placed on the windowsill. This is especially useful for mint, which has very invasive roots, and for any that need to be overwintered indoors.

Sun and Shade

The amount of sun your windowsill receives during the day will determine what type of herbs you can grow there successfully. The Mediterranean herbs especially are sun loving. Rosemary, sage, marjoram and thyme will thrive on a hot sill. Soft leafy herbs often prefer a cooler, shady situation to look and taste their best. Mint requires moist roots, and a pot could share a shady sill with sorrel, chives, lemon balm and parsley.

Left: *This window box is packed with fresh culinary herbs. It contains chervil, coriander, fennel, garlic, purple sage, French tarragon, savory and basil. All these edible herbs can be successfully grown on a warm, sunny windowsill.*

Vegetable and Salad Window Boxes

Most types of vegetable can be grown in a window box, but shallow-rooted, compact and quick-maturing types are most suitable, given the limited space. Many crops also look decorative. A window box is beneficial to tender plants as the house walls provide some warmth and shelter.

Compact but heavy-fruiting tomato plants have been specially bred for growing in containers and you can try these in a window box in full sun. Team them up with other salad vegetables and/or herbs such as compact lettuce, chives and parsley. Tomatoes are thirsty plants and need to be kept moist. Feed them with a proprietary tomato food.

If you have a very sheltered and sunny windowsill, consider growing (bell) peppers, chillies and small-fruited aubergines (eggplants). You can also grow dwarf beans, beetroots (beets) and stump-rooted carrots.

As space in the window box is rather cramped, it is a good idea to sow vegetable seeds elsewhere and transplant seedlings as they are ready, except for those vegetables that are best sown in situ.

VEGETABLES FOR WINDOW BOXES

Carrot
Beetroot (Beets)
Dwarf French beans
Garlic
Lettuce
(Bell) Pepper
Radish
Shallot
Spring onion (scallion)
Tomato

Below: *This salad window box contains compact tomatoes, lettuces, radishes, chives and parsley.*

Fruit Window Boxes

A number of fruits, including apples, lemons and peaches, can be successfully grown in containers, but they all need a large tub or half-barrel. For window boxes, strawberries are the only realistic choice. They grow happily in containers – in fact, they will be less vulnerable to slugs and snails than those grown in the ground – and they make good ornamental plants with their pretty daisy-like flowers, interesting leaves and colourful fruit.

Ordinary strawberries need plenty of sun to ripen, but the much smaller alpine strawberries can produce delicious fruit in light shade. These alpine types also make good edge planting in window boxes.

There are some very heavy cropping types, and you can buy varieties to fruit at different times to extend the season. Some even produce a second crop in the autumn. Generous and regular watering when the fruits are ripening will increase a plant's yield. To ensure a good crop next year, cut the leaves of large strawberries right back after fruiting.

Above: *A window box combination of strawberries, ivy and herbs planted in an agricultural metal basket.*

Above: *Strawberries can be successfully grown in window boxes in full sun. They look decorative as well as having a finer taste than commercial ones.*

Edible Flowers

In addition to herbs, some garden flowers are edible and make unusual but pretty additions to salads and drinks or can be used to garnish other dishes. Edible flowers can also be frozen with ice cubes.

In the kitchen, flowers can be used to colour butter and to scent oil, vinegar and sugar. With the addition of egg white and sugar they are transformed into crystallized flowers, which can grace cakes, cookies, mousses and sweet or savoury roulades.

To keep the plants producing flowers for as long as possible, deadhead regularly. Once a plant has set seed, it will produce fewer and fewer flowers. Wash them before use.

Use nasturtium flowers in salads; they not only look spectacular but also add a lovely peppery flavour. Chive and thyme flowers also make attractive additions to salads. Rose petals and violets make delightful crystallized cake decorations, and lavender can be used in desserts or with chicken cooked on a barbecue.

EDIBLE FLOWERS

Calendula
Chive
Courgette (zucchini)
Daisy
Lavandula
Lemon verbena
Nasturtium
Pansy
Rose
Sweet violet

Below: *Nasturtium, pansies, chives and marigolds* (Calendula) *fill this window box, making a decorative display of edible flowers. They can be used in sweet and savoury dishes.*

Seasonal Tasks

KNOWING WHAT TO DO WHEN IS PART OF THE SECRET OF SUCCESSFUL WINDOW BOX DISPLAYS. THIS QUICK GUIDE SUMMARIZES THE IMPORTANT TASKS ACCORDING TO SEASON. THE JOBS HAVE BEEN LISTED IN THE ORDER THEY GENERALLY WOULD NEED TO BE DONE.

SPRING

Early Spring
- plant herbs in containers for permanent display
- plant strawberries in containers for summer display
- plant edible flower plants in containers for summer display
- sow seed for vegetables under protection

Mid-spring
- plant herbs in containers for permanent display
- plant edible flower plants in containers for summer display
- plant ferns for spring and summer display
- sow seed for vegetables under protection
- sow seed for sunflowers

Late Spring
- sow seed of biennial bedding (polyanthus, wallflowers etc) in seed beds or trays for display next spring
- start overwintered dahlia tubers into growth and plant out in containers when all danger of frost is past
- sow nasturtium seeds, about 4 to 6 weeks before you plant your window box
- feed ferns
- lift tulips after flowering and hang to dry in a cool, airy place
- plant containers for summer display
- plant succulents for summer display
- plant overwintered geraniums (*Pelargonium*) in containers for summer display
- plant herbs in containers for permanent display
- plant vegetables in containers for summer display
- sow seed for vegetables outdoors

Auricula

Tulip

SUMMER

Early Summer
- sow seed of biennial bedding (polyanthus, wallflowers etc) in seed beds or trays for next spring
- sow seed of forget-me-nots outdoors
- sow seed of daisies outdoors
- plant containers for summer display
- plant succulents for summer display
- plant overwintered geraniums (*Pelargonium*) in containers for summer display
- plant chrysanthemums and marguerites in containers for summer display. Place in a bright, sheltered position
- plant sunflower seedlings for late-summer display

Geranium

Summer Continued

- pinch out shoots of chrysanthemums, marguerites and *Osteospermum* to encourage bushy plants
- deadhead bedding plants regularly to ensure new buds develop

Midsummer
- feed greedy plants like geraniums an occasional foliar feed
- cut back lavender heads after flowering
- deadhead bedding plants regularly to ensure new buds develop

Late Summer
- pot up geraniums (*Pelargonium*) and overwinter indoors. Reduce height of each plant by at least half and it will soon send out new shoots
- trim flower stems of perennial plants like *Dianthus* and overwinter in situ
- pot up *Scaevola* and *Convolvulus* and overwinter on an indoor windowsill or in a frost-free greenhouse. Cut plants right back
- pot up *Gazania* and *Osteospermum* and overwinter fairly dry in a frost-free place ready for planting out in the garden in spring
- plant bulbs for spring display
- plant biennial bedding plants in containers for spring display (raised from seed sown during previous year)
- plant bulbs for autumn display

Gazania

Autumn

Early Autumn
- plant bulbs for spring display
- plant biennial bedding plants in containers for spring display (raised from seed sown during previous year)
- plant heathers for autumn display
- buy polyanthus and winter-flowering pansies and plant in containers for winter display
- buy wallflowers and forget-me-nots and plant in containers for spring display
- buy daisies (*Bellis perennis*) and plant in containers for spring display

Crocus

Mid-autumn
- plant bulbs for spring display

Late Autumn
- lift tender fuchsias and overwinter on an indoor windowsill or in a heated greenhouse. Cut back by half.
- pot up *Campanula* and overwinter in a frost-free greenhouse. Cut back
- dig up dahlia tubers after first frosts, cut stems back to 15cm (6in), dry off then overwinter in slightly damp peat in a frost-free shed
- cut back all fern foliage when it begins to die back. Add a fresh layer of bark to protect plants
- move tender succulents indoors for the winter
- plant winter heathers for winter display
- plant tulip bulbs for spring display

Petunia

Winter

- protect vulnerable shoots from frost as necessary
- move frost-vulnerable terracotta containers indoors
- protect taller plants from strong winds
- select seeds from seed catalogues and order for next spring

Ivy

Best Window Box Plants

THIS QUICK REFERENCE CHART CAN BE USED TO SELECT THE MOST SUITABLE PLANTS FOR YOUR WINDOW BOXES IN TERMS OF THEIR REQUIREMENTS AND SEASON OF INTEREST.

PLANT	COMPOST (SOIL MIX)	WHEN IN FLOWER
Ageratum (FS)	standard, moist	midsummer to first frost
Allium sativum (H) (FS)	standard	year-round foliage
Allium schoenoprasum (H) (PS)	standard	summer*
Aloe (t) (FS)	standard	year-round foliage
Aloysa triphylla (fh) (FS)	standard, dryish	late summer*
Anagallis (t) (FS)	standard, moist	summer
Antirrhinum (hh) (FS)	standard, moist	summer into autumn
Arabis caucasica (FS)	standard	late spring
Argyranthemum (hh) (FS)	standard	late spring to early autumn
Argyranthemum frutescens (hh) (FS)	standard	summer
Armeria (FS)	standard	late spring, summer
Arundinaria pygmaea (FS)	standard, moist	year-round foliage
Aster novae-angliae (PS)	standard, moist	late summer to early autumn
Aster novi-belgii (PS)	standard, moist	late summer to mid-autumn
Aubrieta (FS)	neutral, alkaline	spring
Bacopa (syn. *Sutera*) (t) (FS)	standard	summer to autumn
Begonia rex (t) (PS)	neutral, slightly acid	year-round foliage
Bellis perennis (PS)	standard	winter and spring*
Bergenia (PS)	standard	spring/year-round foliage
Bidens (t) (FS)	standard	midsummer to autumn
Borago officinalis (H) (PS)	standard	summer*
Brachyscome (hh) (FS)	standard	summer
Buxus (some fh) (PS)	standard	year-round foliage
Calendula (PS)	standard	summer to early winter*
Calluna vulgaris (FS)	acid/ericaceous	midsummer to late autumn
Camellia (some t) (PS)	acid/ericaceous	winter or spring
Campanula carpatica (PS)	standard, moist	summer
Campanula isophylla (PS)	standard, moist	summer
Chamaecyparis, dwarf cultivars (S)	neutral, slightly acid	year-round foliage

Argyranthemum

Calendula

Calluna

PLANT	COMPOST (SOIL MIX)	WHEN IN FLOWER
Chlorophytum (t) (PS)	standard	year-round foliage
Chrysanthemum (some hh) (FS)	standard	autumn
Colchicum autumnale (FS)	standard	autumn
Coleus blumei (t) (PS)	standard	year-round foliage
Convallaria majalis (FS)	standard, moist	late spring
Convolvulus sabatius (fh) (FS)	gritty	summer to early autumn
Cordyline (t to hh) (PS)	standard	year-round foliage
Cotoneaster conspicuus (FS)	standard	berries autumn into winter
Crassula (t to hh) (FS)	gritty	year-round foliage
Crocosmia (some fh) (PS)	standard, moist	mid- to late summer
Crocus (FS)	gritty	spring
Crocus nudiflorus (fs) (FH)	standard	autumn
Cyclamen (PS)	standard	autumn, winter or early spring
Dianthus (FS)	neutral, alkaline	early summer to autumn
Echeveria (t) (FS)	standard	year-round foliage
*Eranthis hyemalis (*DS)	standard	late winter to early spring
Erica carnea (FS)	acid, slightly alkaline	winter to mid-spring
Erisymum cheiri (FS)	alkaline, neutral	spring
Euonymus fortunei (PS)	standard	year-round foliage
Felicia amelloides (t) (FS)	standard	summer to autumn
Ferns (S)	standard	spring to autumn foliage
Foeniculum vulgare (H) (FS)	standard, moist	spring to autumn foliage
Fuchsia (hardy to t) (PS)	standard, moist	summer to autumn
Galanthus nivalis (PS)	standard	late winter
Gazania (t to hh) (FS)	gritty	summer
Gaultheria procumbens (PS)	standard, moist	summer/fruit autumn to spring
Grasses (PS)	standard, moist	year-round foliage
Hakonechloa (PS)	standard, moist	year-round foliage
Hebe, dwarf cultivars (PS)	standard	summer, year-round foliage
Hedera helix (PS)	preferably alkaline	year-round foliage
Helianthus annuus (FS)	neutral, alkaline	summer
Helichrysum petiolare (hh) (FS*)*	neutral, alkaline	year-round foliage
Heliotropium (hh) (FS)	standard, moist	summer
Heuchera micrantha (FS, PS)	standard	year-round foliage
Hosta (PS)	standard, moist	year-round foliage

Convallaria

Fuchsia

Hedera

Hosta

PLANT	COMPOST (SOIL MIX)	WHEN IN FLOWER
Hyacinthoides (DS)	standard, moist	spring
Hyacinthus (PS)	standard	spring
Iberis (FS)	moist, neutral, alkaline	summer
Impatiens New Guinea Group (S)	standard, moist	summer to autumn
Kalanchoe (t) (PS)	standard	late winter, spring or summer
Lampranthus (t) (FS)	standard	summer to early autumn
Lavandula (some hh) (FS)	standard	summer*
Lilium (FS) (fh, hh)	acid, neutral	summer
Lobelia erinus (t) (PS)	standard, moist	summer to autumn
Lobularia maritima (FS)	standard	summer, early autumn
Lysimachia nummularia (PS)	standard, moist	summer
Melissa officinalis (H) (PS)	standard	summer*
Mentha (H) (PS)	standard, moist	summer*
Muscari armeniacum (FS)	standard, moist	spring
Myosotis (PS)	standard, moist	spring to early summer
Narcissus (DS)	standard, moist when growing	spring
Nemesia (fh to hh) (FS)	moist slightly acid	summer
Nepeta mussinii (PS)	standard	summer
Nerine (some hh) (FS)	standard, moist when growing	autumn
Nicotiana (t) (PS)	standard, moist	summer, autumn
Ocimum basilicum (t) (H) (FS)	standard	summer foliage
Ophiopogon 'Nigrescens' (PS)	slightly acid	year-round foliage
Origanum majorana (H) (fh) (FS)	preferably alkaline	summer*
Origanum onites (H) (fh) (FS)	preferably alkaline	late summer*
Origanum vulgare (H) (FS)	preferably alkaline	midsummer, early autumn*
Osteospermum (t to hh) (FS)	standard	late spring to autumn
Pelargonium (t) (FS)	neutral, alkaline	spring to summer
Petroselinum crispum (H) (PS)	standard, moist	summer
Petunia (hh) (FS)	standard	late spring to late autumn
Phlox (FS, PS)	standard	summer
Portulaca (t to hh) (FS)	standard, dryish	summer
Primula Auricula (PS)	standard, moist	spring
Primula Polyanthus Group (PS)	standard, moist	late winter to mid-spring
Primula vulgaris (PS)	standard, moist	early to late spring

Lobelia

Narcissus

Osteospermum

Plant	Compost (Soil mix)	When in flower
Rosmarinus officinalis (H) (fh) (FS)	standard	mid-spring, early summer
Salvia officinalis (H)	standard	early and midsummer*
Salvia splendens (t) (PS)	standard, moist	summer to autumn
Sansevieria (t) (FS)	neutral, slightly alkaline	year-round foliage
Saxifraga (some fh or hh) (some FS, some PS)	neutral, alkaline; some gritty, some moist	spring, summer
Scaevola (t) (DS)	standard, moist	summer
Schizostylis (FS)	standard, moist	late summer, early winter
Sedum (some fh or t) (FS)	neutral, slightly alkaline	summer, early autumn
Sempervivum (FS)	gritty	year-round foliage
Senecio cineraria (fh) (FS)	standard	year-round foliage
Skimmia reevesiana (S)	moist	autumn and winter buds
Solanum pseudocapsicum (t) (FS)	neutral, slightly alkaline	winter berries
Solenopsis (syn. *Isotoma)* (t) (FS)	standard	spring to late autumn
Sternbergia (fh) (FS)	standard	autumn, winter
Tagetes (hh) (FS)	standard	late spring to early autumn
Thuja, dwarf cultivars (FS)	standard, moist	year-round foliage
Thymus vulgaris (H) (FS)	neutral, alkaline	spring, early summer*
Tradescantia (t) (PS)	standard, moist	year-round foliage
Tropaeolum majus (FS)	standard or gritty	summer to autumn*
Tulipa (FS)	standard	mid- to late spring
Verbena x *hybrida* (t) (FS)	loam-based with sand	summer, autumn
Vinca minor (FS)	standard, moist	mid-spring to mid-autumn
Viola x *wittrockiana* cultivars (PS)	standard	spring to summer or autumn to winter

Vinca minor

Viola

Key

(t) = tender: need minimum 5°C (41F°); they need to be overwintered indoors or in a cool or temperate greenhouse

(hh) = are half hardy and can withstand temperatures down to 0°C (32°F)

(fh) = are frost hardy down to –5°C (23°F)

Unmarked plants are fully hardy

* = edible flowers

(H) = herbs, grown mainly for their leaves

(FS) = full sun

(PS) = partial shade

(DS) = dappled shade

(S) = shade

INDOOR PLANTS

There is a vast choice of houseplants available, ranging from easily cared-for favourites to demanding and unusual exotics, but any selection must depend on how hot or cool you like to keep your rooms and how dry or humid the atmosphere. This chapter contains all you need to know about basic care and dealing with common problems, to help you grow a stunning collection of plants to beautify your home.

Living with Houseplants

HOUSEPLANTS CAN INSTANTLY CHANGE THE ATMOSPHERE OF ANY ROOM IN YOUR HOME, BRINGING THE BEAUTY OF LIVING NATURE INTO YOUR EVERYDAY SURROUNDINGS. MOST REQUIRE VERY LITTLE EFFORT TO KEEP THEM PERFORMING WELL AND LOOKING GOOD FOR MANY YEARS.

Left: Given the right conditions plants will flourish in your home.

GROWING HOUSEPLANTS

Generally, most plants are easy to look after if they are provided with the right conditions, especially light, moisture and nutrition. If well tended they will look attractive, often varying their appearance with seasonal flowers or colourful bracts. Those plants that require exacting conditions not normally found in a home will be high maintenance, and could become a chore to look after, so you may prefer to choose from the wide selection of plants that are easy to care for and require minimum attention.

Above: Pot plants in flower will add colour and warmth to a room.

Most indoor collections found in garden centres and florists consist of a combination of easy-care, long-lasting foliage plants and seasonal plants. Flowering pot plants are often regarded as short-term colour, more like long-lasting cut flowers, but with careful pruning, deadheading and feeding, some can be treated as perennials and will flower again the following year.

HUMIDITY

The amount of heat and light in your home is major consideration. The dry heat caused by central heating can be damaging. Tropical plants especially require moisture in the atmosphere. Fortunately, the majority of houseplants can survive in low levels of humidity, particularly in summer when windows are open. In winter, when heating is turned up, commercial room humidifiers will moisten the air, but a more economic solution would be to select plants that do not need very humid conditions.

Above: Change the colour scheme of a room by introducing a bold group of plants.

Achieving Different Effects

Plants can entirely change the atmosphere of a room, or introduce a new mood or even colour scheme from season to season. Fragrant spring bulbs, pots of herbs, autumnal toned chrysanthemums or a bowl of brightly coloured cyclamen will all add to the mood of their particular time of year.

Some plants are better suited to certain types of interiors than others, and should be compatible in size and shape as well as colour. Small plants that complement fabrics and wallpapers work well with a traditional, cottagey décor. Stark modern interiors can take big, bold "architectural" plants. Be prepared to invest in one or two really good specimens if necessary because they have far more impact than half a dozen cheaper plants.

Shopping for Houseplants

Plants are living, perishable things, and supplies often fluctuate widely according to season and what the commercial growers decide to market.

Whenever possible, buy where the plants are well cared for in surroundings conducive to good growth: warmth, freedom from icy blasts, high humidity (though this is not important for cacti and succulents), and a high level of diffused light or artificial lighting designed for plant growth. Wilting, diseased or dying plants should not be on display.

Look beneath the pot – some roots will have grown through if capillary matting has been used for watering, but masses of long roots indicate that the plant needs to be repotted. Always check the plant for signs of pests and diseases. Turn over one or two of the leaves – pests may be lurking out of sight.

With flowering plants, timing is everything. You may get several weeks of pleasure if you buy a plant just coming into flower rather than one that is already at its peak.

GARDENER'S TIP

Houseplants tend to grow slowly and are sold in a range of sizes. If a room requires a large plant, select one at the right height or slighter smaller than required. Otherwise, you could wait a long time for a small specimen to reach the necessary size.

Left: Mauve flowers look very effective against a light grey or pale blue wall.

Below: Plants benefit from being placed in strong but indirect light. It is a good idea to move them occasionally if light is low.

Colour

Houseplants come in every possible colour. Even foliage comes in many shades of green, in variegated forms, and with silver or bronze tints. Plants can be used to add colour or to complement different decorative schemes.

Heavy, dark green foliage, distinctive in itself, would dominate a softly toned wallpaper or delicate paint effect. Conversely, pale fern fronds or a pastel-and-white flowering plant would enhance a soft colour scheme. While most plants would complement pale plain-coloured walls, placing foliage or flowering plants in front of a patterned wallpaper or furnishings, especially a floral design, could be problematic. If you have patterned paper or fabric, take a piece with you when you buy plants to help you select a complementary green.

SUN-LOVING PLANTS

Ananas
Coleus
Pelargonium
Roses, miniature
Yucca elephantipes

PLANTS FOR SHADE

Asplenium nidus
Dracaena
Fatsia
Hedera helix
Philodendron

Sun and Good Light

In a typical house it is usually difficult to give houseplants enough light for really healthy and even growth, yet ironically a position on a windowsill in full sun will probably injure or kill most of them. Sun through unshaded glass is much more intense than sun in the open – it acts like a magnifying glass and will often scorch vulnerable foliage. Although most plants will benefit from gentler early and late sun, when the intensity is not too great, you need really tough sun-lovers to tolerate the hot midday sun intensified through glass.

Most cacti and succulents are ideal for a windowsill position. *Echinocactus*, *Ferocactus*, *Opuntia*, *Parodia* and *Rebutia* are all readily available.

Succulents such as *Lithops* and *Kalanchoe* are also excellent for hot windowsills. There is more variation in shape and growth habit among succulents than cacti, but if you want yet more variety there are other true sun-lovers you can try.

Some plants that benefit from softer winter sun may be harmed by the harsher summer sun that will scorch tender leaves.

Shade

Plants that tolerate lower light levels are especially useful. They can be positioned by shady windows and within any room, perhaps on a table or sideboard, and still survive for a reasonable time. You can use any plant in these conditions, but after a while most will become sickly and deteriorate. You will then have to move them into better light or buy a new plant.

Foliage

Purely foliage plants are anything but dull. Leaves come in a vast range of greens, many are variegated, some are more colourful than many flowers, and all last much longer. Many also have contrasting textures and shapes.

FOLIAGE PLANTS

Aglaonema hybrids
Asparagus densiflorus 'Sprengeri'
Begonia, foliage
Dracaena marginata
Fatsia japonica
Ficus benjamina 'Starlight'
Hedera helix, variegated
Monstera deliciosa
Philodendron scandens
Sansevieria trifasciata 'Laurentii'
Syngonium podophyllum
Yucca elephantipes

Plants grown for their leaves will form the backbone of most arrangements and groupings. They can also form a backdrop for flowers.

Shape

Interesting shape will compensate for any lack of colour in a leaf. Plants such as philodendrons and *Ficus benjamina* create as much interest as those with bright flowers or brilliant foliage, and they do it in a restrained way that creates the right mood for a room.

Above: *A selection of plants showing interesting foliage and texture.*

Texture

Leaf texture adds variety. There are rough, hairy and puckered leaves, all of which can add extra interest and contrast to a group. Some demand to be touched, providing tactile as well as visual stimulation.

RELIABLE FLOWERING PLANTS

Aechmea fasciata
Begonia, elatior type
Chrysanthemum
Clivia miniata
Exacum affine
Hydrangea
Jasminum polyanthum
Kalanchoe
Pelargonium, Regal
Primula obconica
Saintpaulia
Stephanotis floribunda
Tillandsia cynea
Vriesea

Flowering Plants

Houseplants with flowers are usually a little more difficult than foliage plants to keep long-term. However, they add brilliance and colour that even the boldest foliage plants find difficult to match, and some have the extra bonus of fragrance.

A few flowering plants are available throughout the year (chrysanthemums, kalanchoes and African violets are examples), but most flower in a particular season. This is no bad thing because it prevents your displays becoming predictable or boring. Some are annuals, or treated as annuals, and have to be discarded when flowering is over. These short-term flowering pot plants are especially useful for creating instant displays of stunning colour anywhere in the home. They also make it possible to continue a colour scheme throughout the year using different plants.

Scent

Houseplants allow you to enjoy natural fragrances the year round. Sometimes a single, strongly scented plant is sufficient for an entire room. You will need several in succession, but this gives you the chance to enjoy different kinds of perfume over the seasons.

Above: *Flowering houseplants may need more care, but they give so much pleasure with their colourful blooms and bright green foliage.*

GARDENER'S TIP

Some flowers give heady perfume which can be overpowering, depending on your sensitivity. To make sure you will enjoy their fragrance over the full flowering period, try to buy new plants just as they are coming into bloom.

Above: A miniature rose provides both colour and fragrance.

For late winter and early spring there are numerous varieties of scented hyacinths and narcissi. During autumn, plant up individual pots with hyacinths every fortnight to give you fragrance in late winter.

In summer, many shrubs and plants provide scent. Aromatic pelargoniums (geraniums) start flowering in late spring and will continue into autumn, if placed on a sunny windowsill. You will need several together to make an impact, and grow them where you will brush their leaves as you pass.

Some lilies provide a concentrated perfume from late afternoon into the evening. Plant specially prepared bulbs at intervals during winter to provide scented blooms from summer into autumn.

How This Chapter Works

In this chapter you will find practical advice on choosing plants that will best suit you and your home. *Getting Started* describes the basic tools and equipment you will need for keeping houseplants, with information on the many kinds of containers available. *Caring for Houseplants* covers all the techniques needed for looking after them, including repotting and methods of propagation to increase your stock. *Troubleshooting* discusses common pests and diseases, together with other problems that can affect your plants, and suggests effective ways of dealing with them. Finally, a comprehensive *A–Z of Houseplants* describes a wide selection of recommended plants, giving details of the preferred conditions and care requirements in each case.

SCENTED PLANTS

Hoya bella
Gardenia jasminoides
Hyacinthus
Jasminum officinale
Lilium (oriental hybrids)
Narcissus
Stephanotis floribunda

Getting Started

ONCE YOU HAVE DECIDED WHICH PLANTS YOU WANT TO GROW, YOU NEED TO STOCK UP ON BASIC TOOLS AND EQUIPMENT, INCLUDING THE CORRECT SOIL FOR POTTING, AND TO CHOOSE THE APPROPRIATE CONTAINERS TO DISPLAY YOUR PLANTS TO BEST ADVANTAGE.

TOOLS AND EQUIPMENT

You can look after your houseplants without any special tools. However, the right tools do make the jobs easier, and usually more pleasant. The tools described here won't cost much. Take particular care over the choice of a watering-can and a mister – both should be in daily use, so don't skimp on these.

Canes (stakes) – usually made from bamboo, used for supporting plants.

Dibber – a tool used for making a hole in potting soil.

Fertilizer – food for plants, which comes in various forms.

Knife – useful for taking cuttings and other indoor gardening tasks.

Leaf shines – products for putting a shine on glossy leaves.

Leaf-wipes – tissue-type leaf shine.

Mister – a sprayer producing a fine mist.

Insecticide – for pest control.

Insecticidal plant pins – insecticide-impregnated strips to push into potting soil.

Raffia – a natural tying material.

Rooting hormone – stimulates root formation on cuttings.

Scissors – useful for cutting ties and deadheading.

Water indicator – indicates moisture level in soil.

Watering-can, indoor – one with a long, narrow spout for precision watering.

Wire – plastic-coated to protect stems.

Potting Soil

Plants depend on an appropriate potting soil to provide vital nutrients essential for growth, and act as a reservoir for moisture.

Loam-based potting soil – heavy, but it may be the best choice for some plants. Tall or large plants that are top-heavy may benefit from the extra weight in the pot. Some plants, including most succulents, benefit from the good drainage and reserve of nutrients provided by loam-based mix.

Loam-based mix

Peat-based (peat moss) mixtures – light and easy to handle, but usually require supplementary feeding after a month or so. They can dry out and become difficult to re-wet, and they are more easily overwatered. They can vary greatly in quality. Some gardeners are reluctant to use peat-based products on the grounds of depleting wetland areas. Alternative products are available, including mixes based on coir (waste from coconuts).

Peat-based (peat moss) mix

Orchid mixtures – are unlike any others that you will use. They are free-draining and contain no loam (soil). Bark is a common ingredient.

Orchid mixture

Cactus potting mix – very free-draining, and will contain plenty of grit or other material to ensure that the roots don't become waterlogged.

Ericaceous potting mix – for acid-loving, or lime-hating, plants such as azaleas. Lime or other alkaline materials are not used in the mixture, and the pH is more acidic than in normal soils.

Cactus mix

Water-absorbing granules – sometimes used as an additive to potting soil. They swell when wet and hold many times their own weight of water. They can be useful if you are often away for a few days and find it difficult to water regularly.

Fine gravel – helps with drainage if mixed with the soil when potting up a plant, and can be used as an attractive mulch on the surface of the soil to prevent your plant drying out as quickly.

Fine gravel

Choosing Pots and Containers

Pots and containers can form part of the room décor. The right container will enhance an attractive plant and can compensate for a mediocre one. Part of the fun of growing houseplants is displaying them with imagination. Many everyday items can be used.

The bigger the plant, the smaller the pot or container should be in relationship to it. Small, bushy plants look best in pots that are either roughly their size or slightly smaller. A tall plant, 25–60 cm (10–24 in) in height, looks best in a pot about a quarter of its height. The pot must also be sufficiently heavy to provide a solid base when the soil dries out, otherwise the plant might topple over.

Half pots, which stand about half the height of ordinary pots but have the same diameter, suit cacti which do not have a large root system, as well as azaleas.

Galvanized Metal Containers and Cache-pots

These have a waterproof base and no drainage holes. They are useful for flowering plants that are on display for a short time only and for fast-growing plants that require frequent repotting.

You do need to be careful about watering. Make sure that the plant pot is easily lifted out for watering or place on a bed of crocks or stones.

Glass

These containers allow for imaginative presentation. You can surround the plant pot with visually attractive material such as coloured stones, marbles, sand or a thick layer of moss or pine cones.

Planters and Self-watering Containers

Large containers are ideal for displaying a group of plants. Some planters are self-watering with a reservoir at the

***Below:** Many types of container are suitable for houseplants.*

Glazed ceramic

Terracotta

bottom, which means you can leave several days between watering. Plants generally thrive in these.

Baskets

Many plants look especially attractive in wicker, moss-covered or wire baskets. If you use a basket not specifically intended for plants, line it with a protective sheet of flexible plastic, otherwise water will seep through and spoil the surface underneath. The plastic should not be visible once the basket has been planted.

Ordinary hanging baskets are unsuitable for using indoors because of the problems with drips. Choose one with a drip tray or water reservoir.

Terracotta

Large terracotta containers are good for specimen plants. The weight gives stability to plants with thin trunks and wide, arching branches.

The orange tone of terracotta can be softened by weathering it outside over winter. Or it can be artificially aged by applying a weak solution of a pale-coloured, water-based paint.

Match the drip tray to the pot and make sure that it is internally glazed, otherwise water will seep through and spoil the surface it is resting on. For a plant that requires humidity, choose a drip tray large enough to take stones or water-retaining granules as well as the plant pot.

Glazed Ceramic

Solid coloured ceramic containers are more versatile than patterns and can be useful for linking a plant's foliage with a room's colour scheme.

Many glazed containers do not have drainage holes; to overcome this, quarter-fill a large one with pebbles, cover with a thin layer of charcoal and top with potting soil.

Wire baskets

Wicker basket

Galvanized metal pail

Caring for Houseplants

IF YOU WANT LUSH, HEALTHY HOUSEPLANTS YOU MUST CARE FOR THEM ROUTINELY AND APPLY REMEDIAL TREATMENT AS SOON AS A PROBLEM OCCURS. TO INCREASE AND REJUVENATE YOUR STOCK, SOME PROPAGATION TECHNIQUES WILL BE USEFUL.

WATERING

Some plants require water daily, others, once or twice a week. In winter, some may not need water for weeks. Cacti and succulents resting during winter, for example, should not be kept constantly moist.

Feel the surface of the soil and water when it has dried out but before the plant is affected by lack of water. Don't allow the pot to stand in surplus water as this will waterlog the soil. Most plants benefit from being stood in water for 30 minutes before being returned to their original position.

Above: *Choose a watering-can with a long, narrow spout so that you can control the flow easily. You want the water around the roots, not over the leaves (or on your table or windowsill).*

HUMIDITY

Raising the humidity level will benefit most plants, except sun-lovers. Covering the soil surface with moss, stones or shells will reduce water evaporation. Placing plants on wet pebbles immediately raises the level of humidity around a plant; make sure the roots are not in contact with the water.

Misting plants daily will give a better texture to the leaves and help keep them free of dust, as well as improving humidity for a short time. Use tepid water and ideally mist your plant in the morning so the leaves dry before nightfall.

FEEDING

Slow-release fertilizers feed a plant for months, while controlled-release types release the fertilizer only when the soil is warm enough for most plants' active growth. Granules can be mixed before potting; pellets or sticks can be pushed into the soil around an established plant. Liquid feeds feed the soil for a set period, so when the plant is resting, you can stop feeding it. The amount required depends how vigorously a plant is growing.

Going Away

There are plenty of ways to take care of your plants if you are going away for a week or two.

Move your plants into a few large groups in a cool position out of direct sunlight. Stand them on a tray of gravel, watered to just below the level of the pot bases. This will not moisten the potting soil, but the humid air will help to keep the plants in condition.

Above: Group plants together in a tray or large container and water thoroughly before you go away, leaving a little water in the bottom of the outer container.

Supply the most vulnerable plants with some kind of watering system. There are various proprietary devices on sale, but many of these are suitable if you have a few plants only. Porous reservoirs and ceramic mushrooms are both simple, effective systems, but you need one for each pot.

Wicks, which are inserted into pots placed above a reservoir of water, are suitable for a handful of plants.

Drip feeds, sold for greenhouse and garden use, are good, but expensive.

Capillary matting, sold for greenhouse benches and widely used by commercial nurseries, can be a good way to keep plants moist. It can be used in a sink or bath, and the system works best with plastic pots that have nothing placed over the drainage holes. Water the plants thoroughly first.

For the sink, cut a length of matting to fit the draining area and reach the bottom of the sink. Fill the sink with water, or leave the plug out but let a tap drip on to the mat to keep it moist. If you do the latter, have a trial run to make sure that it keeps the mat moist without wasting water. (If filling with water, stand the plants on the draining area only, not in the water.) Do the same for the bath, but if you leave water in it, place the mat and plants on a plank of wood on bricks.

Above: Capillary wicks will draw water from a reservoir. Make sure the wicks are soaked and put one end deeply into the potting soil. The other end must reach the reservoir base.

Grooming

Regular grooming of your plants will keep them looking good. Apart from picking off dead flowers whenever you notice them, grooming is a weekly task. Most jobs need doing less frequently than this, but by making a routine of tidying up your plants you will detect pests, diseases and nutritional problems that much earlier.

Deadheading

Removing flowers as they fade keeps the plant looking neat, and in many cases encourages the production of more flowers. It also discourages diseases; many fungal infections start on dead flowers. Remove the stalks as well as the flower spikes, using a pulling and twisting motion. Cut whole flower heads or spikes back to just above a pair of leaves.

Foliage

Remove dying and fallen leaves. These will spoil the appearance of a plant and can harbour disease. Most can be pulled off with a gentle tug, but tough ones may have to be cut off.

Dust settles on foliage, and can prevent the plant from breathing properly, and block light. If the leaves are delicate or hairy dust them using a soft paintbrush.

Large, glossy leaves can be wiped clean using a soft damp cloth or sponge or proprietary leaf-wipes. Plants with small glossy leaves may have too many to make the use of leaf-wipes a sensible option. Stand these outside in a shower of light rain in the summer or spray them with water. In winter, plants can simply have their leaves swished gently in a bowl of tepid water.

1 Plants with large, glossy leaves can be wiped clean. Commercially produced leaf-wipes are convenient to use, but check that they don't carry a warning against using them on certain plants.

2 Cacti, succulents and plants with hairy leaves such as *Saintpaulia* are much more difficult to clean. These should be brushed carefully with a soft paintbrush kept for the purpose to remove dust.

PRUNING

The shape of many houseplants can be improved by pinching out the growing tips to prevent them from becoming tall and leggy. Removing the tips of the shoots makes the plant bushier. *Hedera*, *Hypoestes*, *Pilea* and *Tradescantia* are among the many plants that benefit from this treatment. Start when the plants are young, and repeat it whenever the growth looks too thin and long. This is especially useful for trailers: a dense cascade will look better than weedy-looking shoots twice the length. If any all-green shoots develop on a variegated plant, prune to the point of origin.

***Right:** Train new growth of climbing plants before it becomes difficult to bend. Twist stems carefully into position to avoid breaking tender shoots.*

***Above:** If you want a bushy rather than a tall or sprawling plant, pinch out the growing tips a few times while it is still young. This will stimulate the growth of sideshoots and produce a bushier effect.*

Climbers and trailers need regular attention. Tie in any new shoots to the support, and cut off any long ones.

Pruning can also be a good opportunity for propagating your houseplants, as longer shoots can be treated as cuttings to pot up for new plants.

GARDENER'S TIP

Pests and diseases can spread more easily and rapidly from plant to plant when they are in close proximity, and you may be less likely to notice early symptoms on leaves hidden by other plants. Make grooming a regular routine to minimize the danger.

Repotting Plants

Sooner or later most plants need repotting, and it can give an ailing plant a new lease of life. Not all plants respond well to frequent repotting, and some prefer to be in small pots.

Repotting a plant should only be done when the plant needs it. Young plants require it much more frequently than older ones. Once a large specimen is in a big pot it may be better to keep it growing by repotting into another pot of the same size, by top-dressing, or simply by additional feeding when required.

When to Repot

The sight of roots growing through the base does not indicate that repotting is necessary. Check by inverting the pot and knocking the rim on a hard surface while supporting the plant and soil with your hand. It is normal for some roots to run around the inside, but if there is also a solid mass of roots it is time to pot on.

***Above:** A plant with tightly packed roots needs to be potted on.*

How to Repot

1 Prepare a pot that is one or two sizes larger than the original. Cover the drainage hole of a clay pot with pieces of broken pot. Don't cover the holes in a plastic pot that you intend using with a capillary watering mat.

2 Place a small amount of potting soil in the new pot. Knock the pre-watered plant out of its pot and position it so that it is at the right height.

3 Trickle potting soil around the sides. Gently firm the soil with your fingers. Leave a gap of about 1–2.5 cm (½–1 in) between the top of the soil and the rim of the pot. Water thoroughly. Place in the shade for about a week and mist the leaves daily.

Simple Propagation

In the late spring and summer it is possible to multiply some of your plants by means of simple propagation. It is usually best to do this in spring or early summer. Always take several cuttings from the plant in case some fail.

Stem Cuttings

Many plants will respond to this method. Choose a piece of stem 7.5–13 cm (3–5 in) long and cut just below a leaf. Make the cut straight, not at an angle, using a razor blade or sharp knife. Remove most of the leaves from the lower half of the cutting. Stand the cutting in a glass of water in a light position, making sure no leaves are in contact with the water. Pot up the cutting when the new roots are 2.5–4 cm (1–1½ in) long. Change the water as necessary.

The Swiss cheese plant and many philodendrons can become straggly with age. They can be divided into several plants by taking stem cuttings with noticeable root nodules at their bases. Place them in water in good light as before.

Plantlets

The tiny plantlets produced by some plants, including spider plants, mother of thousands and piggyback plants, can be inserted directly into soil or can be rooted in water as for stem cuttings. Wait until a good root system has developed before potting up.

Leaf Cuttings

Take leaf cuttings of African violets, begonias and succulents.

1 Cut a mature leaf, with about 5 cm (2 in) of stalk attached, from the base of a plant. Make a straight cut.

2 Fill a pot with a rooting medium and make a hole using a pencil at a 45-degree angle. Insert the cutting with the back of the leaf towards the outside of the pot and the base just above the soil. Firm gently, then water.

3 Place short canes close to the leaf and place an airtight plastic bag over the pot. Secure with a rubber band. Place in a light position, out of direct sunlight.

Troubleshooting

REGULAR INSPECTION OF YOUR PLANTS WILL ALERT YOU TO ANY SERIOUS PROBLEMS, DISEASE OR INFESTATIONS IN TIME TO TAKE THE NECESSARY REMEDIAL ACTION.

PHYSICAL PROBLEMS

Upper Leaves Turn Yellow: affects lime-hating plants, and is caused by watering with hard water containing too much calcium. Use boiled or filtered water only.

Brown Spots or Patches on Leaves: may be due to insect infestation, too much direct sunlight or splashing water on leaves.

Leaves Curling at the Edges and Dropping: can be caused by too cool an atmosphere, overwatering or a cold draught.

Brown Tips and Edges to Leaves: usually too little humidity and too much direct sun. Can be due to either overwatering or overfeeding.

Wilting Leaves: underwatering, or if soil is waterlogged, then overwatering. In this case the roots will have rotted.

Dull Leaves: Lifeless leaves may require a wipe with a damp cloth. May also indicate too much light or the presence of red spider mites.

Sudden Leaf Fall: may occur after repotting or when a plant has been relocated. Can be the result of a sharp rise or fall in temperature, an icy draught or underwatering.

No Flowers: usually caused by insufficient light. If the flower buds develop but drop before opening, this is probably due to dry air or underwatering. Flowers that develop but fade quickly may be getting too much heat, too little light and not enough water.

Variegated Leaves Turning Green: due to lack of light, which generally results in pale, small leaves and a leggy growing habit.

Rotting Leaves and Stems: probably due to a disease and often caused by overwatering, poor drainage and insufficient ventilation.

Left: *If the potting soil has become very dry, with a hard surface, loosen the surface with a fork to help a dried-out root-ball absorb water.*

Pests and Diseases

Mealy Bug: small insects covered with white fluff that form colonies in leaves and in leaf axils. The leaves eventually turn yellow, wilt and drop off. Wipe off the bugs with alcohol-impregnated swabs, or spray with malathion.

Vine Weevil: a creamy-coloured grub that lives in the soil and eats roots. The adult dark brown beetle chews leaves. If caught early, leaves and soil need spraying with pesticide.

Whitefly: tiny, moth-like flies that deposit a sticky honeydew on the undersides of leaves, encouraging black mould to develop.

Above: Whitefly damage houseplants and look unsightly. They can be killed with a pesticide spray.

Red Spider Mites: almost too small to see, these pests suck sap, causing black spots and yellowed leaves. Infestation is indicated by the presence of fine webs and mottling of the plant's leaves. Remove affected leaves and spray with insecticide.

Aphids (Greenfly): brown, grey or green insects that suck the sap, leaving sticky honeydew that causes leaves to wither. Remove with alcohol-impregnated swabs, and spray with pesticide.

Powdery Mildew: coats the leaves with a white powdery deposit. Remove and destroy affected leaves and spray with a systemic fungicide. Improve the ventilation.

Black Leg (Black Stem Rot): affects stem cuttings, turning the bases black. Destroy affected cuttings. Use a well-draining medium and dip cuttings in a fungicide hormone-rooting powder.

Sooty Mould (Black Mold): fungus that grows on honeydew left by aphids and mealy bugs. Wipe off the mould using diluted soapy water.

Botrytis (Grey Mold): caused by a cool, damp atmosphere with poor air circulation. Remove affected parts and spray with a systemic fungicide.

Above: If whitefly or aphid infestation is mild you may be able to reduce the population by swishing the plant in water.

A–Z of Houseplants

Most of the houseplants in the following pages can be found in garden centres. The selection covers flowering, foliage and scented varieties.

Acalypha hispida

Tall and quick-growing foliage plant with long red tassel-like flowers, in autumn. 'Alba': white flowers.

Temperature: winter 15°C (59°F).
Humidity: high humidity. Mist frequently if room is centrally heated.
Position: good light, not direct sun.
Watering and feeding: never let soil dry out. Feed from spring to autumn.
Care: deadhead. Prune by half in early spring or late summer. Repot in spring or topdress if in large pot.
Propagation: cuttings.

Achimenes hybrids

Short-lived flowers, in pink, purple, yellow, red or white, through summer. Dormant over winter.

Temperature: undemanding when dormant; minimum 13°C (55°F) while it is growing.
Humidity: mist developing flower buds then provide humidity without spraying by standing plant on a tray of wet pebbles.
Position: good light, not direct sun.
Watering and feeding: water with tepid, soft water during growing season, keeping soil moist. Feed regularly.
Care: support the stems or grow in a hanging pot. Stop watering when leaves begin to drop. Leave rhizomes in pot or store in peat or sand in frost-free place. Start into growth or replant in late winter or early spring.
Propagation: division of rhizomes; cuttings; seed (not named varieties).

AECHMEA FASCIATA

Bromeliad with banded foliage. Long-lasting, spiky blue flowers fading to lilac with pink bracts, mid-summer to early winter.

Temperature: winter minimum 15°C (59°F).

Humidity: undemanding.

Position: good light, not direct sun.

Watering and feeding: keep roots moist. Top up water in funnel in summer, but empty it in winter. Feed with weak fertilizer in summer.

Care: mist only on hot days. To stimulate mature plant into flower, enclose in plastic bag with two ripe apples for a few days. Main plant will die after flowering, but produces offsets.

Propagation: offsets (remove when about half height of parent).

AGLAONEMA HYBRIDS

Tolerant clump-forming foliage plants with silvery-grey variegations.

Temperature: winter minimum 15°C (59°F).

Humidity: high humidity. Mist regularly.

Position: Light shade, not direct sun.

Watering and feeding: water freely from spring to autumn, sparingly in winter. Feed from spring to autumn.

Care: repot only when necessary.

Propagation: cuttings; division.

ALOE VARIEGATA

Trouble-free succulents with thick fleshy, banded leaves, occasionally red flowers.

Temperature: cool but frost-free in winter, 5°C (41°F).

Humidity: will tolerate dry air.

Position: full sun.

Watering and feeding: water twice a week in summer. Feed occasionally in summer.

Care: repot in spring every second year.

Propagation: offsets; seed in spring.

ANANAS BRACTEATUS STRIATUS

Foliage bromeliads with spiky, brightly striped, cream-and-pink leaves.

Temperature: winter 15–18°C (59–64°F).

Humidity: undemanding, but mist in very hot weather.

Position: good light. Variegation often better in sun.

Watering and feeding: water freely in summer, cautiously in winter. Feed from spring to autumn.

Care: in summer, occasionally add a little water to the leaf "vase". Encourage mature plants to flower by placing in a plastic bag with ripe apples or bananas.

Propagation: leaf crown on top of fruit.

ANTHURIUM SCHERZERIANUM

Distinctive foliage plant with exotic red blooms spring to late summer.

Temperature: winter minimum 16°C (60°F).

Humidity: high humidity. Mist frequently, avoiding flowers.

Position: good light, not direct summer sun.

Watering and feeding: water freely in summer, sparingly in winter. Soft water if possible. Feed with weak fertilizer in summer.

Care: repot every second year, in spring, using fibrous potting mixture.

Propagation: division.

ASPARAGUS DENSIFLORUS 'SPRENGERI'

Fern-like foliage on arching to pendulous, thread-like stems.

Temperature: winter minimum 7°C (45°F).

Humidity: mist occasionally, especially in centrally heated room.

Position: good light or partial shade, not direct sun.

Watering and feeding: water from spring to autumn, sparingly in winter. Feed from spring to early autumn.

Care: cut back by half if turns yellow or grows too large. Repot young plants every spring, older ones every second spring.

Propagation: division; seed.

ASPIDISTRA ELATIOR

Evergreen herbaceous plant with large dark green leaves growing directly from soil. Tough constitution. 'Variegata': creamy white longitudinal stripes.

Temperature: keep cool, 7–10°C (45–50°F) is ideal.

Humidity: tolerates dry air.

Position: light or shade, but avoid exposing to direct sun.

Watering and feeding: water moderately from spring to autumn, sparingly in winter. Feed from spring to early autumn.

Care: wash or sponge leaves occasionally to remove dust and improve light penetration. Repot when necessary – every three or four years.

Propagation: division.

Asplenium

Useful ferns. *A. bulbiferum*: ferny fronds, small plantlets on mature leaves. *A. nidus*: glossy, undivided leaves forming vase-like rosette, very tolerant.

Temperature: winter minimum: *A. bulbiferum* 13°C (55°F); *A. nidus* 16°C (60°F)
Humidity: high humidity.
Position: shade.
Watering and feeding: water freely from spring to autumn, moderately in winter. Soft water if possible.
Care: dust *A. nidus* periodically. Trim off any brown edges.
Propagation: division; pot up plantlets of *A. bulbiferum*.

Begonia elatior hybrids

Single or double flowers mainly red, pink, yellow, orange and white, all seasons, especially winter.

Temperature: winter minimum 13–21°C (55–70°F) while growing.
Humidity: high humidity is beneficial.
Position: good light, not direct summer sun. Best possible light in winter.
Watering and feeding: water freely while in flower. Feed with weak fertilizer while in bud and flowering.
Care: deadhead regularly. Discard after flowering.
Propagation: propagate from leaf or tip cuttings.

Begonia foliage

Foliage begonias are attractive all year. Several species, all compact, with hairy or puckered leaves in brightly variegated colours.

Temperature: winter minimum 16°C (60°F).
Humidity: require high humidity, but avoid spraying leaves.
Position: good light, not direct sun.
Watering and feeding: water freely from spring to autumn, sparingly in winter.
Care: repot annually in spring.
Propagation: division; leaf cuttings.

Billbergia nutans

Bromeliad with yellow-and-green, blue-edged flowers with pink bracts, in spring.

Temperature: winter minimum 13°C (55°F).

Humidity: tolerates dry air if necessary.

Position: good light, not direct sun.

Watering and feeding: water freely from spring to autumn, sparingly in winter. In summer pour some water into the leaf rosettes. Feed from spring to autumn.

Care: allow offsets around base to grow into a large clump – they will soon flower. Repot when clump fills the pot.

Propagation: offsets (separate when new shoots are half as tall as parent plant).

Browallia speciosa

Bushy herbaceous plant with blue, purple or white flowers. Many varieties. Regular sowing ensures year-round colour.

Temperature: 10–15°C (50–59°F) for longer flowering.

Humidity: undemanding, but mist leaves occasionally.

Position: good light. Tolerates some direct sun, but not through glass at hottest part of the day.

Watering and feeding: water freely at all times. Feed regularly.

Care: grow one plant in a 10 cm (4 in) pot, or three in a 15 cm (6 in) pot. Pinch out growing tips for bushiness. Deadhead regularly. Discard plant after flowering.

Propagation: seed, in late winter or early spring.

Campanula isophylla

Trailing stems with soft blue, star-like flowers in mid and late summer.

Temperature: winter minimum 7°C (45°F) for longer flowering.

Humidity: undemanding, but mist leaves occasionally.

Position: good light, avoid direct summer sun.

Watering and feeding: water freely from spring to autumn, sparingly in winter. Feed regularly.

Care: deadhead regularly. Cut stems back to 5–7.5 cm (2–3 in) at end of growing season.

Propagation: seed; or can take cuttings.

Celosia cristata

Deeply ruffled flowers in red, yellow, orange and pink, in summer and early autumn. The Plumosa group has feathery flower plumes.

Temperature: 10–15°C (50–59°F) if possible.
Humidity: moderate humidity.
Position: good light, avoid direct summer sun through glass.
Watering and feeding: water moderately; vulnerable to under- and overwatering. Feed regularly but cautiously – too much leads to poor flowers.
Care: raise in greenhouse or buy as young plants. Discard after flowering.
Propagation: seed.

Ceropegia woodii

Succulent trailer with heart-shaped leaves, with silver mottling.

Temperature: winter minimum 10°C (50°F).
Humidity: tolerates dry air.
Position: good light, tolerates full sun and partial shade.
Watering and feeding: water sparingly at all times. Feed regularly with weak fertilizer in summer.
Care: shorten bare spindly stems in spring.
Propagation: Seed; layering; stem tuber cuttings.

Chamaedorea elegans

Compact palm with arching leaves growing from base, and tiny yellow ball flowers.

Temperature: winter 12–15°C (53–59°F).
Humidity: mist occasionally, even in winter if the room is centrally heated.
Position: good light, avoid direct summer sun.
Watering and feeding: water generously from spring to autumn, keep just moist in winter. Feed regularly in spring and summer with weak fertilizer.
Care: repot when roots grow through bottom of pot.
Propagation: seed; division.

CHLOROPHYTUM COMOSUM 'VITTATUM'

Arching, linear white-and-green variegated leaves, 30–60 cm (12–24 in) long. Long stalks bear small white flowers and leaf plantlets.

Temperature: winter minimum 7°C (45°F).
Humidity: mist leaves occasionally.
Position: good light, not direct sun.
Watering and feeding: water generously spring to autumn, sparingly in winter. Feed regularly from spring to autumn.
Care: repot young plants each spring, mature ones when roots push the plant out of pot.
Propagation: stem plantlets; division.

CHRYSANTHEMUM YEAR-ROUND

Compact plants for year-round colour, in red, pink, purple, yellow and white.

Temperature: 10–15°C (50–59°F). Tolerates a warm room, but flowers will be shorter-lived.
Humidity: undemanding; mist leaves from time to time.
Position: undemanding.
Watering and feeding: keep moist.
Care: deadhead regularly. Discard after flowering or transfer to garden.
Propagation: None.

CISSUS RHOMBIFOLIA

Vigorous climber with dark green leaves.

Temperature: winter 7–13°C (45–55°F).
Humidity: undemanding, but mist leaves occasionally, especially in summer.
Position: good light, avoid direct summer sun.
Watering and feeding: water generously from spring to autumn, but sparingly in winter.
Care: pinch out growing tips on young plants; tie new shoots to the support. Thin overcrowded shoots in spring.
Propagation: cuttings.

x *CITROFORTUNELLA MICROCARPA*

Glossy, dark green evergreen plant up to 1.2 m (4 ft) high. Clusters of fragrant white flowers, usually in summer, followed by miniature orange fruits.

Temperature: winter minimum 10°C (50°F).

Humidity: undemanding, but mist leaves occasionally.

Position: good light, avoid direct summer sun through glass.

Watering and feeding: water freely in summer, sparingly in winter. Feed regularly in summer, perhaps including magnesium and iron.

Care: pollinate flowers using cotton wool.

Propagation: cuttings.

CLIVIA MINIATA

Evergreen perennial with strap-shaped leaves. Large flower head of orange or yellow funnel-shaped flowers, in early spring.

Temperature: winter minimum 10°C (50°F). Avoid warm winter temperatures.

Humidity: undemanding; mist leaves occasionally.

Position: good light, avoid direct summer sun.

Watering and feeding: water moderately from spring to autumn, sparingly in winter until flower stalk is 15 cm (6 in). Feed from flowering to early autumn.

Care: sponge leaves occasionally. Repot when roots push plant from pot, after flowering. Winter in unheated room.

Propagation: division (after flowering).

COCOS NUCIFERA

Tall and slow-growing palm with visible coconut. Grows to 3 m (10 ft) indoors.

Temperature: winter minimum 18°C (64°F).

Humidity: high humidity.

Position: good light, some full sun, but avoid direct sun through glass during hottest part of day.

Watering and feeding: water freely in summer, moderately in winter. Feed with weak fertilizer in summer.

Care: sponge leaves occasionally; never use leaf shine. Repot young plants in the spring.

Propagation: seed (difficult at home, can be done by a professional plantsman).

CODIAEUM VARIEGATUM VAR. PICTUM

Many varieties with colourful or variegated, glossy, evergreen leaves, many colours.

Temperature: winter minimum 16°C (60°F).
Humidity: high humidity. Mist leaves regularly.
Position: good light, avoid direct summer sun.
Watering and feeding: water generously from spring to autumn, sparingly in winter. Feed regularly in spring and summer.
Care: avoid cold draughts. Repot when outgrown pot.
Propagation: cuttings.

COLCHICUM AUTUMNALE

Corms producing large crocus-shaped, pink flowers in early autumn.

Temperature: undemanding and hardy.
Humidity: undemanding.
Position: light windowsill, preferably out of strong direct sunlight.
Watering and feeding: none required.
Care: place dry corms in saucer of sand or tray of dry pebbles, set in light position and leave to flower. After flowering plant in garden in light shade.
Propagation: buy new corms.

COLEUS BLUMEI (SOLENOSTEMON) HYBRIDS

Perennial sub-shrubs treated as annuals. Variegated leaves in a range of pattern and colour – reds, yellows and greens.

Temperature: winter minimum 10°C (50°F).
Humidity: high humidity. Mist leaves frequently.
Position: good light, avoid direct summer sun.
Watering and feeding: water freely from spring to autumn, keep roots just moist in winter. Use soft water. Feed from spring to autumn.
Care: pinch out growing tips of young plants, several times to obtain really bushy plants. Cut back hard old overwintered plants and repot in spring. If grown from seed, retain most appealing and discard the rest.
Propagation: seed in spring; stem cuttings in spring or summer.

COLUMNEA

Trailing evergreen perennials with red or orange-red flowers, winter or early spring.

Temperature: winter minimum 13°C (55°F).
Humidity: high humidity. Mist regularly.
Position: good light, but avoid direct summer sun.
Watering and feeding: water freely from spring to autumn, sparingly in winter. Feed regularly in spring and summer.
Care: shorten stems after flowering. Repot every second or third year, in humus-rich, fibrous potting mixture.
Propagation: cuttings.

CROCUS

Mainly spring-flowering corms. Plant in autumn for late winter to early spring colour.

Temperature: keep cool.
Humidity: undemanding.
Position: good light indoors.
Watering and feeding: water cautiously.
Care: leave in garden until mid-winter, but protect from excessive freezing and waterlogging. Maintain cool conditions in house until at least a third of developing flower bud is visible. After flowering plant in garden.
Propagation: new corms; offset corms; and seed.

CYCLAMEN

Tuber for autumn to spring colour, in pinks, red, purples, salmon and white.

Temperature: 10–15°C (50–59°F) in winter.
Humidity: moderate humidity. Stand pot on tray of wet pebbles. Mist leaves only.
Position: Good light, not direct sun.
Watering and feeding: water freely while actively growing, gradually reduce after flowering. Feed regularly during active growing and flowering periods.
Care: deadhead regularly, removing entire stalk. When leaves have died, keep cool (perhaps outside) and almost dry until mid-summer. Start watering, repot if necessary (burying tuber to half its depth) and bring indoors if outside.
Propagation: seed.

CYPERUS

Rush-like plants, with leaves radiating from stiff stalks. Tolerates overwatering.

Temperature: winter minimum 7°C (45°F).

Humidity: mist regularly.

Position: good light, avoid direct summer sun.

Watering and feeding: water freely at all times, keeping roots moist. Feed from mid-spring to early autumn.

Care: cut off yellowing stems. Repot in spring.

Propagation: division.

DIEFFENBACHIA MACULATA

Bold oval leaves with ivory or cream markings. Poisonous or irritant sap.

Temperature: winter minimum 16°C (60°F).

Humidity: mist leaves regularly.

Position: partial shade and good light, avoid direct summer sun.

Watering and feeding: water freely from spring to autumn, sparingly in winter. Feed regularly in spring and summer.

Care: wash leaves occasionally. Repot each spring.

Propagation: cane or stem cuttings.

DIZYGOTHECA ELEGANTISSIMA

Graceful evergreen with dark green, almost black, elongated, serrated leaves. Grows up to 1.2 m (4 ft) tall.

Temperature: winter minimum 13°C (55°F).

Humidity: mist regularly.

Position: good light, avoid direct summer sun at hottest part of day.

Watering and feeding: water moderately from spring to autumn, sparingly in winter.

Care: repot every second spring.

Propagation: seed or air layering in spring; tip cuttings in summer.

DRACAENA

Tough, palm-like foliage plants with striking variegation and bold outline.

Temperature: winter minimum 13°C (55°F).
Humidity: mist leaves regularly.
Position: good light, not direct sun.
Watering and feeding: water freely from spring to autumn, sparingly in winter. Never let roots dry out. Feed regularly in spring and summer.
Care: sponge leaves occasionally. Repot in spring if necessary.
Propagation: tip cuttings; air layering; cane cuttings.

ECHEVERIA

Rosette-forming succulents grown for shape and bluish-grey colouring. Yellow, pink or red flowers, from spring through to mid-summer.
Temperature: winter 5–10°C (41–50°F).
Humidity: tolerates dry air.
Position: best possible light. Will tolerate full sun.

Watering and feeding: water moderately from spring to autumn, practically dry in winter. Feed with weak fertilizer in spring and summer.
Care: avoid getting water on leaves. Can use winter-fallen tips as cuttings.
Propagation: tip cuttings; leaf cuttings; offsets; seed.

ECHINOCACTUS GRUSONII

Slow-growing spherical cactus, more cylindrical with age.
Temperature: winter 5–10°C (41–50°F).
Humidity: tolerates dry air.
Position: best possible light. Tolerates full sun.
Watering and feeding: water moderately from spring to autumn, practically dry in winter. Feed with weak fertilizer in spring and summer.
Care: repot only as necessary, using cactus mixture.
Propagation: seed.

Epipremnum aureum

Climber or trailer with heart-shaped glossy leaves, blotched or streaked with yellow.

Temperature: winter minimum 13°C (55°F).
Humidity: undemanding, but benefits from occasional misting.
Position: good light, not direct sun.
Watering and feeding: water freely from spring to autumn, sparingly in winter. Feed in spring and summer.
Care: repot in spring if necessary. To keep plant compact, shorten long shoots.
Propagation: leaf bud cuttings; stem tip cuttings; layering.

Erica

Two species provide indoor winter colour. *E. gracilis*: white-tipped, pink urn-shaped flowers; *E. hyemalis*: white, pink or reddish bell-shaped flowers.

Temperature: 5–13°C (41–55°F) when flowering.
Humidity: mist leaves regularly.
Position: good light. Benefits from winter sun.
Watering and feeding: water freely at all times. Never allow roots to dry out. Soft water if possible.
Care: buy when in flower, then discard.
Propagation: cuttings.

Eustoma grandiflorum

Short-term, compact plant with blue, pink and white poppy flowers, in summer.

Temperature: winter minimum 7°C (45°F).
Humidity: Mist occasionally.
Position: good light, but avoid direct summer sun.
Watering and feeding: water with care. Do not overwater but keep compost moist. Feed regularly once nutrients in potting soil are depleted.
Care: discard when flowering finished.
Propagation: seeds.

EXACUM AFFINE

Masses of small, pale purple or white flowers, from mid-summer to late autumn.

Temperature: 10–21°C (50–70°F).

Humidity: mist leaves regularly.

Position: good light, avoid direct summer sun.

Watering and feeding: water freely. Feed regularly once nutrients in potting soil are depleted.

Care: deadhead regularly. Discard after flowering.

Propagation: seed.

x *FATSHEDERA LIZEI*

Tall-growing foliage plant with shiny, five-fingered leaves. Attractive variegations.

Temperature: winter minimum 3°C (37°F).

Humidity: undemanding in a cool position, but mist occasionally in a warm room.

Position: good light, avoid direct summer sun. Best possible light in winter.

Watering and feeding: water freely from spring to autumn, sparingly in winter. Tepid water if possible. Feed in spring and summer.

Care: repot each spring. Provide support to grow tall, or pinch growing tips each spring for bushy plant.

Propagation: cuttings.

FATSIA JAPONICA

Large, deeply lobed, glossy dark green leaves. Also variegated varieties.

Temperature: winter minimum 3°C (37°F), 13°C (55°F) for variegated types. Keep below 21°C (70°F) if possible.

Humidity: moderate humidity.

Position: good light, avoid direct summer sun. Tolerates shade.

Watering and feeding: water freely from spring to autumn, sparingly in winter. Never let roots dry out. Feed in spring and summer.

Care: sponge leaves monthly. Repot in spring if necessary.

Propagation: cuttings; air layering; seed.

FICUS BENJAMINA

Pendulous shoots with green leaves, up to 2.4 m (8 ft) indoors, useful for focal plant. 'Starlight': variegated leaves.

Temperature: winter minimum 13°C (55°F).

Humidity: mist the leaves occasionally.

Position: good light, avoid direct summer sun during hottest part of day.

Watering and feeding: water freely from spring to autumn, sparingly in winter, using tepid water. Feed in spring and summer.

Care: repot young plants every second year.

Propagation: cuttings; air layering.

FITTONIA VERSCHAFFELTII

Creeping plant with pink-veined, olive-green leaves, about 5 cm (2 in) long.

Temperature: winter minimum 16°C (60°F).

Humidity: high humidity.

Position: partial shade, not direct sun.

Watering and feeding: water freely from spring to autumn, sparingly in winter. Tepid water if possible. Feed from spring to autumn with weak fertilizer.

Care: pinch back straggly shoots. Repot each spring. Does best in a bottle garden.

Propagation: division; cuttings; pot up where rooted.

FUCHSIA HYBRIDS

Compact deciduous shrubs grown for their bell-shaped flowers with flared "skirts", in a range of colours. Grows to 45–60 cm (18–24 in).

Temperature: winter 10–16°C (50–60°F).

Humidity: mist leaves occasionally.

Position: good light, not direct summer sun.

Watering and feeding: water freely from spring to autumn while plant is growing vigorously, otherwise sparingly, and very sparingly in winter if plants are dormant. Feed from late spring through summer.

Care: shorten old shoots just before or as new growth starts; pruning can be severe. Repot every second or third year in humus-rich, fibrous potting mixture.

Propagation: cuttings.

Gardenia jasminoides

Glossy evergreen shrub. Large, fragrant, white flowers, in summer. 45 cm (18 in) houseplant or 1.5 m (5 ft) in conservatory.

Temperature: winter minimum 16°C (60°F).
Humidity: mist leaves regularly.
Position: good light, but avoid direct summer sun during hottest part of day.
Watering and feeding: water freely from spring to autumn, sparingly in winter, never let roots become dry. Soft water if possible. Feed from spring to autumn.
Care: avoid widely fluctuating temperatures when buds forming. Repot every second or third year with ericaceous potting soil.
Propagation: cuttings.

Hedera

Self-clinging climbers or trailers, many varieties, including variegated ones.
H. canariensis: large lobed leaves.
H. helix: small leaves.

Temperature: cool but frost-free.
Humidity: mist leaves occasionally, regularly in summer.
Position: good light or some shade, avoid direct summer sun.
Watering and feeding: water freely in warm weather, moderately in cool temperatures, never let roots become dry. Soft water if possible. Feed regularly from spring to autumn.
Care: repot each spring, unless in a large pot. Pinch out growing tips periodically for a bushy plant.
Propagation: cuttings.

Hibiscus rosa-sinensis

Large-flowered evergreen in many colours, spring to autumn. Up to 75 cm (2½ ft). 'Cooperi': variegated foliage and red flowers.

Temperature: winter minimum 13°C (55°F).
Humidity: mist leaves occasionally.
Position: good light, avoid direct summer sun during hottest part of day.
Watering and feeding: water freely from spring to autumn, sparingly in winter, but never allow roots to dry out. Feed regularly in summer.
Care: deadhead regularly. Shorten long shoots after flowering or in late winter. Once buds form do not turn plant. Repot each spring.
Propagation: cuttings; seed.

HOWEA BELMOREANA

Evergreen palms with thin green stems and arching, pinnate foliage. Can grow to ceiling height.

Temperature: winter minimum 16°C (60°F).

Humidity: mist leaves regularly.

Position: good light, avoid direct summer sun during hottest part of day.

Watering and feeding: water moderately in summer, sparingly in winter. Keep soil just moist. Feed in summer.

Care: sponge leaves occasionally. Don't use leaf shine.

Propagation: seed (difficult).

HOYA BELLA

Fleshy-leaved evergreen climber or trailer. Pendulous clusters of fragrant, white star-shaped flowers, through summer.

Temperature: winter minimum of 18°C (64°F).

Humidity: mist leaves regularly, except when in bloom.

Position: good light, avoid summer sun through glass during hottest part of day.

Watering and feeding: water freely from spring to autumn, sparingly in winter, but never allow roots to dry out.
Feed sparingly when in flower.

Care: provide support if grown as climber. Repot only when necessary and never once flower buds formed.

Propagation: semi-ripe cuttings; also eye cuttings.

HYACINTHUS ORIENTALIS

Indoor bulbs for winter and early spring colour and fragrance, in many colours.

Temperature: hardy. Keep as cool as possible unless advancing flowering.

Humidity: undemanding.

Position: good light once buds begin to show colour. Anywhere once in full flower.

Watering and feeding: Ensure roots do not dry out. Feed only if planting bulbs in garden.

Care: discard after flowering, or plant in garden.

Propagation: buy fresh bulbs each year.

HYDRANGEA MACROPHYLLA

Deciduous shrubs with ball-shaped flower heads in blue, pink or white, usually in spring, but sometimes at other times.

Temperature: winter minimum 7°C (45°F). Move to warm bright position in mid-winter, when you can increase watering.
Humidity: mist occasionally.
Position: good light or light shade. Avoid direct summer sun.
Watering and feeding: water freely from spring to autumn, sparingly in early winter. Soft water if possible. Feed regularly during active growth.
Care: flower colour is affected by the type of potting soil: use ericaceous for blue flowers. Never allow roots to dry out during growing season. Stand outside after flowering. Repot every second or third year with ericaceous potting soil.
Propagation: semi-ripe cuttings.

HYPOESTES PHYLLOSTACHYA

Evergreen with pointed oval leaves covered with red or pink spots or blotches.
Temperature: winter minimum 13°C (55°F).
Humidity: mist leaves regularly.
Position: good light, avoid direct summer sun during hottest part of day.
Watering and feeding: water freely from spring to autumn, sparingly in winter, soil just moist. Feed regularly in summer; spindly growth results from overfeeding.

Care: pinch out leaf tips and cut back straggly shoots. Pinch out flowers – these spoil compact shape.
Propagation: cuttings; seed.

IMPATIENS HYBRIDS

Compact plants with masses of flat flowers in red, orange, pink or white, year-round.

Temperature: winter minimum 13°C (55°F), or 16°C (60°F) if flowering.
Humidity: mist leaves occasionally, avoiding flowers.
Position: good light, avoid direct summer sun.
Watering and feeding: water freely from spring to autumn, sparingly in winter.
Care: pinch out tips of young plants. Cut back lanky old plants, or discard.
Propagation: seed; cuttings.

Jasminum

Woody climbers with very fragrant flowers, suitable for conservatory, usually deciduous. *J. officinale*: white summer flowers. *J. polyanthum*: white winter flowers.

Temperature: winter minimum 7°C (45°F).
Humidity: mist leaves regularly.
Position: good light with some direct sun.
Watering and feeding: water freely from spring to autumn, in winter keep soil barely moist. Feed regularly during active growth.
Care: large pot with support. Prune to contain size if necessary. Avoid high winter temperatures.
Propagation: cuttings.

Justicia brandegeeana

Evergreen grown for long-lasting reddish-brown bracts, available all year. Rarely reaches its potential 90 cm (3 ft).

Temperature: winter 10–16°C (50–60°F).
Humidity: mist occasionally.
Position: good light with some direct sun, but not through glass in summer.
Watering and feeding: water freely from spring to autumn, sparingly in winter. Feed regularly from spring to autumn.
Care: repot each spring, and prune back shoots by one-third.
Propagation: cuttings.

Kalanchoe blossfeldiana

Fleshy-leaved succulent. Flowers in various colours, year-round.

Temperature: winter minimum 10°C (50°F).
Humidity: tolerates dry air.
Position: good light with some direct sun, but avoid direct summer sun during hottest part of day.
Watering and feeding: water freely from spring to autumn, sparingly in winter. Feed regularly from spring to autumn.
Care: discard after flowering.
Propagation: cuttings; seed.

LILIUM HYBRIDS

Indoor bulbs for spring colour and fragrance, in many colours, usually mottled.

Temperature: 3–10°C (37–50°F), avoid high temperatures.

Humidity: mist occasionally.

Position: good light, but avoid direct summer sun.

Watering and feeding: keep soil moist during active growth. Feed regularly.

Care: pot bulb in autumn or winter when bought, with at least 5 cm (2 in) soil beneath and 10 cm (4 in) above. Keep in cool place with soil just moist, ensuring good light once shoots appear. Move in to house when buds show colour. Plant in garden after flowering.

Propagation: buy fresh bulbs each year.

LITHOPS

Prostrate succulents with pairs of fused swollen leaves resembling pebbles.

Temperature: winter minimum 7°C (45°F).

Humidity: tolerates dry air.

Position: good light with plenty of sun.

Watering and feeding: water moderately in summer. Keep dry in winter. Recommence when old leaves split to reveal new ones. Only feed after many years in same pot, with cactus fertilizer.

Care: repot only when the pot filled with leaves.

Propagation: seed.

MARANTA LEUCONEURA ERYTHRONEURA

Squat foliage plants with strikingly marked round oval leaves.

Temperature: winter minimum 10°C (50°F).

Humidity: high humidity. Mist the leaves regularly.

Position: good light, avoid direct summer sun. Best possible light in winter.

Watering and feeding: water freely from spring to summer. Soft water if possible. Feed regularly in summer.

Care: repot every second spring.

Propagation: division.

Monstera deliciosa

Thick-stemmed climber with very large leaves, perforated with age. Can grow to reach the ceiling.

Temperature: winter minimum 10°C (50°F).
Humidity: mist leaves regularly.
Position: good light or shade, not direct sun. Best possible light in winter.
Watering and feeding: water freely from spring to autumn, sparingly in winter. Feed regularly in summer.
Care: provide support. Lightly sponge leaves occasionally.
Propagation: cuttings; air layering.

Narcissus hybrids

Bulbs for late winter and early spring colour. White, fragrant 'Paperwhite' and yellow 'Soleil d'Or' are suitable for forcing.

Temperature: 15–21°C (59–70°F).
Humidity: undemanding.
Position: good light.
Watering and feeding: water moderately while bulbs growing.
Care: grow in pots or in bowls of water supported by pebbles, keeping base of bulb above water.
Propagation: buy fresh bulbs each year.

Nephrolepsis exaltata

Evergreen fern forming a dense clump of pinnate leaves, varying according to the variety.

Temperature: winter minimum 18°C (64°F).
Humidity: mist leaves regularly.
Position: partial shade, not direct sun.
Watering and feeding: water freely in summer, cautiously in winter, keeping roots moist without being wet. Use soft water if possible.
Care: repot in spring if becomes too large for pot. Avoid draughts.
Propagation: plantlets; spores (species only).

Nertera granadensis

Mound-forming, creeping perennial grown for bright orange berries, in autumn.

Temperature: winter minimum 7°C (45°F).
Humidity: mist leaves occasionally.
Position: good light, with some direct sun.
Watering and feeding: water freely from spring to autumn, sparingly in winter. Never allow roots to dry out completely.
Care: can leave outdoors all summer until berries form. Discard after berries finished.
Propagation: division; seed.

Opuntia

Branching cacti, some cylindrical, some with flat pads. Red or yellow flowers.

Temperature: winter minimum 7°C (45°F).
Humidity: tolerates dry air as it is a desert plant.
Position: Best possible light, benefits from direct sun.
Watering and feeding: water moderately from spring to autumn, very sparingly in winter. Feed in summer with weak fertilizer or cactus food.
Care: repot in spring if necessary. Flat pad types do well in ordinary loam-based potting soil, others prefer cactus mixture.
Propagation: cuttings or detach pads; seed.

Parodia

Rounded to cylindrical cacti with bristly spines. Yellow flowers in spring.

Temperature: winter 7–12°C (45–53°F).
Humidity: tolerates dry air as it is a desert plant.
Position: Best possible light, benefits from full sun.
Watering and feeding: water moderately from spring to autumn, leave practically dry in winter. Use soft water if possible. Feed in summer with weak fertilizer or cactus food.
Care: Plants are slow-growing, but if they need repotting use a special cactus mixture if possible.
Propagation: seed.

Pelargonium, regal or Martha Washington

Scalloped leaves and showy, often bicoloured blooms from early spring to late summer.

Temperature: winter minimum 7°C (45°F).

Humidity: tolerates dry air.

Position: good light with some sun. Tolerates full sun.

Watering and feeding: water moderately between spring and autumn. Feed regularly from spring to autumn.

Care: can be kept in leaf if given sufficient warmth. Repot in spring if necessary. Deadhead regularly. Shorten long shoots in autumn. Pinch out growing tip for bushy growth.

Propagation: cuttings; seed.

Pellaea

Ferns with feathery fronds. Tolerate dry conditions, humidity improves growth.

Temperature: winter 13–16°C (55–60°F).

Humidity: mist leaves occasionally.

Position: good light, not direct sun.

Watering and feeding: water moderately at all times, with care. Feed with weak fertilizer in summer.

Care: if repotting, use shallow container or hanging basket.

Propagation: division; spores.

Peperomia

Undemanding compact, slow-growing foliage plants with wide variety of leaf shapes, colouring and size.

Temperature: winter minimum 10°C (50°F).

Humidity: mist leaves occasionally with warm water, not in winter.

Position: semi-shade or good light, avoid direct summer sun.

Watering and feeding: water moderately from spring to autumn, cautiously in winter. Soft water if possible. Feed from spring to autumn.

Care: repot only when necessary to slightly larger pot, in spring, with peat-based mix.

Propagation: cuttings; leaf cuttings.

PHILODENDRON SCANDENS

Climber or trailer with heart-shaped, glossy green leaves. Can reach ceiling.

Temperature: winter minimum 13°C (55°F).
Humidity: mist leaves regularly.
Position: good light, avoid direct summer sun. Tolerates low light levels well.
Watering and feeding: water freely from spring to autumn. Soft water if possible. Feed from spring to autumn; to limit growth avoid nitrogen feeds.
Care: provide suitable support.
Propagation: cuttings; air layering.

PHOENIX CANARIENSIS

Palm with feathery fronds, stiff at first, arching later.

Temperature: winter minimum 7°C (45°F).
Humidity: tolerates dry air.
Position: good light, especially direct sun.
Watering and feeding: water moderately from spring to autumn, sparingly in winter. Feed regularly from spring to autumn.
Care: repot only when becomes pot-bound, in deep container.
Propagation: seed.

PILEA

Bushy or trailing foliage plants. Many textured and with silver or bronze markings.

Temperature: winter minimum 10°C (50°F).
Humidity: mist leaves regularly.
Position: good light or partial shade, avoid direct summer sun.
Watering and feeding: water freely while in active growth. Feed regularly from spring to autumn.
Care: pinch out growing tips of young plants and again a month or two later. Repot in spring.
Propagation: cuttings.

PRIMULA OBCONICA

Rounded, fragrant flowers, in winter and spring. Leaves can cause allergic reaction.

Temperature: winter minimum 13°C (55°F).
Humidity: mist leaves occasionally.
Position: good light, not direct sun.
Watering and feeding: water moderately from autumn to spring, sparingly in summer. Feed regularly during flowering with weak fertilizer.
Care: keep cool during summer.
Propagation: seed.

PTERIS

Ferns with deeply divided fronds. Several variegated varieties.

Temperature: winter minimum: 13°C (55°F) for pale green forms; 16°C (60°F) for variegated ones.
Humidity: mist leaves regularly.
Position: good light, not direct sun. Plain green forms will tolerate poorer light than variegated varieties.
Watering and feeding: water freely from spring to autumn, sparingly in winter. Soft water if possible. Feed regularly with weak fertilizer from spring to autumn.
Care: never allow roots to become dry.
Propagation: division; spores.

RADERMACHERA SINICA

Vigorous, evergreen, bushy foliage plant with individual leaflets, about 60 cm (24 in) tall.

Temperature: winter minimum 13°C (55°F).
Humidity: undemanding.
Position: good light, avoid direct summer sun during hottest part of day.
Watering and feeding: water freely from spring to autumn, moderately in winter.
Care: Pinch out growing tips of young plants.
Propagation: cuttings.

Rebutia

Rounded or oval cacti with bristly spines. Flowers in spring or early summer.

Temperature: winter minimum 5°C (41°F).
Humidity: tolerates dry air, but appreciates humid atmosphere in spring and summer.
Position: good light, full sun.
Watering and feeding: water moderately from spring to autumn, almost dry in winter. Feed in summer with cactus food.
Care: repot in spring if necessary, using cactus mixture.
Propagation: cuttings from offshoots; seed.

Rhododendron

R. x *obtusum* (range of colours) and *R. simsii* (pinks and reds) are good for winter and spring colour. Known as azaleas.

Temperature: winter 10–16°C (50–60°F).
Humidity: mist leaves regularly.
Position: good light, not direct sun.
Watering and feeding: water freely at all times, using soft water if possible. Feed regularly in summer.
Care: repot in ericaceous mixture one month after flowering. Place in garden in sheltered shady spot after all danger of frost is past. Keep watered and fed.
R. simsii must be brought indoors in early autumn.
Propagation: cuttings.

Rosa, miniature hybrids

Miniature bushes or standards make short-term houseplants in various colours.

Temperature: frost hardy. 10–21°C (50–70°F) when plants growing actively.
Humidity: undemanding, but advisable to mist occasionally.
Position: best possible light. Tolerates full sun.
Watering and feeding: water freely from spring to autumn, while in leaf. Feed regularly in summer.
Care: place outdoors when not in flower. Repot in autumn if necessary. Prune in spring. Bring indoors in late spring, or as soon as flowering starts.
Propagation: cuttings.

SAINTPAULIA

Rosette-forming, hairy-leaved perennials with large colour range. Long-flowering with appropriate light intensities.

Temperature: winter minimum 16°C (60°F).
Humidity: high humidity, stand on tray of wet pebbles; misting is unsuitable.
Position: good light, avoid direct summer sun during hottest part of day. Artificial light at least 5,000 lux.
Watering and feeding: water freely from spring to autumn, moderately in winter, allowing surface to dry out a little. Soft water if possible. Don't wet leaves. Feed during active growth, but stop if lots of leaves and few flowers.
Care: will continue flowering with supplemental light, but needs at least one month's rest; lower temperature to minimum, reduce watering and shorten day length. Place the plant in good light to restart growth.
Propagation: leaf cuttings; seed.

SANSEVIERIA TRIFASCIATA 'LAURENTII'

Tough, fleshy, sword-like leaves, dull green with paler cross-banding and yellow edges.

Temperature: winter minimum 10°C (50°F).
Humidity: tolerates dry air.
Position: bright, indirect light, but it tolerates direct sun and some shade.
Watering and feeding: water moderately from spring to autumn, very sparingly in winter. Always allow the soil to dry out slightly before watering. Feed regularly in summer.
Care: repotting is seldom required.
Propagation: division.

SAXIFRAGA STOLONIFERA

Trailing alpine with rounded, broadly toothed leaves, olive green with veining.

Temperature: winter minimum 7°C (45°F).
Humidity: mist occasionally.
Position: good light, not direct sun.
Watering and feeding: water freely from spring to autumn, sparingly in winter. Feed regularly in summer.
Care: trim off long runners if untidy.
Propagation: plantlets (peg down in pots).

SCHEFFLERA ARBORICOLA 'AUREA'

Erect, branched, variegated evergreen with oval leaflets radiating from each leaf stalk.

Temperature: winter minimum of 13°C (55°F).
Humidity: mist regularly.
Position: good light, avoid direct sun.
Watering and feeding: water freely from spring to autumn, sparingly in winter. Feed regularly in summer.
Care: either train as upright, unbranching plant by staking, or remove growing tip to make bushy. Repot annually in spring.

SEDUM

Small, fleshy, branching succulents, some with white, pink or yellow flowers.

Temperature: winter minimum 5°C (41°F).
Humidity: tolerates dry air.
Position: best possible light.
Watering and feeding: water sparingly from spring to autumn, keep nearly dry during winter.
Care: repot in spring, using free-draining potting soil such as cactus mixture.
Propagation: leaf cuttings (for large fleshy leaves); stem cuttings.

SINNINGIA SPECIOSA

Tuberous perennials with large, hairy leaves and bell-shaped flowers in various colours, in summer. It is often sold as *Gloxinia*.

Temperature: minimum 16°C (60°F) during growing season.
Humidity: mist around plant regularly, but avoid wetting leaves or flowers. Provide as much humidity as possible.
Position: good light, not direct sun.
Watering and feeding: water freely once tubers have rooted well. Decrease at end of growing season. Feed regularly in the summer months.
Care: store tubers in the pot in frost-free place, ideally at 10°C (50°F). Repot in the spring.
Propagation: leaf cuttings; seed.

SOLANUM CAPSICASTRUM

Sub-shrubs grown for their autumn to winter fruit (green turning red). Poisonous fruit.

Temperature: winter 10–16°C (50–60°F).
Humidity: mist leaves regularly.
Position: best possible light. Tolerates some direct sun.
Watering and feeding: water freely through growing period. Feed regularly in summer.
Care: buy in fruit or raise in greenhouse until fruit formed.
Propagation: seed; cuttings.

SOLEIROLIA SOLEIROLII

Compact, mounded plant, with tiny leaves, 5 cm (2 in) high. Silver and gold varieties.

Temperature: frost hardy, but 7°C (45°F) is ideal.
Humidity: mist regularly.
Position: good light, not direct sun.
Watering and feeding: water freely.
Care: repot in spring in low, wide container.
Propagation: division.

SPARRMANNIA AFRICANA

Tall and fast-growing evergreen with pale green, downy leaves. White spring flowers.

Temperature: winter minimum 7°C (45°F).
Humidity: mist occasionally.
Position: good light, but not direct summer sun during the hottest part of the day.
Watering and feeding: water freely from spring through to autumn, sparingly in the winter. Feed regularly in spring and summer.
Care: cut back stems after flowering. When repotting, cut back to 30 cm (12 in) if necessary. Young plants may need repotting seveal times a year to accommodate its fast growth. Pinch out growing tips of young plants for a bushy shape.
Propagation: cuttings.

STEPHANOTIS FLORIBUNDA

Climber with glossy, oval leaves. Clusters of fragrant white flowers in summer.
Temperature: winter 13–16°C (55–60°F).
Humidity: mist occasionally.
Position: good light, avoid direct summer sun during hottest part of day.
Watering and feeding: water freely from spring to autumn, sparingly in winter. Feed regularly in summer, in moderation if plant is large.
Care: train to a support. Shorten overlong shoots and cut out overcrowded stems in spring.
Propagation: cuttings.

STREPTOCARPUS HYBRIDS

Perennial with horizontal, stemless leaves and large trumpet-shaped flowers in pink, red and blue, late spring through summer. Leaf sap can cause an irritating rash.

Temperature: winter minimum 13°C (55°F).
Humidity: lightly mist leaves occasionally.
Position: good light, avoid direct summer sun.
Watering and feeding: water freely from spring to autumn, sparingly in winter. Feed regularly in summer.
Care: benefits from dormant winter season, with soil only slightly moist and temperature close to winter minimum. Repot early spring.
Propagation: leaf cuttings; seed.

SYNGONIUM PODOPHYLLUM

Evergreen climber with foot-shaped leaves, arrow-shaped on young plants. Variegated varieties. Will grow to 1.8 m (6 ft).
Temperature: winter minimum 16°C (60°F).
Humidity: mist leaves regularly.
Position: good light, not direct sun. Tolerates low light levels.
Watering and feeding: water freely from spring to autumn, sparingly in winter but do not allow it to dry out completely. Feed regularly in spring and summer.
Care: to retain juvenile leaves, cut off climbing stems at the base. Repot the plant every second spring.
Propagation: cuttings; air layering.

Tillandsia cynea

Rosette of narrow, striped grass-like leaves. Summer flower spike has pink or red bract and purple-blue flowers.

Temperature: winter minimum 18°C (64°F).
Humidity: mist regularly.
Position: good light, not direct summer sun.
Watering and feeding: water freely from spring to autumn, sparingly in winter. Soft water if possible. Apply weak fertilizer to leaves, using mister, or to soil.
Care: can pot in spring.
Propagation: offsets.

Tolmiea menziesii

Bright green foliage plant with heart-shaped leaves. Plantlets develop on base of each leaf blade. Variegated varieties are available.

Temperature: winter minimum 5°C (41°F). Avoid high winter temperature.
Humidity: mist occasionally.
Position: good light or semi-shade, not direct sun.
Watering and feeding: water freely from spring to autumn, sparingly in winter. Feed regularly in summer.
Care: if plant too large and stems congested, cut back in spring. Repot each spring.
Propagation: division; pot up plantlets.

Tradescantia

Trailing foliage houseplants. Several variegated varieties with white or purple tinges.

Temperature: winter minimum 7°C (45°F).
Humidity: mist occasionally.
Position: good light, with some direct sun.
Watering and feeding: water freely from spring to autumn, sparingly in winter. Feed regularly from spring through to the autumn months.
Care: pinch out any unattractive shoots.
Propagation: cuttings.

TULIPA

Some tulips can be forced for winter colour.

Temperature: hardy. Once in flower, the cooler the room, the longer the flowers will last.

Humidity: undemanding.

Position: can be placed anywhere if brought indoors just as flowers open.

Watering and feeding: water moderately while in the home.

Care: in early or mid-autumn, plant bulbs with necks just below soil. Place in sheltered place outdoors and cover with fine gravel or other suitable mulch at least 5 cm (2 in) deep. Keep soil in pots moist but not overwatered. When shoots are 4–5 cm (1½–2 in) tall, place in light at about 15°C (59°F) until buds show colour. Bring into the home. Discard or plant in garden after flowering.

Propagation: buy fresh bulbs each year.

VRIESEA SPLENDENS

Bromeliad with rosette of arching, strap-shaped, banded leaves. Bright red flower bract in summer and autumn.

Temperature: winter minimum 15°C (59°F).

Humidity: mist leaves regularly.

Position: light shade or good light out of direct sun.

Watering and feeding: water freely from spring to autumn, sparingly in winter. Keep "vase" of leaves topped up with water from mid-spring to mid-autumn. Soft water if possible. Feed a weak fertilizer in summer.

Care: discard after flowering, or pot up offsets in ericaceous soil.

Propagation: offsets.

YUCCA ELEPHANTIPES

Rosettes with long pointed leaves growing from a trunk section. Can grow to ceiling.

Temperature: winter minimum 7°C (45°F).

Humidity: tolerates dry air.

Position: prefers good light with some sun but avoid full sun.

Watering and feeding: water freely from spring to autumn, sparingly in winter.

Care: repot small plants as necessary, large ones can remain in same container for many years, but replace top 5 cm (2 in) of potting soil.

Propagation: use sideshoots from the plant as cuttings.

Common Names of Plants

aconite *Aconitum*
African daisy *Arctotis*
African lily *Agapanthus*
African marigold *Tagetes erecta*
Algerian iris *Iris unguicularis*
alyssum *Lobularia maritima*
annual pepper *Capsicum annuum*
arum lily *Zantedeschia aethiopica*
auricula *Primula auricula* hybrids
autumn crocus *Colchicum autumnale, Crocus nudiflorus*
avens *Geum*

baby blue-eyes *Nemophila menziesii*
baby's breath *Gypsophila paniculata*
balsam poplar *Populus balsamifera*
Barberry *Berberis sargentiana*
basil *Ocimum basilicum*
bay *Laurus nobilis*
bear's breeches *Acanthus*
beauty bush *Kolkwitzia amabilis*
bedding geranium *Pelargonium*
beech *Fagus sylvatica*
bellflower *Campanula*
bells of Ireland *Moluccella laevis*
bergamot *Monarda*
betony *Stachys*
black-eyed Susan *Rudbeckia*
bladder senna *Colutea*
blazing star *Liatris*
bleeding heart *Dicentra spectabilis*
blue daisy *Felicia*
blue fescue *Festuca glauca*
bluebell *Hyacinthoides*
borage *Borago officinalis*
Boston ivy *Parthenocissus tricuspidata*
box *Buxus sempervirens*
bridal wreath *Francoa*
broom *Cytisus, Genista*
bulrush *Typha latifolia*
burnet *Sanguisorba*
busy Lizzie *Impatiens*
buttercup *Ranunculus*
butterfly bush *Buddleja davidii*

calamint *Calamintha*
calico bush *Kalmia latifolia*
California lilac *Ceanothus*
Californian poppy *Eschscholzia*
campion *Silene*
candytuft *Iberis*
Canterbury bells *Campanula medium*
Cape figwort *Phygelius*
cardoon *Cynara cardunculus*
carnation *Dianthus*
castor oil plant *Ricinus*
catchfly *Lychnis*
catmint *Nepeta* x *faasseni*
chamomile *Chamaemelum nobile*
cherry *Prunus*
cherry pie *Heliotropum*
China aster *Callistephus chinensis*
Chinese pink *Dianthus chinensis*

chives *Allium schoenoprasum*
Christmas box *Sarcococca*
Christmas cactus *Schlumbergera*
cineraria *Senecio cineraria*
cinquefoil *Potentilla*
climbing hydrangea *Hydrangea petiolaris*
coleus *Solenostemon*
columbine *Aquilegia*
comfrey *Symphytum*
common bugle *Ajuga reptans*
coneflower *Echinacea, Rudbeckia*
contorted/corkscrew hazel *Corylus avellana* 'Contorta'
coral flower *Heuchera*
cornflower *Centaurea cinerea*
cotton lavender *Santolina chamaecyparissus*
cowslip *Primula veris*
crab apple *Malus*
cranesbill *Geranium*
creeping Jenny *Lysimachia nummularia*
creeping zinnia *Sanvitalia*
cuckoo flower *Cardamine pratensis*
Cupid's dart *Catanache*
curry plant *Helichrysum italicum*

daffodil *Narcissus*
daisy *Bellis perennis*
daisy bush *Olearia*

dame's violet *Hesperis matronalis*
daylily *Hemerocallis*
deadnettle *Lamium*
dittany *Dictamnus*
dog's tooth violet *Erythronium*
dogwood *Cornus*
Dutchman's pipe *Aristolochia*

elder *Sambucus*
elephant ears *Bergenia*
evening primrose *Oenothera speciosa*

false castor oil plant *Fatsia japonica*
feather grass *Stipa*
fennel *Foeniculum vulgare*
feverfew *Tanacetum parthenium*
firethorn *Pyracantha*
flag *Iris germanica*
fleabane *Erigeron*
floss flower *Ageratum*
flowering currant *Ribes sanguineum*
flowering flax *Linum grandiflorum*
flowering quince *Chaenomeles*
forget-me-not *Myosotis*
foxglove *Digitalis purpurea*
French marigold *Tagetes patula*
fritillary *Fritillaria*
furze *Ulex*

garlic *Allium sativum*
gay feather *Liatris*
gentian *Gentiana*
geranium *Pelargonium*
giant thistle *Onopordum*
ginger mint *Mentha* x *gracilis* 'Variegata'
globe amaranth *Gomphrena globosa*
globe thistle *Echinops*
globeflower *Ranunculus ficaria*
godetia *Clarkia*
golden privet *Ligustrum ovalifolium* 'Aureum'
golden rod *Solidago*
gorse *Ulex*
grape hyacinth *Muscari*
guelder rose *Viburnum opulus*
gum *Eucalyptus*

harebell *Campanula rotundifolia*
Harry Lauder's walking stick *Corylus avellana* 'Contorta'
hart's tongue fern *Asplenium scolopendrium*
hawthorn *Crataegus*
hazel *Corylus*
heartsease *Viola tricolor*
heath *Erica carnea*
heather *Calluna vulgaris*
heliotrope *Heliotropium*
hellebore *Helleborus*
hemp agrimony *Eupatorium*
Himalayan poppy *Meconopsis*
holly *Ilex aquifolium*
hollyhock *Alcea rosea*
honesty *Lunaria annua*
honey bush *Melianthus*
honeysuckle *Lonicera*
honeywort *Cerinthe major*
hop *Humulus lupulus*
hornbeam *Carpinus betulus*
houseleek *Sempervivum*
hyacinth *Hyacinthus orientalis*

iceplant *Sedum spectabile*
Indian bean tree *Catalpa bignonioides*
ironweed *Vernonia*
ivy *Hedera*

Jacob's ladder *Polemonium*
Japanese anemone *Anemone* x *hybrida*
Japanese maple *Acer palmatum*

Japanese quince *Chaenomeles*
japonica *Chaenomeles*
jasmine *Jasminum*
Jerusalem cross *Lychnis chalcedonica*
jessamine *Jasminum*
Jew's mallow *Kerria japonica*

kaffir lily *Schizolstylis coccinea*
katsura tree *Cercidiphyllum*
king fern *Dryopteris pseudomas* 'Cristata'
kingcup *Caltha*
knapweed *Centaurea*
knotweed *Persicaria*
kolomikta vine *Actinidia kolomikta*

lad's love *Artemisia abrotanum*
lady fern *Athyrium*
lady's mantle *Alchemilla mollis*
larkspur *Consolida ambigua*
lavender *Lavandula*
lemon balm *Melissa officinalis*
lemon verbena *Aloysa triphylla*
leopard's bane *Doronicum*
lesser celandine *Ranunculus ficaria*
lesser stitchwort *Stellaria graminea*
Leyland cypress x *Cupressocyparis leylandii*

lilac *Syringa*
lily *Lilium*
lily-of-the-valley *Convallaria majalis*
lilyturf *Liriope muscari*
lime tree *Tilia*
loosestrife *Lysimachia*
love-in-a-mist *Nigella*
love-lies-bleeding *Amaranthus*
lungwort *Pulmonaria*
lupin *Lupinus*

Madonna lily *Lilium candidum*
mallow *Lavatera, Malva*
maple *Acer*
marguerite *Argyranthemum frutescens*
marigold *Calendula*
marjoram *see* pot marjoram, sweet marjoram
marsh marigold *Caltha palustris*
mask flower *Alonsoa*
masterwort *Astrantia*
meadow buttercup *Ranunculus acris*
meadow cranesbill *Geranium pratense*
meadowsweet *Filipendula*
medlar *Mespilus germanica*
Mexican orange blossom *Choisya ternata*
Mexican sunflower *Tithonia*
Michaelmas daisy *Aster*
mignonette *Reseda odorata*
mile-a-minute plant *Fallopia baldschuanica*

milfoil *Achillea millefolium*
milk thistle *Silybum marianum*
mint *Mentha*
mock orange *Philadelphus*
money flower *Mimulus*
monkshood *Aconitum*
montbretia *Crocosmia*
morning glory *Ipomoea*
Mount Etna broom *Genista aetnensis*
moutan *Paeonia*
mullein *Verbascum*
myrtle *Myrtus*

nasturtium *Tropaeolum majus*
New England aster *Aster novae-angliae*
New Zealand flax *Phormium*
night-scented stock *Matthiola longipetala*

old man *Artemisia abrotanum*
oregano *Origanum vulgare*
Oregon grape *Mahonia*
ornamental onion *Allium*
ornamental rhubarb *Rheum*
ornamental vine *Vitis*
ox eye *Heliopsis*

pampas grass *Cortaderia selloana*
pansy *Viola* x *wittrockiana* cultivars
parsley *Petroselinum crispum*
passion flower *Passiflora caerulea*
pennyroyal *Mentha pulegium*
peony *Paeonia*
periwinkle *Vinca major, V. minor*
Peruvian lily *Alstroemeria*
pimpernel *Anagallis*
pineapple broom *Cytisus battandieri*
pink *Dianthus*

plantain lily *Hosta*
plumbago *Ceratostigma willmottianum*
poached-egg flower *Limnanthes douglasii*
polyanthus *Primula*
poppy, field *Papaver rhoeas*
poppy, opium *Papaver somniferum*
Portugal laurel *Prunus lusitanica*
pot marigold *Calendula*
pot marjoram *Origanum*
prickly poppy *Argemone*
potato vine *Solanum crispum*
primrose *Primula vulgaris*
privet *Ligustrum*
purple coneflower *Echinacea purpurea*
purple loosestrife *Lythrum salicaria*
purple velvet plant *Gynura aurantiaca*
purslane *Portulaca*

quince *Cydonia oblonga*

red-hot poker *Kniphofia*
red orache *Atriplex*
red valerian *Centranthus ruber*
rock cress *Aubrieta deltoidea*
rock rose *Cistus, Helianthemum*
rose *Rosa*
rose of Sharon *Hypericum calycinum*
rosemary *Rosmarinus officinalis*

rue *Ruta graveolens*
Russian sage *Perovskia*

sage *Salvia officinalis*
St John's wort *Hypericum*
saxifrage *Saxifraga*
scabious *Scabiosa*
scented geranium *Pelargonium fragrans*
scorpion weed *Phacelia*
sea buckthorn *Hippophäe rhamnoides*
sea holly *Eryngium*
shoo-fly flower *Nicandra physalodes*
Siberian wallflower *Erysimum* x *allioni*
silk tassel bush *Garrya elliptica*
slipper flower *Calceolaria*
smoke bush *Cotinus coggygria*
snake's-head fritillary *Fritillaria meleagris*
snapdragon *Antirrhinum*
sneezeweed *Helenium*
snowberry *Symphoricarpos*
snowdrop *Galanthus nivalis*
snowflake *Leucojum*
Solomon's seal *Polygonatum*
sorrel *Rumex acetosa*
southernwood *Artemisia abrotanum*
Spanish broom *Spartium junceum*
speedwell *Veronica*
spider plant *Chlorophytum comosum*
spiderflower *Cleome*
spindle *Euonymus*
spotted laurel *Aucuba japonica*
spurge *Euphorbia*
squirrel tail grass *Hordeum jubatum*
stag's horn sumach *Rhus typhina*
star jasmine *Trachelospermum jasminoides*
statice *Limonium*
stock *Matthiola*
stonecrop *Sedum*
sun rose *Cistus, Helianthemum*
sunflower *Helianthus annuus*
Swan river daisy *Brachyscome iberidifolia*
sweet alyssum *Lobularia maritima*
sweet bay *Laurus nobilis*
sweet box *Sarcococca*
sweet briar *Rosa eglanteria*
sweet marjoram *Origanum majorana*
sweet pea *Lathyrus odoratus*
sweet rocket *Hesperis matronalis*
sweet rush *Acorus calamus*
sweet violet *Viola odorata*
sweet William *Dianthus barbatus*

tamarisk *Tamarix*
Texan bluebell *Eustoma grandiflorus*
thyme *Thymus vulgaris*
tickseed *Coreopsis tinctoria*
toadflax *Linaria*
tobacco plant *Nicotiana alata*
Torbay palm *Cordyline*
torch lily *Kniphofia*
tree mallow *Lavatera*
tree peony *Paeonia*
tulip *Tulipa*

turflily *Liriope*
turtle's head *Chelone*

velvet sumach *Rhus typhina*
Venus' navelwort *Omphalodes linifolia*
violet *Viola*
viper's bugloss *Echium vulgare*
Virginia creeper *Parthenocissus quinquefolia*
virgin's bower *Clematis flammula*

wake robin *Trillium grandiflorum*
wallflower *Erysimum cheiri*
wandering Jew *Tradescantia*
wattle *Acacia*
whitewash bramble *Rubus cockburnianus*
wild bergamot *Monarda fistulosa*
willow *Salix*
willow-leaved jessamine *Cestrum parqui*
windflower *Anemone*
winter aconite *Eranthis hyemalis*
winter cherry *Solanum pseudocapsicum*
winter green *Gaultheria procumbens*
winter heath *Erica carnea*
winter jasmine *Jasminum nudiflorum*
winter-sweet *Chimonanthus*
witch hazel *Hamamelis mollis*
woad *Isatis tinctoria*
wood anemone *Anemone nemorosa*
wood lily *Trillium*
wormwood *Artemisia*

yarrow *Achillea*
yew *Taxus baccata*

Index

Abeliophyllum distichum 143
Acacia 124, 125, 143, 150
Acalypha hispida 282
Acer 39
Achillea 19, 32, 40
Achimenes 282
Acorus calamus 131
Aechmea fasciata 283
Agapanthus 36
Aglaonema 283
Ajuga reptans 14
Alchemilla mollis 82–3, 88
Allium 33
Aloe variegata 283
Amaryllis belladonna 117
Ananas bracteatus striatus 283
Anaphalis triplinervis 37
Anchusa 36
Anemone 81, 90, 91
  A. blanda 42
  A. japonica 40
  A. nemorosa 29
Angelica archangelica 153
annuals 52–5, 56–7, 64–5
  bedding schemes 58–60
  climbers 61
  colour 62–3
  hanging baskets 180
  scent 118–19, 138
Anthurium scherzerianum 284
Antirrhinum 19, 52, 73
Aquilegia 14, 75
architectural plants 89
Artemisia 88
Arum italicum pictum 31
Asparagus densiflorus 'Sprengeri' 284
Aspidistra elatior 284
Asplenium 285
Aster 39, 40, 96–7

Astilbe 95
autumn 38–41, 96–7, 140–1
  hanging baskets 184–5
  window boxes 236–7

bedding plants 30, 58–60, 243
beds 30, 36, 40
  island beds 77, 120
Begonia 32–3, 285
Bellis perennis 30
Berberis 135
Bergenia 99
berries 39
Betula 45
biennials 52–3
  scent 118–19, 138
Billbergia nutans 286
borders 10–11, 30–1, 40
  perennials 76–7
  white 36–7
Browallia speciosa 286
Buddleja 39, 120, 121, 140
bulbs 10–11, 28, 33, 38–9, 42
  scent 116–17, 134
Buxus 59, 79, 146, 149, 150
buying plants 170, 264

Calceolaria 18
Calendula 19
Calluna vulgaris 24–5, 45, 120
Camellia 26, 29
Campanula isophylla 286
  C. lactiflora 40
Canna 33, 38, 41
capillary matting 275
Catananche 32
Celosia cristata 287
Cephalaria gigantea 40
Ceratostigma willmottianum 39
Cercidiphyllum 125, 141
Ceropegia woodii 287
Cestrum parqui 85, 110, 139
Chamaedorea elegans 287
Chamaemelum nobile 114, 145
Cheiranthus 134
children 74, 78–9

Chimonanthus 111, 142
Chlorophytum cosmosum 288
Choisya ternata 26, 120, 132
Chrysanthemum 39, 40, 153, 288
  lifting 137
Cistus 34, 149
x *Citrofortunella microcarpa* 289
Citrus 132, 133, 149
Clematis 35, 37, 87, 122, 128, 129, 135
Cleome 60
climbers 35, 37
  annuals 61
  perennials 86–7
  scent 128–9, 135
  supporting 86
Clivia miniata 289
Cobaea scandens 61
Cocos nucifera 289
Codiaeum variegatum pictum 290
Colchicum 38, 290
Coleus blumei 290
colour 10–11, 14–17, 40, 44–5
  hanging baskets 188–9
  perennials 100–1
  window boxes 244–5
Columnea 291
conifers 43, 125, 132, 144, 150
  plantings 26–7, 120
containers 11, 54, 145, 153, 148, 224
  houseplants 272–3
Convallaria majalis 81, 84, 123, 130, 135
Cordyline 79, 89
Cornus 43, 44, 45
Cortaderia selloana 41
Corylopsis 43
Cosmos atrosanguineus 123
Cotinus 12
Crambe cordifolia 130
Crataegus 125
Crinum 38, 117
Crocosmia 33, 36
Crocus 28, 31, 42, 116, 134, 291
Cupressus sempervirens 148–9

cuttings 279
Cyclamen 42, 81, 117, 291
Cydonia oblonga 141
Cyperius 292
Cytisus 122

Dahlia 11, 17, 32, 38, 41, 140
Daphne 43, 142, 143
deadheading 23, 173, 276
Delphinium 32, 92, 93
Dendranthema 40
design 59
Dianthus 109, 112, 120, 123, 136, 146, 147
  D. barbatus 56, 138
Dicentra 28–9, 91, 92
Dieffenbachia maculata 292
Digitalis 14, 21
Dizygotheca elegantissima 292
Doronicum 29
Dracaena 293
Dracunculus vulgaris 84
dry sites 83

Echeveria 293
Echinocactus grusonii 293
Echium 36
edible flowers 118, 119, 208–9, 250–1, 255
Elaeagnus 26, 141
environments 74, 113
Epipremnium aureum 294
Eranthis hyemalis 31, 42, 44, 72, 99
Erica 24–5, 37, 45, 135, 136, 294
Erigeron karvinskianus 92
Erodium manescani 92
Erysimum 19, 30, 93
Erythronium 28

Eucalyptus 109, 110, 111, 125
Eucryphia glutinosa 39
Euphorbia 81
E. polychroma 29, 91
Eustoma grandiflorum 294
evergreens 26
Exacum affine 295
Exochorda x *macrantha* 29

x *Fatshedera lizei* 295
Fatsia japonica 295
Ficus benjamina 296
Fittonia verschaffeltii 296
focal points 16, 17
foliage plants 12–13, 15, 39, 58, 63, 80, 88–9, 94, 267
hanging baskets 180–1, 192–3
scent 141
window boxes 246–7
Forsythia 29
forward planning 95, 170, 177, 221
Freesia 117
Fritillaria meleagris 28
fruit 250
window boxes 254
Fuchsia 34–5, 39, 179, 296

Galanthus nivalis 31, 42, 44
Gardenia jasminoides 297
Genista 137, 138, 149
Geranium 36, 79, 86
G. macrorrhizum 81, 130
G. pratense 92
Gladiolus 153
grasses 25, 41, 45, 63, 80, 120
gravel 148
grooming 276
ground cover 87
scent 130
Gunnera 83
G. manicata 89
Gypsophila 23, 32, 36

Hamamelis 43, 142
hanging baskets 55, 160–7, 210–11
autumn 184–5
colour 188–9
herbs 204–5
planting 171
pruning 173
scent 194–5
vegetables 202–3
watering 169, 172
Hebe 26, 37
Hedera 27, 297
Helenium 32, 94
Helianthemum 34
Helianthus 39, 96
Helichrysum 21, 139, 150
Heliotropum 109, 119
Helleborus 28, 31, 42, 91, 98, 99
H. foetidus 72
Hemerocallis 123
herbs 126–7, 139, 250
hanging baskets 204–5
window boxes 251, 252
Hesperis matronalis 30, 139, 147
Hibiscus 39, 297
Hosta 13, 40, 80, 152–3
houseplants 264–9
care 274–9
problems 280
Houttynia cordata 130, 131
Howea belmoreana 298
Hoya bella 298
Humulus lupulus 86, 128
Hyacinthus 28, 30, 31, 116–17, 134, 151, 153, 298
Hydrangea 34, 39, 299
Hymenocallis 117
Hypericum 109, 111
H. calycinum 34
Hypoestes phyllostachya 299

Impatiens 23, 55, 60, 299
Inula 32
Ipomoea 61
Iris 28, 30, 88, 95, 116
I. reticulata 98, 134
I. unguicularis 42, 85, 98, 143

Jasminum 43, 113, 129, 146, 300
Juglans 141
Juniperus 27, 148
Justicia brandegeeana 300

Kalanchoe blossfeldiana 300
Kniphofia 16, 36

Laburnum 114
Lathyrus odoratus 61, 118, 119, 147
Laurus nobilis 126, 132, 150
Lavandula 79, 109, 113, 126, 139, 146, 149, 150
L. stoechas 127
Leucojum 28
light 12, 266–7
Lilium 32, 36–7, 95, 112, 117, 147, 150–1, 152, 301
Liriope muscari 39
Lithops 301
Lobularia maritima 30, 138, 151
Lonicera 128, 129, 143, 146
Lunaria annua 53
Lupinus 32, 92
Lythrum salicaria 73

Magnolia 29, 110, 112, 124–5, 132, 135, 140–1
Mahonia 121, 143, 153
Malus 111, 125, 135, 141
Maranta leuconeura erythroneura 301
Matthiola 110, 119, 138, 139,141

Meconopsis 75
Melissa officinalis 126
Mentha 114, 126, 130, 131
Mespilus germanica 141
Monarda 85, 112
Monstera deliciosa 302
moving plants 96–7
Muscari 28, 31, 116, 134
Myosotis 11, 15, 28, 30
Myrtus communis 120

Narcissus 28, 31, 42, 116–17, 134, 302
Nemophila menziesii 17
Nepeta 80, 85
Nerine 38
Nertera granadensis 303
Nicotiana 110, 139, 140, 147, 151
Nigella 20
Nymphaea 131

Ocimum basilicum 126
Oenothera speciosa 21, 108
Olea europea 150
Opuntia 303
orchids 109, 115, 163
Osmanthus 39, 135
Osteospermum 18, 23

Paeonia 32, 112, 122–3, 133, 139, 146–7
P. mlokosewitschii 29
Papaver 32, 36
P. somniferum 15
Parrodia 303
Pelargonium 32, 53, 55, 114, 132, 133, 179, 304
Pellaea 304
Penstemon 32, 36, 98
Peperomia 304
perennials 28–9, 32–3, 39, 42
borders 76–7
choosing 70–5, 102–5
climbers 86–7

colour 100–1
foliage 88–9
scent 84–5, 122–3, 134–5, 136–7
Perovskia 109, 111
Persicaria affinis 87
Petunia 55
Philadelphus 34, 112, 113, 137
Philodendron scandens 305
Phlox 32, 84
Phoenix canariensis 305
Phormium 12
Phuopsis stylosa 84
Pieris 29
Pilea 305
pinching out 173
plants for
hanging baskets 212–15
scent 154–7
shade 81, 221
sun 80
window boxes 258–61
ponds 95
Populus balsamifera 125
potting soil 271
Primula 11, 15, 28, 30, 98, 123, 130
P. obconica 306
P. vulgaris 31, 42, 72, 90, 91
propagation 279
pruning
hanging baskets 173
houseplants 277
Prunus 125, 135
Pteris 306
Pulmonaria 28, 81, 90, 91, 98, 99
Pyracantha 39

Radermachera sinica 306
Ranunculus ficaria 91
Rebutia 307
repotting 278
Reseda odorata 109, 138
Rhododendron 16, 26, 29,134, 307
Rodgersia 88
Rosa 35, 36, 122, 128, 307
hanging baskets 178–9
scent 109, 111, 112, 113, 114, 120, 122, 129, 133, 136–7, 140, 146
Rosmarinus 113, 114, 126, 132
Rubus 43
Rudbeckia 39, 40, 96
Ruta graveolens 127

Saintpaulia 308
Salix 11, 43, 45
Salvia 126, 127
Sansevieria trifasciata 308
Santolina 126, 153
Sarcococca 142
Saxifraga stolonifera 308
scent 84–5, 108–15, 124–5, 130, 132–3, 141, 154–7
annuals 138–9
bulbs 116–17, 134
climbers 128–9, 135
hanging baskets 194–5
houseplants 268–9
night 110, 115, 139
perennials 84–5, 122–3, 134–5, 136–7
shrubs 120–1, 134–5 136–7, 142–3
window boxes 248–9
Schefflera arboricola 309
Schizostylis coccinea 39, 97
Scilla sibirica 30
Sedum 39, 97, 309
S. spectabile 40, 133
seedheads 33
shade 81, 162–3, 252, 267
shrubs 29, 34–5, 39, 43
scent 120–1, 134–5, 136–7, 142–3
Sinningia speciosa 309
Skimmia 111, 113, 120, 132, 134–5, 144, 146
soil, potting 271
Solanum capicastrum 310
Soleirolia soleirolii 310
Sophora 138

Sparrmannia africana 310
spring 28–31, 90–1, 134–5
hanging baskets 176–7
window boxes 230–1
Stachys 88
S. byzantina 80
stems 43
Stephanotis floribunda 311
Sternbergia 38
strawberries 206–7, 254
Streptocarpus 311
style 74–5, 144–5, 162, 220
cottage 28, 78, 146–7
formal 30, 79, 150–1
informal 30, 78–9
Japanese 114–15, 140–1
Mediterranean 83, 148–9
modern 152–3
summer 32–7, 92–3, 94–5, 136–7
hanging baskets 178–83
window boxes 232–5
sun 80, 162–3, 221, 252, 266–7
supporting plants 229
Syngonium podophyllum 311
Syringa 29, 121, 135

Tagetes 19
taste 250
texture 200–1, 268
Thuja 112
Thymus 109, 110, 114, 126, 139
Tilia 125, 138
Tillandria cynea 312
Tolmiea menziesii 312
tools 270
Trachelospermum jasminoides 113, 129
Tradescantia 312
trees 39
scent 124–5, 135, 138
Trillium grandiflorum 28
Tropaeolum majus 19, 60, 61, 118, 119
Tulipa 11, 28, 30, 31, 109, 116, 134, 313

vegetables 250
hanging baskets 202–3
window boxes 251, 253
Verbascum 19
Verbena 41
Vernonia 39, 96
Viburnum 43, 45, 121, 132, 134, 142
Viola 11, 19, 30, 52, 86, 109, 112, 130
V. odorata 42, 98
Vriesea splendens 313

water plants 95, 131
weeds 87
Weigela florida 30
wildflower plantings 79
wildlife 97, 110
window boxes 218–21, 256–61
autumn 236–7
colour 244–5
compost (soil mix) 226–7
edible plants 250–5
foliage plants 246–7
planting 228–9
plants 258–9
scent 248–9
spring 230–1
summer 232–5
types 222–5
watering 235
winter 238–9
winter 42–5, 98–9, 142–3
hanging baskets 186–7
window boxes 238–9
Wisteria 128, 129
woodland plantings 81, 91

year-round colour 10, 24–7, 99, 240–3
Yucca 79, 153, 313

Zantedeschia aethiopica 83
Zinnia 21